CAMBRIDGE

Brighter Thinking

The Quest for Political Stability: Germany, 1871–1991

A/AS Level History for AQA
Student Book

Nick Pinfield

Series Editors: Michael Fordham and David Smith

:ROUP

)R

CAMBRIDGE
UNIVERSITY PRESS

University Printing House, Cambridge CB2 8BS, United Kingdom

Cambridge University Press is part of the University of Cambridge.

It furthers the University's mission by disseminating knowledge in the pursuit of education, learning and research at the highest international levels of excellence.

www.cambridge.org
Information on this title: http://www.cambridge.org/9781107566088 (Paperback)
http://www.cambridge.org/9781107566118 (Cambridge Elevate-enhanced Edition)

First published 2015

A catalogue record for this publication is available from the British Library

ISBN 978-1-107-56608-8 Paperback
ISBN 978-1-107-56611-8 Cambridge Elevate-enhanced Edition

Additional resources for this publication at www.cambridge.org/ukschools

Cambridge University Press has no responsibility for the persistence or accuracy of URLs for external or third-party internet websites referred to in this publication, and does not guarantee that any content on such websites is, or will remain, accurate or appropriate. Information regarding prices, travel timetables, and other factual information given in this work is correct at the time of first printing but Cambridge University Press does not guarantee the accuracy of such information thereafter.

Message from AQA

This textbook has been approved by AQA for use with our qualification. This means that we have checked that it broadly covers the specification and we are satisfied with the overall quality. Full details of our approval process can be found on our website.

We approve textbooks because we know how important it is for teachers and students to have the right resources to support their teaching and learning. However, the publisher is ultimately responsible for the editorial control and quality of this book.

Please note that when teaching the A/AS Level History (7041, 7042) course, you must refer to AQA's specification as your definitive source of information. While this book has been written to match the specification, it cannot provide complete coverage of every aspect of the course.

A wide range of other useful resources can be found on the relevant subject pages of our website: www.aqa.org.uk

Contents

About this Series

Cambridge A/AS Level History for AQA is an exciting new series designed to support students in their journey from GCSE to A Level and then on to possible further historical study. The books provide the knowledge, concepts and skills needed for the two-year AQA History A Level course, but it's our intention as series editors that students recognise that their A Level exams are just one step to a potential lifelong relationship with the discipline of history. This book has further readings, extracts from historians' works and links to wider questions and ideas that go beyond the scope of an A Level course. With this series, we have sought to ensure not only that the students are well prepared for their examinations, but also that they gain access to a wider debate that characterises historical study.

The series is designed to provide clear and effective support for students as they make the adjustment from GCSE to A Level, and also for teachers, especially those who are not familiar with teaching a two-year linear course. The student books cover the AQA specifications for both A/AS Level. They are intended to appeal to the broadest range of students, and they offer challenge to stretch the top end and additional support for those who need it. Every author in this series is an experienced historian or history teacher, and all have great skill in conveying narratives to readers and asking the kinds of questions that pull those narratives apart.

In addition to high-quality prose, this series also makes extensive use of textual primary sources, maps, diagrams and images, and offers a wide range of activities to encourage students to address historical questions of cause, consequence, change and continuity. Throughout the books there are opportunities to criticise the interpretations of other historians, and to use those interpretations in the construction of students' own accounts of the past. The series aims to ease the transition for those students who move on from A Level to undergraduate study, and the books are written in an engaging style that will encourage those who want to explore the subject further.

Icons used within this book include:

 Key terms

 Speak like a historian

 Voices from the past/Hidden voices

 Practice essay questions

 Chapter summary

About Cambridge Elevate

Cambridge Elevate is the platform which hosts a digital version of this Student Book. If you have access to this digital version you can annotate different parts of the book, send and receive messages to and from your teacher and insert weblinks, among other things.

We hope that you enjoy your AS or A Level History course, as well as this book, and wish you well for the journey ahead.

Michael Fordham and David L. Smith
Series editors

1 The Kaiserreich, 1871–1914

In this section, we will examine the structure of the German Empire, including how it was governed, what its economic basis was and the nature of its society. We will look into:

- Political authority: the extent and make-up of the German Empire in 1871; the 1871 constitution; the role of emperor and chancellor; political groupings and parties and their ideologies

- Government and opposition: Kaiser Wilhelm I and government under Bismarck; their personalities and policies; the role of the Reichstag; the struggle between autocracy and democracy; the development of parties and political opposition

- Government and opposition: Kaiser Wilhelm II and his chancellors; personalities and policies; the place of the Reichstag; the struggle between autocracy and democracy; the development of parties and political opposition

- Economic developments: industrial expansion; old and new industries; agriculture; trade and wealth

- Social developments: the class hierarchy; elitism and the culture of militarism; the condition of the working people

- The political, economic and social condition of Germany by 1914.

Political authority

The extent and make-up of the German Empire in 1871

On 18 January 1871 the German Empire (**Kaiserreich**) was born. The origins of this new force in European diplomacy lay in a decisive military victory over France in the Franco-Prussian War (1870–71). The National Day of the new empire or *Reich* commemorated the crushing German victory in that war at the battle of Sedan on 1 September 1870.

Germany was now united. In theory, this was by voluntary agreement among the rulers of the various states that were now gathered into the new empire: the kings, grand dukes, dukes and princes, together with the senates of the Free Cities of Hamburg, Bremen and Lübeck. In practice, Prussia was by far the most powerful of the parts that made up the empire.

- Prussia's king became the German emperor, Wilhelm I.
- Prussia's chief minister, and the political architect of the new empire, Otto von Bismarck, became chancellor of the new empire.
- Prussia's capital, Berlin, became the empire's capital city.
- Prussia occupied about two-thirds of the empire's land area and held about three-fifths of its population.

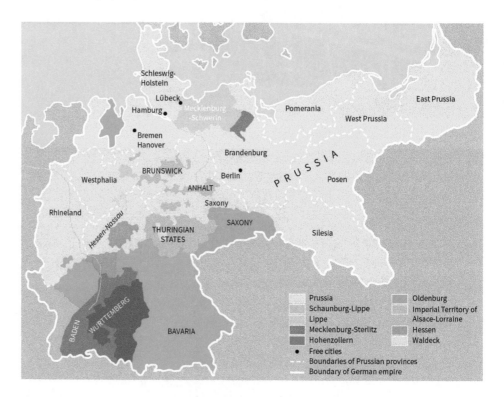

Figure 1.1: The German Empire in 1871. Note the size of Prussia, but also the fact that Prussia is itself made up of several different units, making it to some extent a federal kingdom within a federal empire. The borders are by no means those of modern Germany, but include a large chunk of modern Poland.

Prussia had led the movement to abolish hundreds of internal customs **tariffs** that had become barriers to trade. This allowed the free movement of goods within

Hidden voices

Hildegard von Spitzemberg (1843–1914)

Von Spitzemberg was the daughter of a politician in the south German state of Württemberg. A **Protestant** herself, she married a Catholic diplomat and accompanied him when he was sent to be Württemberg's ambassador to the Prussian capital. Although initially unenthusiastic, she became an admirer of Prussia and a friend of Bismarck's. In a country where women could not vote or stand for public office, she was nevertheless involved in politics as a 'salon hostess', inviting influential men to meet and discuss issues of the day in her home.

What a peace treaty for us Germans! More magnificent and glorious than ever! United into one Reich, the greatest, the most powerful, the most feared in Europe; great by reason of its physical power, greater still by reason of its education and the intelligence that permeates it! Every German heart hoped for it, none suspected that its dreams would be fulfilled, in this way, so soon and so magnificently.[1]

Discussion points

1. What does von Spitzemberg's response to the victory in the Franco-Prussian War tell us about **nationalism** in Germany?
2. What kind of country and what kind of political policy are implied in the *first* part of her description of the new empire as 'greatest', 'powerful' and 'feared'?
3. Now comment on the *second* part of the description, 'education and intelligence'.

---

their own territories. They were joined by other German states, notably in the Customs Union or ***Zollverein*** of 1834, but some states had joined before that, while others only joined later. Prussia went on to exploit the iron ore and coal found in its western territories of the Ruhr valley and Saarland to develop its economy strongly in the 1850s and 1860s.

However, the German Empire was more than just an extension of Prussian power over the smaller states. Constitutionally it was an unusual combination of apparently conflicting principles, all of them deeply rooted in the new state:

- Conservatives tended to back federalism;
- **Liberals** supported the unitary principle;
- The Prussian political establishment emphasised the military nature of the new empire.

Let's take those three terms in order.

The empire was a federation, in which each member state sought to retain a voice in discussions and decisions. Accordingly, the main executive body was a Federal Council or **Bundesrat**. This council was made up from ambassadors from the various states and its meetings were always held in private. It had considerable power and prestige. All laws needed its consent and it could veto any proposed changes to the Constitution. It had powerful committees in such areas as foreign affairs. As chancellor, Bismarck usually presided over Bundesrat meetings. Many Conservative politicians were reluctant to see any of the different states' traditional rights overridden by a centralising (and essentially Prussian) government.

Key term

Chancellor: A figure with authority over certain organisations, such as a head of government.

For Liberals, unification was a move towards a more modern German state. As a concession towards their ideas of the unity of the new empire, there was also a democratic national assembly or *Reichstag*, elected by universal adult male suffrage (all men over 25 had a vote). At the time, this was known as 'universal suffrage'; today we would call it 'universal male suffrage'. The Reichstag shared legislative power with the Bundesrat and also shared the right to review non-military government expenditure. Members were also involved in campaigns for further **reform**.

However, it was a military victory that had helped to create the empire and, as you will discover, the backbone of the empire was its army, an army that was a fundamentally Prussian institution. This plain political fact was to have the enormous influence over the history of the country as a monarchy, as a republic and then as a tyranny.

The 1871 Constitution

The new empire needed a new constitution. Bismarck provided one by adapting that of the Prussian-dominated North German Confederation (1867–71) to suit the new unified German state. The 1871 Constitution was designed to protect the traditional rights of the crown, as well as the special powers of the army and the bureaucracy, from any liberalising threats. The most notable aspect of this was the complete separation of military and civilian affairs. The army, of which the **Kaiser** (German emperor) was commander-in-chief, was granted a budget that was only to be subjected to democratic review by the Reichstag every seven years. This recognised what was seen as the special part played by (largely Prussian) military might in the unification of Germany, known in the phrase of the day as **Nationalwerdung** (becoming a nation).

This state of affairs should be seen against the backdrop of a military establishment and bureaucratic tradition looking back towards the autocratic regimes of the 18th century in German states. This was especially the case in the north, where Prussia was the dominant power. In the south, especially in Bavaria, democratic political parties were more advanced.

The 25 states that made up the federal empire retained a degree of authority to run their own local affairs. There were still kings in Bavaria, Saxony and Württemberg, and grand dukes in Baden and Hesse.

At a federal (national) level, there were two new institutions of government:

- The *Bundesrat* (Federal Council) had 58 members drawn from all the states of the empire. The largest group, unsurprisingly, was from Prussia, which sent 17. The next largest was from Bavaria which sent 6, then Saxony with 4 and so on. If 45 members of the Bundesrat could agree, then the Federal Council could rewrite the constitution. This meant that there was the appearance of a liberal ability to reform, but it gave Prussia's group of 17 the ability to block all change.
- The 397 members of the *Reichstag* (National Assembly or Parliament) were chosen in elections in which all men who were German citizens and at least 25 years old could vote in a secret ballot. The members were elected for a five-year term. The Reichstag was required to approve the federal budget and all legislation.

The roles of emperor and chancellor

The leadership of the empire was in the hands of the Prussian king in his new role as kaiser (emperor). In this role, he had considerable powers.

- He was commander-in-chief of the armed forces, so he gave the orders.
- He appointed all ministers, including the chancellor; he could also dismiss them whenever he chose.
- He could issue decrees and ordinances, which were like laws but did not have to go through the Reichstag.

The national anthem of the empire was personally dedicated to the emperor. The imperial flag was red, black and white, the personal colours of Wilhelm's family. Thus, the new state clearly placed the emperor at the centre of things.

Appointed by the emperor and responsible (answerable) to him, the **Reichskanzler** (imperial chancellor) was also a powerful figure.

- He presided over the Bundesrat, which meant that he ran it.
- He had to sign the emperor's decrees and ordinances in order for them to be legal.
- He was in charge of all aspects of government.

Despite this, the job's title 'chancellor' seemed to suggest that it was not a powerful role. The name was lower in standing than 'prime minister', for example. This was part of the means for reassuring the member states that they, and their prime ministers, retained much of their old authority. Just as the emperor's first minister was a chancellor, not a prime minister, so the institutions were referred to as federal agencies, not ministries or government. The first chancellor, Bismarck, never referred to himself as an imperial minister, and nor did any of his successors (until the upheavals of 1918).

Bismarck held on to his old jobs as prime minister and foreign minister of Prussia until close to the end of his time in office as chancellor of the empire, regarding them as essential to his political power.

Political groupings and parties and their ideologies

In the Reichstag, the biggest political party was the **National Liberals** or *National-liberale partei*. In the first federal elections, they won 125 seats, making them the largest single party. They increased their representation to 155 seats in the 1874 election.

The party had its origins in a grouping of deputies in the Prussian **Landtag** (state parliament) in the 1860s and had supported Bismarck's foreign policies, including the move towards German unification. They mostly supported the government, especially on matters of social reform. They drew their own support from the *Grossbürgern*: wealthy landowners in central Germany, rich businessmen and northern merchants.

Liberalism was a major force in the Kaiserreich. Understandably, given its supporters, the movement supported a free-market approach to economics and the rule of law. It opposed **revolutionary** politics but campaigned for political

ACTIVITY 1.1

Was Prussia just too dominant a part of a united Germany?

Create a spider diagram showing the areas in which Prussia occupied a position of power in the Kaiserreich. Conduct some research to find out what checks there were on Prussian power.

reform including increasing democratisation. Liberalism contained both more and less radical groupings. Sometimes these divisions led to parties forming, splitting or merging, a volatility that undermined its political effectiveness. Liberals supported Bismarck's social and political reforms, and his attack on the Catholic Church.

The other main liberal group was the **Progressives**. They too had begun in the Prussian *Landtag* but, unlike the National Liberals, they had a history of opposing Bismarck. They were not able to accept Bismarck's refusal to give way and grant regular Reichstag oversight of the huge expenditure on the army (some 90% of the total government budget) or the responsibility of government ministers to the democratic body. The Progressive party actively opposed the government in the Reichstag on these issues.

They campaigned for a parliamentary democracy on the British model, with the monarchy's role strictly limited and power lying in the elected national assembly. Initially opposed to state intervention, the party became more enthusiastic about legislation for social welfare. The Progressives drew their support from the intelligentsia, artisans, the lower ranks of the civil service and businessmen.

While Conservative political groups in the Reichstag never enjoyed the electoral support given to the Liberal groups, this was more a function of the weakness of the Reichstag during this period than anything else. Many important powers were held by the assemblies in the individual states, the *Landtage*, and in these Conservatives often had a majority. This was the case, for example in Prussia, which was home to three-fifths of the German population.

A good example of the Conservative groups was the *Reichspartei* (Empire Party, but usually known as the **Free Conservatives**) in Prussia. Mainly speaking for heavy industry, this party drew its support from Berlin, the Rhineland and Silesia.

The **Conservatives** were supported by the landed interest in East Prussia and Mecklenburg. They had even less party organisation than the liberal parties and relied instead on their patriarchal and traditional powers in these rural areas. They were unenthusiastic about change and had not supported unification, unlike the Free Conservatives.

Sometimes nicknamed the 'throne and altar' party, Conservatives supported a powerful monarchy, a strong army and the Protestant church, believing in the right of the authorities to govern. They tended to support Bismarck, but were unimpressed by the reforms he had introduced to meet Liberal demands. They paid attention to agricultural voters and opposed anything that might harm farmers' interests. They sought to protect the rights and traditions of the different states that made up the new empire, and opposed moves to centralise power. Conservatism was also **anti-Semitic**.

The second largest party in the Reichstag was the **Centre Party** or *Zentrumspartei*. It had been founded in 1870 to represent the interests of **Roman Catholics** in Germany. Its founders were noblemen from Silesia and the Rhineland, but it was based on religion, not class or region. It drew support from smallholders in south and west Germany, as well as from farmers and the Catholic urban working class in western Germany.

Because of its nature and purpose, it did not fit easily into a conservative-liberal spectrum, representing a coalition. This included a working-class wing which wanted more government intervention, with social and economic reforms, and a more middle- and upper-class wing with social-conservative views. It took a strong interest in education and defended Catholic schools. Initially in conflict with Bismarck (who regarded them as potential traitors), they became his allies in opposing Socialism.

Government and opposition: Wilhelm I

Wilhelm I and Bismarck: their personalities and policies

Wilhelm I was in his mid-seventies in 1871. When only ten he had joined the Prussian army as an officer and he saw active service in his teens, fighting the French and winning an Iron Cross. Bismarck described him as an old-fashioned, courteous, infallibly polite gentleman of the Prussian military caste.

Wilhelm survived two assassination attempts in 1878, in the second of which he was seriously wounded. Bismarck used this opportunity to push an anti-**socialist** law through the Reichstag, even though the assassin himself had been expelled from the Social Democratic Party.

Wilhelm I died in 1888 and was succeeded briefly by his ill son Friedrich, who died after just 99 days as emperor. He was succeeded in turn by his son Wilhelm, later in the same year.

Unlike her husband Wilhelm I, **Empress (*Kaiserin*)** Augusta received a full and liberal education, including lessons in drawing and music. When they first met in 1826, she was Princess Augusta von Sachsen-Weimar-Eisenach, and half his age at just 15. They married in 1829. She was bored by military and court life, and disliked Bismarck a great deal. He returned her feelings, accusing her of having undue influence on the kaiser. Augusta especially disliked Bismarck's foreign policy, believing that under his influence Prussia had been aggressive and without principles. She was tolerant of Catholicism, something which conflicted with Bismarck's suspicion of Catholic influence in German society and his belief that loyalty to the Vatican undermined the German political unity for which he was working. The chancellor, who had so praised the emperor, showed his hostility to Empress Augusta, saying that Wilhelm I's good sense was occasionally undermined by 'female influences'.

In 1864 Augusta founded the National Women's Association, which looked after the wounded, and corresponded with Florence Nightingale. She blamed Bismarck for the outbreak of the Franco-Prussian war (1870–71) and founded a school for the destitute daughters of German officers in 1873. She only became reconciled with Bismarck towards the end of her life, in the light of his support for her grandson, who would become Wilhelm II.

Otto von Bismarck was the son of a **Junker** (a Prussian country gentleman) from east of the river Elbe. The Junkers were famous for their conservative values, hostility to change, solid virtues and deep Lutheran Protestant faith. They dominated the officer class in the army and the bureaucracy.

Tall and slim in his early years, Bismarck later became corpulent from eating and drinking enormous quantities. He had a high-pitched, soft voice and he claimed to detest public speaking. Far more intelligent and well-read than was usual among Junkers, he became interested in politics in his early thirties, convinced that he had the ability to stem the tide of liberal thinking and to preserve the powers of the Junker in Prussia and, after 1871, in a unified Germany.

Bismarck was a complex man. As a politician he was ruthless and could be cruel. On the other hand, he was no fanatic or ascetic. He enjoyed a happy family life and was not without a sense of humour. He knew when compromise was necessary. The product of a Prussian grammar school, he knew Latin and Greek and spoke and wrote fluently in French and almost as well in English. Later he learned Russian. He often expressed himself in abrupt ways, coldly and harshly, sometimes even disdainfully.

His fall from power in 1890 caused a sensation in Germany and beyond. He did not agree with the increasing interest taken by Wilhelm II in social policy such as improving conditions for industrial workers. His 30 years as first Prussian then German political leader had seen great achievements, not least as architect of a united Germany.

Kaiser Wilhelm I and government under Bismarck

Throughout the period of his chancellorship, Bismarck pursued a policy of building German unity around Prussian leadership. As part of this he identified those groups which were powerful enough, or which might become powerful enough, to threaten national unity and social stability.

The first such group was the Roman Catholic Church. About a third of Germany's citizens were Catholic. In 1871, the year of German unification, a meeting of the Catholic First Vatican Council declared that the Catholic leader, the Pope, was unable to make a mistake when declaring something to be a doctrine of the Church. This was widely believed to mean that popes could never make mistakes, something the First Vatican Council hadn't actually said. Such a declaration seemed to make the Pope an autocratic leader whom Catholics would obey in everything, making the Protestant German nationalist Bismarck question their loyalty to the empire.

Catholics were also suspected of being supportive of German-speaking, Catholic Austria. As Austria was a country which Prussia had fought as recently as 1866, this also contributed to the political belief that Catholics were not dependable citizens. These suspicions led to the **Kulturkampf** (literally 'culture struggle'), refer to the section on 'The struggle between autocracy and democracy'.

The second group to draw Bismarck's fire were those Poles who lived in eastern Germany. The German Empire was a nation of several languages: there were speakers of French in Alsace-Lorraine and Danish speakers in North Schleswig, while, in the east, over 5% of the population were Polish speakers. A principle of

Speak like a historian

Bismarck's biographer Jonathan Steinberg discusses what the basis of Bismarck's authority was. He quotes Max Weber, one of the founders of sociology, who offered three reasons for our obeying the state:

Tradition: 'the authority of the "eternal yesterday"';

Charisma: 'the absolutely personal devotion and personal confidence in revelation, heroism, or other qualities of individual leadership … the elected war lord, the plebiscitarian ruler, the great demagogue, or the political party leader';

Law: 'the belief in the validity of legal statute … this is domination as exercised by the modern "servant of the state"'.[2]

Discussion points

1. Which of these three do you think best defines the kind of leader you think Bismarck was?
2. Steinberg's own conclusion was that Bismarck combined the first and the third, tradition and law. What aspects of Bismarck's career do you think led Steinberg to this conclusion?

the Prussian constitution was 'self-administration': the different communities in the wider state had a degree of autonomy. But a major concern for Bismarck was that the German nation might be diluted by these minorities. Bismarck's biographer Otto Pflanze records that in 1873 he declared his regret that the empire had not driven the entire pro-French population out of Alsace-Lorraine and resettled the area with Germans.

Bismarck's personal dislike of Germans whose first language was Polish was notorious. He felt that building a sense of national identity for a unified Germany was to be his most important task and anything that got in the way of this was, for him, immediately suspect. Poles spoke a different language and they were Catholics: how dependable were they as citizens of the empire?

The German government adopted a policy of Germanisation. Between 1871 and 1873, it pushed through a Germanising education system for the Polish-speaking regions. It encouraged German settlement in Polish-speaking areas and banned the speaking of Polish; children who spoke it in school were punished. Pflanze notes that, having given instructions for the expulsion of **Jesuits**, other Catholic priests, journalists and all 'politically-active' people from Posen, in 1872 the chancellor began to argue in favour of expelling *all* Poles who could not prove citizenship.

The 1876 Language of Government Act made German the language for conducting all public business, with the exception of school boards and local councils. In 1886, the emperor opened a session of the Prussian *Landtag* as King of Prussia and spoke about the importance of Germanising the eastern regions. Two weeks later, Bismarck gave what is called his 'great Polish speech' on the subject of the supposed 'danger' from Poles. The speech was published and half a million copies were distributed around Germany; his office was inundated with letters and telegrams of support. The plan was to buy up Polish-owned land and lease it to Germans. German teachers were to be encouraged to work in the east, and at the same time Polish officials and military recruits were to be deployed in the west of the country to make them more German. In the same year, the government decided that it was time for the temporary exceptions to the Language of Government Act to lapse and in 1887 it abolished the use of Polish for teaching.

The third group that seemed to Bismarck to threaten the Reich were Socialists and Social Democrats. Like the Catholic Church, they were part of an international movement. As a result, German citizens looked abroad for inspiration and leadership. In 1869 the Social Democratic Party (SPD) had been formed out of various previous reform parties. (Strictly speaking, the party only changed its name to the *Sozialdemokratische Partei Deutschlands* in 1890 but for the sake of simplicity we refer to them as the SPD throughout.) It published its programme in 1875, calling for the state to take control of industry and for workers to share in their workplace's profits.

Bismarck responded with a two-pronged approach. On the one hand, he pushed through the Anti-Socialist Laws of 1878, which permitted elected SPD deputies in the Reichstag (though not officially as SPD – they had to stand under other labels) but other than that banned socialist organisations, including trade unions and political parties and associations.

On the other hand, he developed his own programme of social reform to undermine the appeal of the SPD and other groups. In 1883, the state began to provide a sickness benefit to men who could not work because of illness. The following year, in 1884, the Accident Insurance Law was passed, meaning that workers injured at work would be compensated. Then in 1889 an old-age pension

 Voices from the past

Otto von Bismarck (1815–98)

Bismarck dominated German (and much of European) politics in the second half of the 19th century. He was in no doubt that politics was about power. He built up the power of the king within Prussia, of Prussia within Germany and of Germany within Europe. Domestically, he allied himself with Liberals against Catholics, and then with Catholics against Socialists, according to his judgement of where the major threat to Prussian interests lay at the time. In his foreign policy, he engineered military successes against Prussia's neighbours, Denmark, Austria and France. However, he spent much of his career using diplomacy to avoid wars breaking out and to keep Germany from becoming involved when they did.

Germany does not look to Prussia's liberalism, but to her power … The great issues of the day are not decided through speeches and majority resolutions – that was the great error of 1848 and 1849 – but through blood and iron.[3]

Discussion points

1. What does the remark about Germany tell us about Bismarck's sense of Prussia's role?
2. Comment on Bismarck's contrast between 'liberalism' and 'power'.
3. What does Bismarck mean by 'blood and iron'? What comparison or contrast would you make with Hildegard von Spitzemberg's 'education and intelligence'?

scheme was introduced for workers aged 70 or over. As with the introduction of universal male suffrage for the Reichstag, this made Germany one of the most liberal states in Europe.

The role of the Reichstag

There had been revolutions in many parts of Europe in 1848. The German revolutions were crushed and the decade that followed was conservative and repressive. However, strong economic growth in German states in the late 1850s and 1860s encouraged the formation of political organisations whose aim was to win the support of public opinion. There were new public demonstrations in 1866, this time against Prussian policy towards Schleswig-Holstein.

These kinds of popular involvement in political debate had concerned autocratic governments. However, Bismarck had shrewdly allowed for the democratic spirit that they expressed by including in the 1871 Constitution a Reichstag that was elected by universal male suffrage. The Reichstag voted on the national budget and legislation. As a result, contemporaries regarded Germany as having one of the most advanced political systems in Europe.

Such apparent liberalisation dismayed some conservatives. Junkers in particular, regarded Bismarck as having betrayed the interests of his own class.

However, the Reichstag which the constitution had established was no more than a nod towards democracy. Bismarck intended to limit its powers to discussing government policy and then approving it (what we call 'rubber-stamping' today). at the time of German unification and the publishing of the 1871 Constitution, the Reichstag was a significant institution but naturally it did not have a home. The assembly initially met in the Prussian *Landtag* (state parliament) building, and then in buildings in Berlin's Leipziger Straße, including what had been a porcelain factory. The deputies not surprisingly petitioned for a parliament to be built, though Bismarck opposed the idea. A competition was held in 1872 for designing the proposed building.

However, even when the principle of a monumental new building had been agreed, there was a debate over where to put it. In the event, nothing was done for another ten years, while discussions and disputes continued between the emperor, the chancellor and the deputies. Another competition was held ten years after the first one in 1882 and, in 1884, the foundation stone was laid by Wilhelm I on a site in what was then Königsplatz and in modern Berlin is called Platz der Republik. He never saw the building used: he died in 1888 and the deputies only took up residence in 1894.

This had been more than an argument about architecture. It had also been a dispute about the significance of the Reichstag as an institution. If the assembly was of permanent political importance, it needed the equivalent of a palace in which to deliberate. On the other hand, if it was temporary, or unimportant, then it could meet anywhere. Wilhelm I took the role of constitutions and parliaments seriously. Before becoming King of Prussia he had been regent for his older brother, who had had a stroke, and he insisted on taking his oath of office on the constitution, whereas his brother's advice had been to throw the constitution aside. By the time the first debates took place in the new Reichstag building, however, his grandson was emperor, and Wilhelm II had far less respect for the institution.

- It could not initiate legislation: that was the business of government, the emperor and his ministers, notably the chancellor.
- It did not appoint or dismiss the chancellor or any other government ministers, who were all appointed by the emperor.
- It had little or no influence on foreign policy, which was in the hands of the emperor and chancellor.
- It had little or no influence on military spending and could not even demand to know how the money was being spent.

Furthermore, the kaiser had the power to dissolve the assembly with the agreement of the Bundesrat whenever it suited the government. (In practice this was done by the chancellor.)

This constitutional framework had dressed an autocratic body in modern democratic clothes, enabling autocratic Prussian rule to continue in a united Germany. It was not really until 1914 that the balance of power shifted and governments increasingly began to need to take account of the Reichstag.

The struggle between autocracy and democracy

Conservatives in many states opposed change and reform, particularly where it affected the traditional rights of the individual states. Accordingly, when Bismarck wanted to enact reforms, he often turned for support to the National Liberals. This included pushing through centralising government measures. For example, in 1876 a *Reichsbank* was created and the legal system was standardised and modernised. The creation of a national currency, the **Goldmark**, was another such measure, as it involved replacing the different states' own currencies.

A second area in which liberals supported Bismarck was in the *Kulturkampf*, the campaign against the Catholic Church which ran from 1871 to 1878. In an attempt to appeal to the two-thirds of the population of united Germany who were Protestant, Bismarck sought to break the power of the Catholic Church. Although his campaign was mainly focused on Prussia, it brought Catholics throughout Germany and at all levels of society together in defence of their traditional rights.

The three main issues of the *Kulturkampf* were marriage, education and nationalism. In 1871 Bismarck enacted a law (the **Pulpit Law**) that prevented priests from making any political comment. A year later, in 1872, the **Jesuit** order was banned from German soil. The Jesuits were independent of the regular Church structure, were bound to spiritual contemplation and were prominent in education. They had a sinister reputation among non-Catholics. At the same time religious administration of any school in Prussia was also prohibited. Catholics were dismayed and protested loudly.

The **May Laws** of 1873 were a further move in the struggle. These laws removed the training and appointment of the clergy from church to state. Now there was even more resistance from the Catholic Church. Later that year Wilhelm von Ketteler, the Catholic Bishop of Mainz, and founder of the Centre Party in 1870, publicly condemned the May Laws. He was arrested and sentenced to two years in prison.

In 1875 Bismarck had the **Congregation Laws** passed. These abolished all religious orders – monks, friars and nuns – and stopped all state subsidies to the Catholic Church. The same year also saw the removal of the right to marriage in a Catholic church. A civil ceremony was now to be the only legal process. Many clergy resisted. There were many arrests and removals. Monasteries were closed and priests were arrested and exiled. Many Catholic **parishes** found themselves without priests.

German nationalism, perceived as being based on Protestant values, Prussian military achievements and Liberal politics, had a weaker appeal to Catholics. Perhaps one-third of all Germans looked to Rome for spiritual guidance rather than to Berlin. Much of the eastern part of the Reich was land that had historically been part of Poland, and it was still substantially Polish in language and culture. Most Germans of Polish origin, as well as majorities in Alsace, Lorraine, the Saarland and the Rhineland in the west, and Silesia and Bavaria in the south, were Roman Catholics. The Catholic nobility in the eastern parts of Germany were especially powerful and Bismarck would not tolerate that. His dislike of the Polish minority in Prussia was well known. In Polish nationalism he detected a threat to the growth of German nationalism that had been brewing ever since the opposition to the Napoleonic occupation of German lands in the early 19th century.

The development of parties and political opposition

The elections of 1874 demonstrated the risks run by Bismarck when he took on the Roman Catholic Church. The Centre Party increased its representation in the Reichstag as Catholics expressed their anger at moves against the Church by voting for their party in ever larger numbers. Initially, Bismarck continued on his chosen path with the changes of 1875 already mentioned. However, his allies in the struggle could be seen attacking not merely the Catholic Church but all religion: this was not the outcome Bismarck wanted at all.

He now began to realise that the Centre Party, with its growing representation in the Reichstag, could be a useful balance to the Liberals and Socialists. He therefore started to soften his stance on the Catholic Church. The death of the long-serving Pope Pius IX in February 1878 and the appointment of Pope Leo XIII, a less abrasive and confrontational figure than his predecessor, gave Bismarck an opportunity to back down without losing authority. The anti-Catholic Liberals left his governing political coalition, giving him a freer hand to compromise.

The most lasting effect of the *Kulturkampf* was the emergence of the moderate Centre Party as a major element in German politics. Formed in 1870, it became the second largest party in the Reichstag in the elections of 1871 with 63 seats. In 1874, an increased vote gave them 91 seats and subsequent elections saw their size grow to more than 100 seats.

However, as with the other political groupings in the Reichstag, the Centre Party was slow to develop any party apparatus. Even so, it had an active press, an annual meeting of Catholics (*Katholikentag*) and many associations for charitable or social purposes. It articulated the views of the large Catholic minority in the Kaiserreich and it now had the political influence to make those views heard at the highest levels of government.

Meanwhile, Socialists and Social Democrats were also organising. Two different parties with roots in the revolutionary activity of 1848 had been founded in the 1860s, merged in 1875 and became a significant force in the Reichstag. The party was ably led by August Bebel (1840–1913), a deputy in the Reichstag for 42 years.

There were two attempts by political radicals to assassinate Wilhelm I in May and September 1878. The government blamed the Socialists and Social Democrats for their supposed influence on the assassin. In response Bismarck introduced the Anti-Socialist Laws (the full title in German means 'Law against the dangerous activities of **social democracy**'), a series of acts designed to curb but not eliminate the SPD.

The first law was approved by the Reichstag in October 1878. It banned any Social Democratic meeting that might spread socialist ideas, outlawed trade unions and closed down 45 Social Democrat newspapers. The SPD got round most of these restrictions by, for example, having their newspapers printed outside Germany and having their political candidates stand as Independents.

The Liberal *Deutscher Nationalverein* (German National Union) was founded in 1859 and included such prominent citizens as the historian Theodor Mommsen and the engineer Werner Siemens. The Conservative *Preußische Volksverein* (Prussian People's Union) was founded in 1861. Both were forerunners of national political parties. The early 1860s also saw the foundation of the German Labour Party by the Silesian lawyer Ferdinand Lassalle; it drew its support from Berlin, Frankfurt and the Rhineland. Although it was a party in favour of radical change, Lassalle was no friend of the Liberals, regarding them as a **bourgeois** movement whose reforms would benefit the **middle classes**, not the workers. As well as being a radical, he was a German nationalist and came to regard monarchy as an institution potentially better able to protect the working classes

Voices from the past

August Bebel

Among other issues, August Bebel was a pioneer in **women's rights** and wrote a booklet on the subject in 1879. In it he wrote:

The Socialist Party is the only one that has made the full equality of women, their liberation from every form of dependence and oppression, an integral part of its programme, not for reasons of **propaganda** but from necessity. For there can be no liberation of mankind without social independence and equality of the sexes.[4]

Discussion points

1. What connections is Bebel making between socialism and women's equality?
2. What vision of society does Bebel's list of abstract nouns suggest: equality, liberation, social independence?

than any bourgeois political party. Questioned by Bebel in the 1870s, Bismarck acknowledged that he had had secret meetings with Lassalle to discuss politics. It is now generally acknowledged that these meetings may have influenced Bismarck first in his introduction of universal male suffrage and later in the social reforms of the 1880s.

Membership of these political groups was relatively small. The *Nationalverein*, the largest such group, never had more than 25 000 and Lassalle's Labour Party had as few as 1000 members. The political parties of the Kaiserreich were not mass movements but were mostly vehicles for bourgeois and aristocratic networking.

The autocratic rule of the kaiser through Chancellor Bismarck was not, therefore, without opposition, both formal in the Reichstag and informal through pressure groups and associations. Nevertheless, with a characteristic mixture of shrewdness and ruthlessness, Bismarck was usually able to brush this opposition aside. He was helped by the widespread public support for the kaiser and the calculated weakness of the democratic institutions he had devised.

Government and opposition: Kaiser Wilhelm II

Kaiser Wilhelm II and his chancellors: personalities and policies

Bismarck

Wilhelm II was just 29 when he was crowned following his grandfather's and then father's deaths. He was a grandson of Queen Victoria and was at her bedside at Osborne House when she died in 1901. His cousins included the Russian **Tsar** Nicholas II and the UK's King George V, both of whom attended the wedding of his daughter Victoria Louise to a Hanoverian prince in Berlin in 1913.

Wilhelm II has been described in various ways. His biographer Lamar Cecil calls him 'bombastic and impetuous' and 'a curious mixture of bombast and affability'. The new kaiser referred to himself as a 'modern man', though his taste in art was resolutely conventional and he detested all modern trends in painting. Perhaps he had in mind his interest in public education and social welfare. He was also interested in science and technology, which led to the foundation of the Kaiser Wilhelm Society for the Advancement of Science under his patronage.

Wilhelm II's succession in 1888 brought many political changes to the Kaiserreich. The new kaiser clashed with Bismarck from the moment he inherited the throne from his sick father. He felt that Bismarck was too conservative and out of touch, especially on social policy.

In 1889, Bismarck planned to use military force against striking coal miners in Silesia. Wilhelm II did not want the start of his reign to be marked with German blood and threw out the idea. At a time when many European monarchs were becoming ornamental figureheads in ruling the various states, the new kaiser wished to assert his authority. In this he was different from his grandfather, who had been content to be guided by his chancellor. He told his cousin Nicholas II that as emperor he had a 'divine right' to rule.

ACTIVITY 1.2

Find out more about Ferdinand Lassalle. Why did Bismarck have a series of meetings with him?

ACTIVITY 1.3

The historian Golo Mann says of Wilhelm II that he was 'a good actor'. What do you think he means?

Create a mind map showing aspects of Wilhelm's personality and connecting where possible to actions, attitudes and policies.

Influenced by the British example, Wilhelm II wanted to find overseas colonies, something in which Bismarck had no interest

Caprivi

Bismarck resigned as chancellor in March 1890 and from then on Wilhelm II was careful to appoint chancellors who would share more closely his own interests, such as in industrial matters, and be less confrontational than Bismarck. The one he chose in 1890 was General Leo von Caprivi, a career army officer without any particular political links but of unquestioned loyalty to the kaiser. There were, certainly, contrasts between the relatively liberal policies of Caprivi and the more reactionary ones of Hohenlohe and von Bülow, over domestic matters of tariff and social policies for example, but in general Kaiser Wilhelm II achieved a break from Bismarck and his grandfather.

As chancellor from 1890 to 1894 Caprivi began to introduce what has been called the 'New Course' (*NeuerKurs*) both in Germany and overseas. Like Bismarck, he was also appointed as Minister President of Prussia as well as Foreign Secretary so that he was well placed to set off on this new policy course. It was new because it marked a clear change from the policies of Bismarck and reflected both the interests in industrial matters at home and the colonising instincts of Wilhelm II.

One notable change under Caprivi was that the Reichstag did not renew the Anti-Socialist Laws, which were allowed to lapse. While Bismarck had been chancellor, they had been renewed four times.

Within Germany Caprivi sought to support German trading and industrial interests by lowering import duties on wheat, rye, cattle and timber. This antagonised the powerful rural landowners, especially the Junker interests in the east of Germany, who wanted the protection of high import duties for their agricultural produce.

He also built on Bismarck's legislation of the 1880s by introducing a number of reforms in industrial working conditions, banning the employment of children under 13 and restricting the working day for 13- to 18-year-olds to ten hours each day. Working hours for women were reduced to 13 each day, Sunday working was banned and a guaranteed minimum working wage was introduced. Industrial tribunals were established to deal with disputes over these matters.

In 1890 the kaiser decided to refuse the Russian request to renew the 1887 Reinsurance Treaty. Caprivi acceded to the emperor's decision and opted for the Triple Alliance with Austria-Hungary and Italy. (Russia allied herself instead with France: this was to have consequences in 1914.) Caprivi also attempted to repair relations with the Centre Party, whose votes in the Reichstag would have been useful, by trying to introduce some Catholic faith schools into the educational system and to heal the bruises of the *Kulturkampf* period. However, this was opposed by many Protestants and by the Social Democrats, and his attempts failed.

This failure to achieve better relations with the Catholic Church and their political voice, the Centre Party, led to Caprivi's downfall. Protestant politicians insisted that he be deprived of his post as Minister President of Prussia; that post went to Botho zu Eulenburg. The tension between Chancellor Caprivi and Minister

President Eulenburg made the situation unworkable and both were dismissed in October 1894.

Hohenlohe

Caprivi was followed as chancellor by the 75-year-old Chlodwig, Prince of Hohenlohe (1894–1900). Although brought up a Bavarian Catholic, he was not a supporter of the louder Catholic cause in Germany. He belonged to a princely house in Hesse and had been Prime Minister of Bavaria (1866–70), Foreign Secretary (1880) and Imperial Lieutenant of Alsace-Lorraine (1885–94). He was thus aristocratic, fatherly, an experienced politician and diplomat. This seemed to make him an ideal candidate for the post of chancellor, where it was essential to handle the Reichstag on the one side and the emperor on the other.

However, the emperor was surrounded by flatterers whose access to the monarch and influence on him far outweighed Hohenlohe's. An elected member of the Reichstag, Hohenlohe visited it rarely and preferred to leave most of the business of governing to his Secretaries of State. He endlessly attempted to agree with the kaiser. Although he did not agree with Wilhelm's plan to deal harshly with the SPD, he supported passage of the 1894 federal law against subversion and the 1897 Prussian law against the Socialists. Eventually he recognised that he was entirely unable to persuade Wilhelm of anything, resigned the chancellorship in October 1900 and died in Switzerland the following year.

Von Bülow

Hohenlohe was succeeded as chancellor in 1900 by his foreign secretary, Bernhard, Prince von Bülow (1900–09). A charming, educated former diplomat, the latter spent much of his time agreeing with Wilhelm II and flattering him. When he was in Berlin, von Bülow would ride in a park called the Tiergarten and then spend the rest of the morning with Wilhelm II, whom he addressed with unfailing politeness and respect.

In the Reichstag von Bülow largely enjoyed the support of the Conservatives and Centrists but, like Bismarck, knew how to turn to the National Liberals when he needed them. He contributed to the improvement of social conditions, introduced some political reforms, and rationalised the Reich's finances, introducing direct federal taxes. Measures that liberals could support, these were also reforms that pleased the emperor who wanted to see an improvement in industrial working conditions and a strengthening of the Reich's central authorities.

His downfall came as a result of the publication in the British *Daily Telegraph* in 1908 of some unwise remarks that the kaiser made on a visit to London. The newspaper article reporting them had been sent to the kaiser before publication and von Bülow had been supposed to check it first but failed to do so. Instead he passed it back unread to the kaiser, advising that it was fine to publish.

The views in the embarrassing article offended the French, the Russians and many Germans. Von Bülow blamed the German Foreign Office for failing to check the article but the Kaiser decided that it was the chancellor's fault. When von Bülow's government lost a vote in the Reichstag in June 1909 regarding the financing of ship construction, the opportunity was there for the chancellor to offer his resignation.

Von Bülow's performance as chancellor had been disappointing given his evident intelligence and ability. Much of his energy seems to have been used for his own political survival. He did make some effective speeches to the Reichstag and there were some progressive reforms during his time as chancellor but overall he achieved a good deal less than had been expected.

Bethmann Hollweg

Von Bülow's Secretary of State for the Interior had been Theobald von Bethmann Hollweg. The latter was appointed chancellor following von Bülow's resignation in 1909, retaining the post until 1917.

An experienced and able bureaucrat, he was no politician. He tried to manage the Reichstag by attempting to pacify both the Right and the Left, taking what he called 'a diagonal course', but in the end he satisfied neither. The kaiser's biographer Lamar Cecil describes Bethmann as having little support from the Reichstag deputies and little respect from the emperor, who did not consult him on important decisions.

Bethmann had no party political affiliation, but was by nature mildly liberal. He assumed that the system of monarchical rule and a democratic assembly was about right, but was unenthusiastic about the Reichstag and its deputies. His moves to reform the system were accordingly unenthusiastic as well. Wilhelm II and his Reichstag took different views on armaments, constitutional reform and fiscal policy, and Bethmann Hollweg made little headway in establishing a dialogue. By 1917 he was willing to put forward more radical proposals for political reform, but by this time power had passed into the hands of the general staff and the war lords. Lacking their support, and having no mandate in the Reichstag, Bethmann Hollweg's resignation was inevitable.

Bethmann was in favour of keeping Britain content but was overruled by the kaiser whose generals and admirals were in favour of expanding the army and building up the Imperial Navy. The policy of building warships was particularly associated with Grand Admiral Alfred von Tirpitz, Secretary of State of the Imperial Navy Office from 1897 until 1916. Unfortunately for Bethmann Hollweg, the kaiser was enthusiastic about navies and sided with Tirpitz. Years later Wilhelm wrote:

I had a peculiar passion for the navy. It sprang to no small extent from my English blood. When I was a little boy … I admired the proud British ships. There awoke in me the will to build ships of my own like these some day, and when I was grown up to possess as fine a navy as the English.[5]

Despite differences of personality and emphasis, Wilhelm II's chancellors after Bismarck had two things in common:

- None had a party affiliation. They all ranged in general political sympathy between moderate Liberalism and Conservatism.
- None were anything like as powerful as Bismarck. Wilhelm II made sure of that.

The place of the Reichstag

According to the kaiser's biographer John Röhl, Germany under Wilhelm II concentrated power in the hands of the kaiser. Given his active enthusiasms and his often impulsive attitudes, Wilhelm II regarded the Reichstag as a barrier to his own autocratic power. Many of the elected Reichstag deputies increasingly resented his tendency to ignore the Reichstag and the Foreign Office. The October 1908 *Daily Telegraph* interview (see section 'Von Bülow') illustrates the point. This mistrust was reinforced by his unwillingness to support extra-parliamentary pressure groups such as the Pan-German League or the Navy League. Chancellor von Bülow described his role as being, 'the executive tool of His Majesty, so to speak, his political Chief of Staff'. This was clearly different from the roles played by Wilhelm I and Bismarck.

Wilhelm II was an active ruler, initiating legislation in a way that his grandfather never did. Tirpitz recognised that 'genuine enthusiasm among the people and therefore also among their parliamentary representatives is lacking for the vigorous development of our forces at sea'. But the fact that neither the voters nor the Reichstag were enthusiastic had little effect on the government: the Fleet Acts were pushed through the Reichstag.

This did not mean that the Reichstag could be ignored. The constitution gave it a role to play and chancellors had to know how to manage it. Bismarck had been able to gather conservative and liberal support when he needed it. Von Bülow similarly built up support in the Reichstag. In the 'Blue–Black Bloc' (1900–05) he brought together Conservatives and the Centre Party to ensure a majority would vote for the legislation the government presented to the assembled deputies. When he fell out with the Centre, he gathered Conservative, National Liberal and Left Liberal deputies into the 'Bülow Bloc' (1907–09). As the SPD gradually became stronger, so creating government majorities became harder. Von Bülow saw legislation voted down when the Centre and the SPD combined against him, forcing him to fight the 1907 election to get a more cooperative Reichstag. This issue became a permanent problem for Bethmann Hollweg who struggled to put together supportive majorities of deputies.

The struggle between autocracy and democracy

Tariff policies were a specific domestic issue between successive Imperial governments and the Reichstag. The Alliance of Rye and Iron of 1879, which had proved beneficial to the large landowners and industrialists, was replaced in 1902 by a new tariff law which restored high duties on imported grain. In social policy, the 1903 Sickness Insurance Law and the increasingly repressive measures taken against minorities from 1900 onwards, such as those of Polish origin in the east and French origin in the west, were both contentious social issues. These were the focus of the struggle between Imperial government and the Reichstag.

The growth of the SPD in the Reichstag to become the largest political party after the 1912 federal elections was another major factor in this struggle. By the outbreak of World War I in August 1914, divisions in German society were becoming much more marked.

The Navy League sought to get the German public to realise the importance of the Imperial Navy in an age of growing national strength and the acquisition of colonies overseas. It did this in many ways, through adventure books, magazines and cards to collect. The wearing of sailor suits by young boys became popular.

By the end of 1898 the League had some 30 000 fee-paying members and by the outbreak of war in 1914 it had around a million. It had by then become the largest pressure group in Germany and was very influential.

The 'Fleet Laws' issue was clearly an important element in the background to the outbreak of war in 1914. But it was also a telling example of the struggle between autocratic and democratic forces. American historian Isabel Hull has called Imperial Germany a 'thinly veiled **autocracy**', a military despotism designed to protect Prussian institutions – the monarchy, the Junker class and the army – from the forces of progress, including **industrialisation**, **urbanisation** and the rise of Social Democracy. In this struggle it was the task of government continually to convince industrialists and businessmen that their interests were better served in alliance with landowners and the court than with the growing working-class movement of the SPD. John Röhl however argues that although the kaiser was an ideological autocrat ('the sworn enemy of Liberalism, Democracy, Catholicism and Socialism'), it would be a mistake to regard Wilhelm II's rule as strictly autocratic. He could issue decrees and intervene at will in political decision-making. But despite its inadequacies as a parliamentary system, the forces of German democracy were gradually growing stronger, supported by economic change.

The development of parties and political opposition

The empire was not a unitary nation under either Wilhelm I or his grandson, and this division affected the way in which the Reichstag worked. Ethnic and national minorities had a small but influential presence in the Reichstag. The imperial government was responsible for defence, civil and criminal codes of law, customs, banking, coinage, communications and foreign policy. But individual states still preserved important rights, notably in direct taxation, education, justice, agriculture, local government and relations with the Church. Many deputies were reluctant to support centralising government initiatives as these took powers away from the regions which they represented. Deputies from ethnically or linguistically distinct areas were not sympathetic to government policy on Germanisation. However, the very diversity of opinion meant that it was difficult for the government's critics and opponents to create majorities in Reichstag votes.

Under the Anti-Socialist Laws (1878), socialist groups had been illegal and meetings to promote socialism had been banned, so when SPD members stood in local and national elections, they did so as independents. The socialists had only a small proportion of the vote in 1871 (just 3.2%). Following the lifting of the ban in 1890, however, and with the party re-launched as the SPD, the grouping's vote rose to 23.3% in 1893 and 39% in 1912.

August Bebel became a leading figure in the Social Democratic Movement and was President of the SPD from 1892 until his death in 1913. As a Reichstag member he was active in debates there. The party included both more and less radical members. One of the best known of the radicals was Rosa Luxemburg, who aligned herself with the party's left wing. In the 1910 elections, even the SPD moderate Gustav Noske responded to the Kaiser's claim of 'divine right' to rule by arguing for the monarchy's overthrow and the founding of a republic.

We should remember that, even when freed from the straitjacket of the Anti-Socialist Laws, the SPD's political power was not great. It could not prevent the Fleet Laws being passed. Later, it was unable to oppose the outbreak of the First World War, and the issue was so divisive that the party ended up splitting, with Luxemburg being among the minority that left to pursue a more radical anti-imperialism, anti-militarist agenda.

In addition to the SPD, there were a number of small but vigorous radical left-wing groups. These alarmed more conservative Germans because they brought back memories of the revolutions of earlier in the century. Accordingly, although the parties and associations on the Left had little effective power, Conservatives (and Liberals) were sufficiently afraid of them to support the government's repressive measures against the Left.

At the time of the 1871 Constitution, Germany's population stood at about 41 million people and there were 382 deputies in the Reichstag, increased to 397 in 1873. In the years that followed, the population grew to about 65 million by 1914, and large numbers left the rural areas for the towns and cities. However, the number of deputies remained the same and they represented the same constituencies. This meant that the countryside was increasingly overrepresented and the urban areas were increasingly underrepresented. Given that those were the areas where support for the Social Democrats was strongest, this meant that they were struggling with a constitution where they were systemically disadvantaged.

The government's attempts to destroy socialism failed and the Anti-Socialist Laws had been abandoned. The SPD built up a membership of one million people and, despite the disadvantages built into the German electoral system, by the First World War it was the largest party in the Reichstag.

Economic developments

Industrial expansion

Germany's economic history in the century before unification had been one of slow development. The economic historian Clive Trebilcock argues that Germany's growth was generally slow and quite uneven up to the 1850s in agriculture, industry, banking and foreign trade, leaving the country well behind her neighbours and competitors: France, the Netherlands and Britain.

However, from the 1850s Germany began to industrialise. The *Zollverein* (Customs union) of 1834 had unified the domestic market. The railways began to link the major cities to Germany's coal and iron centres. Canals were also being dug. All this assisted increasingly rapid growth.

Compared with Britain, for example, Germany came relatively late to industrial development. There were advantages to this. Factories were newly built full of the latest machinery and informed by the most up-to-date manufacturing thinking. There were few declining or redundant industries. Unification and industrial growth went hand in hand.

Industrial expansion was supported by a population explosion from about 41 million people in 1871 to about 65 million in 1914. Cities and larger urban areas experienced rapid growth in their size and population. Of course, this demographic change was not universal or evenly spread across Germany. Less happened in the north-east, in East Prussia and Pomerania, for example.

In contrast, rapid development and major social change occurred in the industrial areas in the west such as Westphalia, the Ruhr area and the Rhineland, Saxony in central Germany, the big cities such as Berlin and Hamburg, and also Bremen and Lübeck. In Hamburg, for example, the population tripled in little more than a generation, between 1875 and 1910.

These processes transformed Germany between 1871 and 1914 into a more densely populated country as well as a more urban one. Population growth led to more tax payers providing funds for the government, a bigger domestic market for manufactured goods and a rising standard of living for most people.

Old and new industries

Economic growth in the German states had been rapid in the 1850s and 1860s, especially in areas controlled by Prussia such as the Ruhr valley and the Saarland. After unification in 1871, the production of capital goods grew much more rapidly than did that of consumer items such as textiles.

The coal industry was already well established in Germany, with pits being sunk in the 18th century when coal seams were discovered near the Ruhr, Inde and Wurm rivers. Coal production saw a dramatic increase during the Kaiserreich from 30 million tons in 1871 to 60 million tons in 1889 and 190 million tons in 1913. For steel, an industry dependent on the availability of coal as well as iron ore, there was a similar spectacular increase, from 1.7 million tons in 1880 to 7.3 million tons by 1900. Merchant shipping also increased rapidly, from 1.5 million tons in 1880 to 2.6 million tons by 1900. This growth was good for major ports such as Hamburg but also suggests a lively and growing export and import trade. It was the same story for lignite and iron ore. Exports of manufactured goods also increased rapidly.

An unintended consequence was the increased dependence on migratory, especially foreign, workers. In areas of rapid growth, there were a lot of jobs available, which attracted people from different parts of Germany and from abroad. For example, Poles could be found working in the coal fields of the Ruhr. Whenever there were industrial disputes and strikes, Bismarck's first thought was that the migrant workers were behind them.

The rapid industrial growth was supported by an increasingly effective transport network. The railway system grew significantly: in 1880 there were some 29 270 miles of rail track but by 1900 that had grown to 34 800 miles. The improved transport allowed raw materials to be brought to factories and then manufactured goods to be taken from factories to customers. For innovative companies such as Carl Zeiss, the safe and secure transport of their delicate precision instruments could not be safely entrusted to bumpy roads. The Weimar–Gera railway was opened in 1876 linking Jena with Weimar some 25 miles away to the west, with further links to Frankfurt, Germany's largest transport hub.

Railway construction in turn supported the growing iron and steel industry. The railways need iron and steel for the construction of railway track, as well as the trains and rolling stock.

In addition, an enhanced railway network was an important strategic means for the military to be able to deploy troops rapidly across Germany. Many much smaller businesses also benefited – bakers, tailors and watchmakers, for example. It allowed for much better movement for ordinary people too, visiting relatives or

Hidden voices

Hamburg dockworkers

Hamburg was a prosperous, bustling city in north-west Germany. A port on the River Elbe, it was an embarkation place for both passengers and goods of all kinds. Its warehouses were usually full of imported goods and raw materials. For centuries it had been an important trading city, a leading member of that group of cities on the coast of Germany called the *Hansa*. It was a Free City (Freistadt), meaning that it wasn't part of one of the old duchies or kingdoms, and was independently minded. The busy docks provided plenty of jobs and as an important trading city it opposed any plans that might restrict exports and imports.

Hamburg's mayor in 1903 (and three times thereafter) was Johann Burchard, a typical member of a prominent Hansa banking family. (A fine picture of one of these patrician Hansa families can be found in Thomas Mann's novel *Buddenbrooks* (1901), which draws heavily on his own family in Lübeck, another Hansa city.)

He was born in Bremen, also a Hansa city, but had moved to Hamburg and was a Senator there from 1895 until his death in 1912. His family were not noble – that was not Hansa style – but they were influential, wealthy and well connected. In particular, Wilhelm II was a distant relative and Burchard acted as an advisor to the emperor on trade matters. He defended the independence of Hamburg but at the same time recognised the need for a unified Germany.

In the Hamburg Senate he supported universal education and believed that fine art should be accessible to all. Trade with Britain was important to Hamburg, so Burchard believed in maintaining good Anglo-German relations, agreeing in this policy area with Chancellor von Bülow.

In 1892 a serious outbreak of cholera occurred. Approximately 8000 died and a polluted sewage system was identified as the cause. This, combined with the rapid growth in the population of Hamburg, swelled by the **immigration** of Russian Jews, provided the necessary stimulus for reform. As a result, the city saw a period of major improvement to its systems. Burchard played his part in this as the city government diverted significant funds from trade to social need. A much improved sewage system, the provision of clean drinking water, better housing and new parks and other green spaces all transformed Hamburg into a far better place to live.

Figure 1.2: Hamburg dockworkers c. 1900.

Discussion point

Do you think that industrial growth in Germany 1871–1914 was caused by population growth? Or do you think the increasing population was itself the result of industrialisation?

going on shopping trips to a nearby town or city. The overall effect of all of this was a major contribution to the industrial growth in imperial Germany.

In Berlin, the construction of an underground railway network (*Untergrundbahn* or *U-Bahn*) began in 1896 and the first line was opened in 1902. This line ran from east to west under the city and linked Warschauer Brücke and Knie, with a branch to Potsdamer Platz. The provision of a rapid transport network in many German cities was a major factor in their growth in this period, allowing the development of suburbs linked to city centres so that workers could commute to work without having to negotiate busy and crowded streets.

Alongside the railways, an important stimulus to steel production in this period was Admiral von Tirpitz's drive to expand the navy. The construction of warships for the Imperial Navy took place at three *Kaiserliche Werft* (imperial shipyards): Wilhelmshaven, Kiel and Danzig, which worked exclusively on the construction and repair of warships. These naval shipyards became especially busy when the arms race with Britain to build Dreadnought-type battleships began in earnest in 1907. Apart from the large amount of steel involved, the powerful diesel engines required by these sorts of battleships helped to develop the engine-making business in Germany. Many jobs were created in the region and local supplies of all kinds were needed, stimulating demand in this part of the north-west coast of Germany.

Agriculture

Not all of Germany was caught up in industrial development. Of the country's 45 million people, about 25–27 million worked in agriculture and forestry. On the great landed estates of the areas east of the River Elbe, life went on in its own patriarchal way, little changed from feudal times. Progressive landowners adopted modern agricultural methods, with mechanisation, crop rotation, the use of fertilisers, new tools and selective breeding. But many less progressive ones stuck to the traditional practices, which were inefficient but which they knew and trusted. For those landowners who did adopt modern methods and so boosted production, there was a rapidly growing market in supplying the booming cities and towns with the products of their fields and woods.

 Hidden voices

Carl Zeiss

Among new concerns, perhaps the most spectacular growth was in the electrical and chemical industries, and in optics and precision instruments. A good example is Carl Zeiss of Jena.

This company was founded by the physicist and mathematician Ernst Abbe in 1889 and named after his friend, the lens-maker Carl Zeiss, who had died a year before. The company initially produced precision lenses for microscopes and later for cameras. It was also an innovator in glass manufacture. An unusual feature of the company was that the Carl Zeiss Foundation both owned and administered it. Their foundation document emphasised the social responsibility of the company to their workers and put their welfare at the heart of their commercial activities. This concern for workers' rights was ahead of its time – an innovation in labour relations to match the technical innovation of its precision products. Their workforce was highly skilled and trained, and loyal to the company that looked after them so well.

While stationed as an army reservist at the Hanseatic city of Greifswald in north-east Germany, Bismarck had studied agriculture at the town's university. He sympathised with the agrarian politics of the Junker class from which he came himself. Prussia's Junkers had almost a monopoly of power and influence in areas east of the Elbe. The army and higher civil service were dominated by their sons. They were strongly in favour of the monarchy and of **authoritarian** government and regarded themselves as the firm foundation of Prussia and Germany.

A major economic issue for them was the question of tariffs (import duties payable when foreign goods entered the country – something which naturally put up the price of imports). Under Bismarck, Prussia and then Germany had favoured free trade. After all, the unification of the empire had been preceded by a process of creating free trade across the region. The chancellor's allies in the Reichstag were supporters of free trade as the basis of German prosperity. However, the Junkers lobbied hard to protect the prices of their produce from cheaper overseas imports by having high tariffs and they used their considerable political influence to make sure they were introduced.

When the *Gründerkrise* (literally the 'founder crisis', meaning a crisis during the *Gründerzeit* or 'founding years') hit Germany, Bismarck distanced himself from the free-trade policies of his former Liberal allies. In 1879, in response to a well-organised political campaign against the threat to German farmers from cheap agricultural imports, he brought in tariffs to protect German agriculture from foreign competition.

When Bismarck presented the measure to the Reichstag, he naturally talked up its virtues in terms that the Junkers and others in the rural lobby would understand and omitted to mention the Liberal ideas. He asserted that it would lead to greater prosperity.

With the protection of a new tariff on imported grain, many German farmers also diversified and began to grow more root crops, including sugar beet. There was a move to more intensive farming and by 1914 German agriculture had become one of the most efficient systems in Europe. The process must not be exaggerated, however: many farms were small and relied on family members for labour.

Trade and wealth

The years following unification, 1871–73, saw rapid expansion in Germany. The liberalised laws on companies allowed a number of new businesses to be set up. Finance for industrial development after 1871 was mostly provided by giant German banks, such as the Deutsche Bank, the Dresdner Bank and the Berlin Handelsgesellschaft. These remained close to industrial concerns throughout the period. They often worked together in cartels and there were often bankers on the boards of major German companies.

The victory in the Franco-Prussian War created considerable social confidence, and payment of war **reparations** by the defeated France meant the arrival of new capital. The stock market saw increasing levels of speculation in the growth industries, including the rapidly expanding transport companies. The introduction of the new currency of the Goldmark put Germany on the gold standard. At the

Key term

Gründerkrise: German word meaning 'founder crisis'; an economic downturn during the Gründerzeit or 'founding years', the years immediately after the 1871 unification.

same time, however, abandoning silver currency caused a drop in the price of silver, which hit those countries whose silver currencies were suddenly worth less. Those countries' problems affected their neighbours and trading partners.

Of course, German expansion did not proceed at a steady pace. There was a major panic in 1873, part of an international crisis, leading to the *Gründerkrise*. This was the first major downturn to affect the German economy since increasingly rapid industrial development had begun in the 1850s.

Over-investment led to the collapse of finance houses. The unification euphoria was wearing off and the cyclical nature of even rapid economic growth was not well understood. In addition, bad economic news from the US began to affect European markets. In 1873, the Vienna Stock Exchange in Austria crashed, businesses went bankrupt and some banks failed. This reduced the ability of the banking system to lend money to industry. At the same time, France reached the end of her war reparations, which meant that another source of capital for Germany had been shut off. Far from expanding, the German economy now went into a period of contraction. The economic causes were not well understood and the period of difficulty increased anti-Semitism, as many small investors blamed the Jews for their losses in the crash.

There was a call for the protection of some German industries and Bismarck was keen to ensure that his supporters among the industrialists and landowners continued to feel secure. At the sight of the economy in difficulty, the chancellor responded by abandoning the principles of free trade which had helped keep the National Liberals as his allies. He established **protectionist** import tariffs instead. In doing so he found himself better able to call on more conservative parties such as the Centre Party for support, something which ending the *Kulturkampf* helped make possible.

Key term

Inflation: A process by which prices go up over time, making goods and services more expensive on a year-by-year basis.

The banking regulatory framework established by successive imperial governments was generally supportive of industrial expansion and of the banks that provided the necessary funding. The state sought to control the supply of money to the German economy through the Reichsbank, the central bank of imperial Germany. This was founded in 1876 and its first president was Hermann von Dechend, a senior Prussian civil servant. In the period from 1876 to 1914 the Reichsbank produced a stable currency called the Goldmark. Government expenditure was fairly constant in this period, with significant increases in social welfare expenditure (especially after the accession of Wilhelm II in 1888) being balanced by considerable cuts in military expenditure. There was little or no inflation, averaging at 0.48% per year from 1871 to 1914, and unemployment was low at 1–2%.

For much of the period, the prices of essential foodstuffs were fairly stable. As Germany was not able to grow enough food to feed her growing population, much depended on an efficient import system. This explains why not everyone was as in favour of tariffs as the agrarian lobbyists. The need to import meant that major ports such as Hamburg had to maintain the flow of imported agricultural produce. For the government, it was always a delicate balancing act to be fair to both farmers and consumers. Imposing import tariffs to protect producers from the competition resulting from cheaper overseas imports meant inevitably higher food prices in the shops. After Bismarck's fall from power in 1890, the protectionist tariffs were partly withdrawn.

There is some evidence that the power of the consumer was increasing at this time. There were a number of well-organised, disciplined and peaceful protests by consumer groups in the final years of the Kaiserreich but, unlike the more desperate food riots of the 18th century, there was no violence. In any case, these later protests were against the prices for meat and milk rather than that for bread.

For the majority of Germans, therefore, the Kaiserreich years were prosperous, stable ones. For most of the population this was in itself a vindication of authoritarian monarchic rule. But not for all, as witnessed by the growth of Social Democratic support.

There were always those on the margins of society in the Kaiserreich who did not benefit from increased social-welfare spending and who could only find jobs working at well below the minimum guaranteed wage. Their lives are seldom recorded. Nor do they often feature in official statistics. In the late 19th century a new trend in poverty alleviation became evident. Under Father Lorenz Werthmann the German Caritas Association was founded in south-west Germany. Independent of a government still cautious about the influence of the Catholic Church, it had two main aims: the national coordination of welfare efforts and research into a

Voices from the past

Eugen Gutmann

Eugen Gutmann (1840–1925) was a German banker and as such involved in the financing of German industry. He became the effective founder and chief executive of the Dresdner Bank. The bank was formed in the 1860s from a consortium of private banks and smaller finance houses but it was the unification of Germany in 1871 that provided the opportunity for exceptional economic growth. The banks of imperial Germany were essential to this growth, providing the necessary loans. This was inevitably a fairly risky business and some banks failed. Others, like the Dresdner Bank, flourished.

When Gutmann and his colleagues opened the doors of their bank in Dresden in December 1872 they were still a modestly sized provincial finance house. However, by acquisition, shrewd risk-taking and good management they emerged by the 1880s as the second largest bank in Germany, behind the mighty Deutsche Bank.

In 1884 the Dresdner Bank moved its headquarters from Dresden to Berlin, although the legal base remained in its home city. The Berlin branch was now

much larger than the original one in Dresden with its 30 employees. The bank continued to grow, opening a branch in London in 1895 and ten other branches throughout Germany. By 1900 it had 27 branches, the greatest number of branches of any bank in Germany, 23 being in Berlin. In 1905 a close relationship was formed with the large US bank J. P. Morgan, which allowed easier purchase of US securities by German investors. In the meantime, in 1899, the Gutmann family had converted from Judaism to Christianity.

Figure 1.3: Eugen Gutmann

science of charity. Alongside Protestant and non-denominational groups, Caritas set about addressing the needs of the most vulnerable portion of German society.

Social developments

The class hierarchy

Nobility and ruling class

It is remarkable that the German, especially Prussian, nobility was able to retain much of its traditional power when throughout Europe this was disappearing. It managed to survive the end of the Holy Roman Empire in 1806 and the revolutions of 1830 and 1848. Although this was the century of industrialisation, of Nationalism and Liberalism, the Imperial Court in Berlin was the centre of political authority in Germany. Even powerful figures such as Otto von Bismarck could not long survive imperial displeasure.

The nobility had dominated both the army and government and its bureaucracy in the princely states that made up most of the empire. Under Bismarck, a particular effort was made to appoint noblemen to key posts in government. In Prussia it was almost inevitable that the local representative of the national government (*Landrat*) be a local member of the nobility. The nobility took these leadership roles as of right, because they were the king-emperor's closest allies and supporters by virtue of birth, and their social position gave them the political authority to carry out the jobs' responsibilities.

This local control, especially in such areas as East and West Prussia, Mecklenberg, Silesia and Pomerania, ensured the continuation of traditional values. The longstanding social system was certainly paternalistic but shouldn't be dismissed as autocratic: it could include genuine concern for the welfare of the nobility's estate workers, for example.

Industrialisation, urbanisation, rapid population growth and the economic crisis of 1873 combined to threaten the status of the nobility. Nevertheless, the Prussian Conservatives, who took the lead in speaking politically for the rights of the nobility, were aided by the protection that Bismarck provided from competition from imports of cheaper foreign grain and by a tactical alliance with some leading industrialists – the coalition of 'Rye and Iron Alliance'. They managed to persuade a majority of the German population that the paternalistic values of the nobility were an important safeguard for the nation against the menace of disorder.

Middle classes

The middle classes were a large and varied group in German society. In general a distinct feature of the German situation was the apparent willingness of this group to accept the traditional influence of aristocratic and paternalistic norms of social behaviour. At the highest levels of the middle classes, there was an aspiration not to destroy the feudal powers of the nobility but to join that class, often through marriage. Meanwhile, industrialisation had brought great wealth to a few. So we can see that this transfusion of new blood and cash helps to explain the survival of the old nobility.

The middle classes had lived through rapid social, economic and political change. Unsurprisingly, the fear was that still further change would lead to disorder and even revolution.

As the Kaiserreich began to oversee more and more areas of daily life, the civil service in this period became ever more pervasive. Careers in this area, working for the state, had mostly been filled by persons of middle-class status. However, middle-class civil servants found it harder and harder to obtain the senior posts in the administration or the judiciary, which often went to those of noble origin. For the younger sons of the nobility, who had no prospect of inheriting a landed income, these posts offered a solid and secure income.

Academics, university professors and school teachers all counted as civil servants. This educated elite was determined to protect their social status and became increasingly nationalistic and imperialist as time went on. It was not uncommon for them to hold commissions in the army reserve, bringing them even closer to the prevailing militaristic trend of the times in the Kaiserreich. Included in this group were members of the liberal professions – lawyers and doctors, for example. They tended to vote for Conservative or right-wing Liberal political parties and

 Voices from the past

Maria von Bunsen

Maria von Bunsen was a young German noblewoman. She recorded her introduction at court for a ball in 1882 or 1883:

The following winter [1882–83] we experienced the court and the court balls. For the parents, it was a real exertion. But I am thankful to them for the sacrifice; a celebration like this at the Berlin court combined splendour, historical tradition, and a kind of fantastic beauty.

As far back as Unter den Linden, the column of carriages advanced slowly; at every stop there were benevolent or cheeky remarks from the packed crowd and excited constables on horseback. Diplomats and dignitaries had special passes, overtaking us on the side; such patronage annoyed the rest of us, as our coachmen had only the regular tickets attached to their hats. At last, we drove through the massive portal and found ourselves in the courtyard; the light barely allowed us to make out the deep grey of the walls, the mass of snow, the rows of palace guards. It was difficult to make any headway, but eventually the coach came to a halt in front of a brightly lit door; the carriage door was thrown open, and our own servant took the overcoats. Slowly we walked up the stairs and warmed ourselves in front of flickering fireplaces. A vast, magnificent series of halls opened up. They had not changed much over the centuries: walls covered with damask and featuring ancestors' portraits; heavy chairs, carved and gold-plated, dating from the time of the first king. Each door was guarded by two *Gardes du Corps*. They were specially chosen rich farmers' sons; the white and red uniforms spanned their marvellously built figures perfectly. Ladies rustled closely by, with diamonds on their bare shoulders; Excellencies walked by, with their stars and medal ribbons, but they [the *Gardes du Corps*] just stood there, massive and still, wearing their silver eagle helmets, their sabres drawn … [5]

Discussion points

1. In short, which aspects in particular does Maria von Bunsen particularly focus on? What do they suggest about the nature and significance of the event?
2. Von Bunsen notes the presence of different individuals and groups. She mentions diplomats, dignitaries, ladies and excellencies, but also constables, coachmen, palace guards, servants, the imperial bodyguard (*Gardes du Corps*) and finally the watching crowd. Make notes on what this mix tells us about Wilhelmine society.

were increasingly enthusiastic members of nationalist pressure groups such as the Navy League.

The state education system in Germany was extensive. Free elementary and secondary education was available to all, and there was generally a greater emphasis on science, mathematics and technology than was common in other European countries. The elite secondary schools, with their selective entry, were called 'gymnasia'. An extensive and established national network of universities catered for the brightest pupils. Some of these were old and prestigious; those at Heidelberg, Tübingen, Freiburg, Berlin and Munich had a worldwide reputation.

As well as people who had benefited greatly from industrialisation (such as Robert Bosch, Carl Zeiss or Werner Siemens), the middle classes included many people of more modest means. This group did not see themselves as a liberalising force in German politics and society. On the contrary, they enthusiastically accepted the autocratic government of the day and fully endorsed its aims.

The same is true for those still lower down the social scale. Artisans, small industrialists, shopkeepers, farmers, railway workers and others had all had their lives changed by the social and economic progress of the late 19th century. The railway was expanding fast and providing increasing employment. The first Prussian railway line was opened in 1838; the king, Wilhelm I, was unimpressed by the innovation. By the 1870s, however, when Bismarck was considering nationalising the system, it ran to over 17 500 miles. By the eve of the war in 1914, that distance had grown to over 35 000 miles of track. The postal service was another major employer, with responsibility for a growing network after 1890. The assumption by the state of responsibility for many aspects of life such as roads, lighting, drainage and social services provided additional employment.

 Voices from the past

Leonhard Tietz

Tietz's story illustrates well both the commercial opportunities of the period and the new freedom to buy consumer items from department stores.

Leonhard Tietz started business in 1879 with a single small shop in Stralsund (a small town in western Pomerania on the Baltic Sea) selling thread, woollen goods, trimmings and buttons. Focusing on high turnover on small profit margins and requiring cash payment, he prospered, forming a local cooperative to buy goods at a better discount. He was one of the first to offer a money-back guarantee for defective items. He expanded his market, opening a number of branches in the Rhineland: between 1899 and 1909 he opened 11 branches in western Germany and in 1891 moved his company headquarters to Cologne.

He always rented premises in the best parts of town and continued to sell haberdashery items.

In 1895 Tietz even built his own small electricity works, enabling him to have arc lights and plentiful lighting in his stores. They were brightly lit, exciting places to shop, even offering lifts to their customers free of charge. The saleswomen (there were few salesmen) wore black dresses and the German public flocked to the Tietz stores.

The range of goods for sale expanded and Tietz began to talk to some of the most famous architects of the day about designing new department stores. Inspired by a trip to Milan he constructed a gleaming store in the centre of Cologne, followed by another in Düsseldorf in the Ruhr. These large new buildings featured picture windows and his trademark bright lighting and were in the latest Art Nouveau style.

Women's rights

The women's rights campaign was in full flow in Germany during this period. The General German Women's Association had been formed in 1865 and campaigned for access to higher education (universities) and to the professions (lawyers, doctors, accountants and so on), for married women's property rights, for the reform of male sexual conduct and eventually for the vote (which they would achieve in 1919).

In 1894 the many groups of women's rights activists were amalgamated into the League of German Women's Associations. The first president of the League was Auguste Schmidt. By 1901 this umbrella organisation had some 70 000 members in 137 associations and by 1914 this had risen to 250 000. The Movement for Women's Rights certainly had an influence over policy and law-makers. In 1908 a Reich Association Law was introduced, giving women the right to engage in political activity. Before that time, women had been banned from political activity and attending public meetings, though in practice the law had not been consistently enforced and many women had been active even before the law was passed.

The introduction of the Civil Code or *Bürgerliches Gesetzbuch* in 1900 standardised all the rules across the German states. In many cases this worsened a woman's position over property, inheritance and parental rights. In particular, the husband had sole authority over children.

Kinder, Küche, Kirche (children, kitchen, church): these 'three Ks' were seen by many as the proper set of priorities for a woman. To this basic phrase '*Kaiser*', '*Keller*', '*Kammer*' and '*Kleider*' (emperor, cellar, room and clothing) were sometimes variously supplemented or substituted. The list clearly implies domesticity, with the addition of piety or patriotism.

The women's movement in Germany was mainly middle class in membership, as it was in many countries. Most working-class women lacked the time to attend rallies or meetings, being much more concerned with the daily struggle to survive. In Germany as in Britain the movement had a radical wing that tended to regard the policies of the leadership as too cautious. Also, as in Britain, political activity was suspended in 1914 with the outbreak of war.

Despite restrictions, the Kaiserreich contained a range of striking individuals that contradict our assumptions. Both Käthe Kruse and Leonhard Tietz showed entrepreneurial drive. Auguste Schmidt, first president of the League of German Women's Associations, demonstrated organisational flair. Alice Salomon was one of several social reformers. If you take these together, a picture of the Kaiserreich as a dynamic, reformist, socially mobile country emerges, far from the stereotype of a socially rigid, authoritarian and militaristic one that is sometimes presented.

Elitism and the culture of militarism

A marked feature of the Kaiserreich from 1871 until 1914 was the special status in society given to the army by all classes in Germany. This was in part because of earlier victories by the Prussian army over Napoleon I, then the defeat of the Austrians and finally (and crucially) that of the French in the Franco-Prussian War.

The latter victories had indeed been a driving force of German unification in 1871. But, in addition, what were seen as military virtues – discipline, order, obedience – were also what were deemed necessary by the majority for the security of the new state, unsettled as it was by strong population growth and rapid industrialisation.

Only the Social Democrats in the Reichstag opposed this special status. It is fair to say that, as the Social Democrat vote grew, so too did the numbers of voters who opposed **militarism**. However, even at their peak, just 4 million voted for the Social Democrats – substantial, but still a minority.

The 1871 Constitution fixed the size of the peacetime army at 1% of the population. The first emperor, Wilhelm I, regarded any oversight of the military budget by the Reichstag as an infringement of his royal powers but reluctantly conceded ineffective powers every seven years as proposed by Bismarck.

Prussian Junkers dominated the officer caste in the army. The Junker families of East Prussia felt that uniquely in Germany they represented the right sort of virtues that would ensure the survival and prosperity of the German nation. Their younger sons, those with little prospect of inheriting a landed estate, would often join the army instead. Even with the rapid military expansion in the years before 1914, when there were not enough younger sons of Junkers to be recruited, they still dominated the senior ranks and the most fashionable regiments.

Military service for three years was compulsory for all except those who were exempt for some reason. This service was seen as an opportunity to teach blind obedience to those in authority and to encourage monarchic feelings.

 Hidden voices

Käthe Kruse

Käthe Kruse was born in Breslau in 1883, the illegitimate daughter of the town's chief accountant and a local seamstress. She surmounted poverty and social exclusion, took acting classes and got a job at Berlin's Lessing Theatre in 1900. After touring under the stage name of Hedda Simon, she met the sculptor Max Kruse in 1902, becoming his partner. He already had four children by a previous marriage but he had three more with her.

Deciding that the mass-produced dolls available in shops were hideous, she began to make her own. In 1910 her dolls were first put on public sale at the local Tietz department store. With orders from the USA, she set up a workshop in Berlin and hired staff. By 1914 hers was an established name in the manufacture of dolls.

Figure 1.4: Käthe Kruse with some of her dolls c. 1955

Figure 1.5: German Cavalry Division 1912.

The Kaiser was Commander-in-Chief of the Imperial Army. However, under the 1871 Constitution, the Commander-in-Chief of the Bavarian army was the King of Bavaria and his forces only came under imperial direction in wartime. There was also a Minister of War but effective operational control was taken by the Chief of

Hidden voices

Alice Salomon

Another prominent social reformer of the Kaiserreich was Alice Salomon (1872–1948). She is best known as one of the founders of social work as a profession, for which she believed women were uniquely qualified. In many ways a traditionalist, she was appalled at what she saw as the corrosive effects of urban life and of the immorality that she saw all around her. A firm believer in marriage, she felt that the working environment for women was an unsuitable one.

From 1902 to 1906 she studied economics at the Friedrich Wilhelm University in Berlin. She went on to achieve a doctorate in 1908, with a final dissertation on pay inequality between women and men. The same year she opened a school for social work (Soziale Frauenschule) in Berlin. This pioneer of social work as a profession especially suitable for women developed her views despite her socially conservative opinions. She saw a need around her and had the determination to see her plans through.

Figure 1.6: Alice Salomon

the German General Staff. For 25 years this post was filled by one family: that of Moltke.

Field Marshall Helmuth von Moltke the Elder was Chief of the General Staff first for the Prussian army from 1857 to 1871, and then for the Imperial Army of the Kaiserreich from 1871 to 1888. He is usually credited with turning the army of Prussia into a modern, well-organised and successful fighting force, and with creating new methods for directing armies in the field.

Von Moltke defies the caricature of the Prussian army officer. Born in northern Germany as the son of a Danish army officer, he survived relative poverty and joined the Prussian army in 1822, rising rapidly in the military hierarchy. He was a cultured man, loving opera, poetry, art and theatre; he also spoke seven languages. He became something of a literary celebrity when his book on his Turkish travels was published in 1840. He was a fierce nationalist and no Liberal. Shocked by the disorder of the 1848 revolutions, he was loyal to the King of Prussia and then to the German emperor. Von Moltke's success in beating the French in the Franco-Prussian War (1870–71) ensured his enduring reputation as a brilliant military leader.

His nephew, Helmuth von Moltke the Younger, was Chief of the Imperial General Staff from 1906 until the outbreak of war in 1914. On the death of his uncle in 1891 he became aide-de-camp to Wilhelm II and so a member of the imperial inner circle. Critics alleged that he only obtained the post of Chief of the General Staff in 1906 on the death of Alfred von Schlieffen because of his name and personal friendship with the kaiser.

In 1914 von Moltke had a disagreement with the kaiser, who had been told that Britain might not be a combatant, thus allowing Germany to concentrate her forces against Russia on the Eastern Front. This turned out to be a false interpretation of the British position but the kaiser had already instructed von Moltke to change his carefully laid mobilisation plans at the last minute and send almost all his forces east. Von Moltke refused but, even though the kaiser later relented when his advice about British intentions turned out to be incorrect, von Moltke had become ill and resigned his post in September 1914, to be replaced by Erich von Falkenhayn.

Army links with Germany's rapidly developing industrial base were strong ones, ensuring the continuity of supply and exploitation of the latest technical innovations for military use. These links included powers to regulate the availability of credit to industry, the supply of raw materials and even control over patents for new technologies. The importance of the growing railway network for the rapid deployment of troops was not forgotten and every army corps had a trains unit that specialised in rail transport. This integration of the military and the industrial was a central element in late 19th-century German social and economic development and a key aspect of its militarism.

To a large extent, the organisation of the army reflected the organisation of society. Before the 1890s, recruitment to the officer corps was dominated by the sons of Junkers. Although social class and rank were thus closely connected, by 1900 the upper ranks of the army were open to talented officers who were neither

Junkers nor from the nobility. This was particularly true of those areas which were less fashionable, such as the engineers and the artillery.

The armed forces were supported by a nationwide system of reserve forces that could be mobilised quickly. Every young man was drafted into the army at the age of 18.

The condition of the working people

The rapid industrialisation of the period meant a large increase in the workforce. This in turn created a growth in the membership of trade unions, from 344 000 in 1891 to over 3 000 000 by 1914. Such an increase – nearly tenfold – indicates both the speed and the extent of industrialisation. It also suggests that the workforce wanted to have protection and people to negotiate on their behalf with employers. Not many workers could rely on benevolent employers as could the workers at Carl Zeiss in Jena. In general, though, employers in imperial Germany accepted that the best work could only be done by a reasonably contented workforce and the increasing power and influence of the trade unions was not lost on employers.

Rapid industrialisation in many parts of Germany in the last decades of the 19th century also resulted in increasing support for left-wing parties, suggesting a growth in working-class political consciousness. It may also have been a natural response to the hostility of the government and society, especially in conservative rural areas.

Kaiser Wilhelm II took a personal interest in improving working conditions. Soon after he came to the throne in 1888, he disagreed sharply with Bismarck when the chancellor proposed sending troops against striking coal miners in Silesia. He was also supportive of his chancellor's social-welfare legislation in the 1880s. Government involvement in many aspects of everyday life was apparent. Certainly the annual government budget for the provision of social welfare to include education, health and insurance rose markedly during the Kaiserreich.

The working class in imperial Germany is less well documented and less thoroughly studied than the monarchy, nobility and even middle classes. This is not surprising as the lives of ordinary people rarely leave a mark as individuals. As a class, the working people were kept relatively stable and secure because of the development of trade unions, stable food prices and high employment, low inflation and increased social-welfare spending. Nevertheless, rapid industrialisation brought unsettling major social change.

Organised labour did not function to any extent in rural areas and the traditional employment of domestic service (still a major source of employment at this time) was also almost entirely un-unionised. It should not be forgotten that German serfs were only freed in the late 18th and early 19th centuries, and rural labourers and smallholders remained the largest social group in Germany until the 1890s. This group experienced the unsettling twin effects of the largest population increase in Germany and an ever-increasing flight from the land. Many migrated to the fast-growing cities.

Employment opportunities for women were limited in the Kaiserreich. The coal and steel industries employed no women on the shop floor, nor were women to be

Speak like a historian

Corelli Barnett

The leading military historian Corelli Barnett explains about the Prussian army reserve system that became the system for the German Imperial Army after 1871:

the Prussian system … was based on service of only three years with the colours … and four years in the reserve. The Prussian standing army had become simply a training cadre for the intake of conscripts. The Prussian armies' organisation for peace and war was virtually the same. Prussia was divided into army-corps districts for the purposes both of administration and of recruitment. On the outbreak of war the command organisations of the district became that of a corps in the field. 'Localisation' of the Army and its recruitment gave the districts pride and interest in their 'own' corps.[7]

Discussion points

1. What does the organisation of the army tell you about the structure of the German state and society?
2. What do you see as the strengths and weaknesses of the system Corelli Barnett describes?

seen on the dockside in Hamburg or other major ports in Germany. However, they remained important contributors to agriculture because many farms were worked by families.

Huge increases in the vote for the Social Democrat Party, the main political voice of the working class, and a spectacular increase in trade union membership between 1893 and 1914 cannot hide the fact that a majority of the population from all classes still supported a traditional society for Germany with its strict moral code and militaristic preference.

The political, economic and social condition of Germany by 1914

At the end of June 1914, the heir to the imperial throne of Austria-Hungary was assassinated. Archduke Franz Ferdinand was shot by a Serb nationalist while visiting Bosnia's capital, Sarajevo. This act of **terrorism** set off a series of political developments which led to increasing diplomatic tension. Russia mobilised its forces: as the process was old-fashioned and inefficient, it took so long to get an army ready that mobilisation had to start early if Russia were not to be defeated before it had even put an army in the field. As mobilisation was tantamount to a declaration of war, Austria-Hungary mobilised defensively. Germany, Austria's ally since the change of diplomatic tack under Caprivi, mobilised – and so it went on. War went rapidly from being unthinkable to inevitable.

August 1914, when the first shots of the war were fired by armies, found a Germany which was unusual in Europe, in that it:

Speak like a historian

Golo Mann

The historian Golo Mann was the son of the novelist Thomas Mann. He argued that the social analysis of Karl Marx is of little use to an understanding of the society of the Kaiserreich:

It was simply not true in the age of Bismarck, in the age of William [Wilhelm] II, that German society consisted of a very few capitalists and very, very many wretched proletarians.[8]

Discussion point

Conduct some research into German society in this period. How well does a division of it into capitalists and proletarians describe the structure of society? Make notes on the ways in which this division is useful, and the ways in which society was different from that two-part structure or more complicated than it suggests.

- had been unified as the result of a military victory only a generation earlier
- had a strongly growing population
- was undergoing rapid industrialisation and urbanisation
- retained a traditional and paternalistic social structure.

It was confident, wealthy and stable with an effective national consensus, a large and well-trained army, and a strong militaristic tradition.

It should also be noted that social welfare was relatively well developed in the Kaiserreich and that the state took over responsibility for many aspects of everyday life. Insurance schemes were also promoted and, in general, with steadily rising wages, the subjects of the kaiser were materially well off.

In the 1870s and 1880s Germany had acquired colonies in east and west Africa, as well as in the Pacific, as befitted the world's second-largest trading nation. Tirpitz's Navy Bill of 1898 had set in train a major expansion of the Imperial Navy and identified Britain as the main rival and likely enemy. The building of 19 pre-Dreadnought Wittelsbach class battleships had been approved but, following the outbreak of the **Second Boer War** in October 1899, a second Navy Bill had doubled the number of new battleships to 38. By 1914 German naval expenditure was £20 million (Britain's was about £45 million at the same time).

The naval building programme was hugely popular in Germany. The Navy League – formed to popularise the idea of world naval power for Germany – had 78 000 members in 1898 and 600 000 in 1901. By 1914, 1.1 million people were part of the League.

Rapid expansion had also taken place in the army, with the military budget more than doubling from 1910 to 1914. Germany was able to mobilise more than 13 million men in the summer of 1914.

In general, the war had wide popular support. Departing soldiers were given an enthusiastic send-off and some troops put flowers in the muzzles of their rifles. Confidence in victory was high:

- Germany (largely in the form of Prussia) had a record of beating its enemies, including defeating the French in two wars in the 19th century.
- The German economy was strong.
- The German army was powerful.
- Germany had become the world's second trading nation after Britain.
- Germany's population of around 65 million was larger than that of France or Britain.

This was not the case for all, however. The revolutionary left-wing analysis of events was clear: the war (like all wars) was driven by the ruling class and the capitalist system; the workers (who had nothing to gain from it) would be ordered to shoot one another when they would do better to shoot their bosses. In principle, the Socialist movement in all countries opposed the war. In fact, the different national parties tended to support their own country.

Rosa Luxemburg was still politically active. For some years she had believed that the workers of all countries should unite in opposition to the war that she feared was coming to Europe. When war broke out in August 1914, however, the SPD supported the government, much to Luxemburg's dismay.

A radical colleague of Luxemburg was Karl Liebknecht. The son of one of the 1875 SPD leaders, he had abstained when the SPD first voted in favour of funds for the war, and then became the only member of the Reichstag to vote against the war in 1914. Liebknecht had already been imprisoned for his campaigning. His pamphlet *Militarismus und Antimilitarismus* (*Militarism and Antimilitarism*) had brought him an 18-month jail sentence; while still serving his term, however, he was elected to the Prussian *Landtag* (parliament). He joined the Reichstag in 1912. Despite opposing the war, he did not vote against the granting of war loans on 4 August 1914 but abstained in order that the SPD vote should not be divided. Four months later, on 2 December 1914, he did vote against further loans; he was the only member of the Reichstag to do so. This level of unity (despite the doubts held by a number of individual deputies) says a great deal about the state of Kaiserreich politics.

Luxemburg organised an anti-war strike in Stuttgart and, with Liebknecht and others, founded the Spartacus League (Spartacus was the gladiator in ancient Rome who led a revolt against the government). The league published a newspaper, which was quickly declared illegal. Luxemburg also campaigned against conscription and urged soldiers to disobey orders. Both she and Liebknecht were put in prison for their political activities but, even so, Rosa Luxemburg continued to argue against the war.

Voices from the past

Rosa Luxemburg

Rosa Luxemburg was born in 1871 in the Russian-controlled part of Poland. She joined the left-wing Polish Proletarian Party 15 years later, the start of a lifetime career as a radical political activist. She had to flee to escape detention in 1889 and went to Switzerland, where she attended Zurich University, studying economics and politics. In 1898 she married Gustav Lübeck, obtaining German citizenship and moving to Berlin. She joined the Social Democratic Party (SPD), aligning herself with its left wing. She was critical of what she felt was its conformist parliamentary approach. She taught Marxism and economics at the SPD training school in Berlin and met Lenin in London in 1907.

Her 'Junius' pamphlet of 1915 was written in prison. (Lucius Junius Brutus was the founder of the Roman Republic.) In it she called for an immediate end to the fighting:

> The world war serves neither the national defence nor the economic or political interests of the masses of the people whatever they may be. It is but the product of the imperialist rivalries of the capitalist classes of the different countries for world hegemony and for the monopoly in the oppression and exploitation of areas still not under the heel of capital.[9]

Luxemburg and her associate Liebknecht were both murdered in the brutal suppression of the Spartacist Revolt in Berlin in January 1919.

Figure 1.7: Rosa Luxemburg c. 1900.

Discussion point

Luxemburg uses a lot of political vocabulary in this short passage. Make a list of the technical terms, define them and see how they apply to the specific situation of August 1914.

German mobilisation had begun by January 1914 and made use of 11 000 trains. The railways had been factored into the German High Command's 'Schlieffen Plan' (named after Count Alfred von Schlieffen, the head of the German General Staff in 1905) for war with France. Their use is a reminder of the military significance of Germany's massive railway expansion of recent decades. The process was a complex one but was made easier by the fact that Germany (unlike Britain) had been conscripting its young men into the army for some time. The country also had a well-developed system of trained army reserves to call on.

Annotate the timeline, adding brief comments on the significance of the events.

Timeline

1871	Creation of the German Empire
	Introduction of new constitution
	Federal elections
	Pulpit Law passed
1872	Jesuits banned
1873	May Laws passed
	Creation of a national currency, the Goldmark
	Gründerkrise
1874	Federal elections
1875	Congregation Laws passed
1876	Language of Government Act
	Reichsbank (central bank of imperial Germany) founded
1878	Two attempts to assassinate Wilhelm I
	Anti-Socialist Laws passed
1879	Introduction of tariffs to protect German agriculture from foreign competition
1883	The state begins to provide a sickness benefit
1884	Accident Insurance Law passed
	Wilhelm I lays foundation stone of Reichstag building
1886	Government decides to let temporary exceptions to the Language of Government Act lapse
1887	Government abolishes use of Polish for teaching
1888	Death of Wilhelm I
	Accession and death of Friedrich
	Wilhelm II becomes kaiser aged 29
1889	Old-age pension scheme introduced for workers aged 70 or over
1890	Resignation of Bismarck after 30 years as Prussian then German chancellor
	General Leo von Caprivi appointed
	Wilhelm II and Caprivi do not renew the Reinsurance Treaty with Russia
	Anti-Socialist Laws lifted
	Social Democrats re-launched as the SPD

1894	Caprivi dismissed
	Chlodwig, Prince of Hohenlohe appointed chancellor
	Reichstag moves into new home
1898	German Navy League founded
	Tirpitz presents the First Fleet Act to the Reichstag
1900	Second Fleet Act doubles the number of new battleships
	Hohenlohe resigns
	Bernhard, Prince von Bülow appointed chancellor
1908	*Daily Telegraph* affair
1909	Von Bülow resigns
	Theobald von Bethmann Hollweg appointed chancellor
1913	Death of August Bebel
1914	Reichstag votes to grant war loans
	Germany mobilises
	Outbreak of First World War

Practice essay questions

1. To what extent did any of the Chancellors after 1890 exercise the authority that Bismarck had exercised?
2. To what extent was the increasing support for socialist groups caused by rapid industrialisation in Germany from 1890?
3. 'The growth of the railway system was the key economic development in Germany in the two decades following unification.' Assess the validity of this view.
4. With reference to these extracts and your understanding of the historical context, which of these two extracts provides the more convincing interpretation of the issue of reform in the Kaiserreich?

Extract A

Bismarck is reported to have said, 'the citizen who has a pension for his old age is much more content and easier to deal with than one who has no prospect of any'. He also remarked sometime after the social insurance scheme had been introduced that his 'idea was to bribe the working classes'. Clearly, when Bismarck introduced social reform legislation in the early 1880s, it was not his intention solely to improve the working and living conditions of the workers. Rather, he was additionally concerned to maintain the stability of the system, and head off the threat of unrest, by showing that the state could offer more to the workers than the Social Democrats could. He was implacably opposed to measures such as reducing the length of the working day, restricting female and child labour, and imposing a minimum wage since such reforms, though undeniably of benefit to the workers, would have alienated the industrialists upon whom Bismarck relied for support. The reforms implemented in the 1880s were hailed as progressive by other industrial nations but in practice they were of limited value.

Source: Abrams, Lynn, *Bismarck and the German Empire, 1871–1918*, Routledge, 2006

Extract B

Would it have been possible, for instance, to reintegrate the industrial workers into state and society with pomp and ritual rather than with genuine political reform? Was not the dynastic cult propagated by the Kaiser – the cult of 'Wilhelm the Great' the 'Hero Emperor' – the least appropriate method for winning over to the Hohenzollern monarchy the Catholic third of the population or the Bismarckian or democratically oriented middle classes? What is certain is that, given the exposed position into which it thrust itself, each and every setback, whether at home or abroad, represented a direct threat to the very survival of the monarchy. And with it the whole of court society ran the risk of losing 'everything' too.

Source: Röhl, John C.G., *The Kaiser and His Court: Wilhelm II and the Government of Germany*, Cambridge University Press, 1996

Chapter summary

You should now understand the means by which the German Empire came into being and the consequences for the nature of that empire, the roles played by the two emperors, Bismarck and other chancellors, and the way in which the country's society and economy were changing. You have learned that:

- following victory in the Franco-Prussian War, a new German Empire is declared in 1871
- it has a constitution and a national assembly (Reichstag), but democratic control over government is weak
- politics is dominated by the chancellor Bismarck, from the state's foundation to his resignation in 1890
- while Wilhelm I is content to govern through his chancellor and supports Bismarck, his grandson wants to be more directly involved in decision-making and has five chancellors in the pre-1914 period
- the country undergoes rapid economic growth, with industrialisation and urbanisation, but the increasing wealth is hit by more than one economic crisis, of which that of 1873 is the most famous
- growth brings prosperity to many in the middle and working classes but the class hierarchy is unchanging and society is strongly affected by Prussian militarism.

End notes

[1] *The diary of Hildegard von Spitzemberg.*

[2] Steinberg, Jonathan, *Bismarck: A Life*, Oxford University Press, 2012

[3] Steinberg, *Bismarck: A Life*

[4] Title page of August Bebel's booklet *Die Frau und der Sozialismus (Woman and Socialism),* 1879

[5] Kaiser Wilhelm II, autobiography, *My Early Life*

[6] Bunsen, Maria von, *The World I Used to Know,* Thornton Butterworth, 1930

[7] Barnett, Corelli, *Britain and Her Army 1509–1970: A Military, Political and Social Survey,* Faber and Faber, 1970

[8] Mann, Golo, *The History of Germany since 1789,* Pimlico, 1996

[9] Luxemburg, Rosa, *'Junius' pamphlet,* 1915

2 Empire to democracy, 1914–29

In this section, we will be studying how Germany began the First World War a stable monarchy but ended it a republic in the middle of a revolution. The republic then had to survive a number of attempts to seize power, frequent changes of government and a period of hyperinflation. We will look into:

- Political authority: the political impact of the First World War on Germany; political change and breakdown by 1918; the 1918 revolution; the establishment of democratic government in the Weimar Constitution
- Government and opposition to 1924: post-war political problems; attempted coups and the opposition of Left and Right; the working of the Weimar government; its strengths and weaknesses
- Government and opposition, 1924–29: the impact of the Ruhr invasion and the leadership of Stresemann; degree of governmental change; the degree of opposition
- Economic developments: the impact of war; post-war economic problems and policies; reparations; hyperinflation; Dawes and Young Plans and foreign loans; industrial growth; agriculture
- Social developments: the effect of war on German society; social and cultural changes in Weimar Germany
- The political, economic and social condition of Germany by 1929.

Political authority

The political impact of the First World War on Germany

The First World War began amid an atmosphere of apparent national unity. The parties in the Reichstag either supported the war or at least did not oppose it. The British historian Benjamin Ziemann argued in a recent book that Germans believed their country to be facing what a popular slogan of the time called a 'world of enemies'. The politics of the day became less a matter of debate and more one of emotions, excitements and promises; many people (and their political leaders) accepted the ideas of sacrifice and fate.

Even the Social Democratic Party (SPD) voted in the Reichstag to approve military expenditure. In 1914 the party split. Most members and representatives stayed within the SPD and were prepared to support the Kaiser and his government in wartime, but a faction would not do so. They left the SPD to form the Independent Social Democrats or *Unabhängige Sozialdemokratische Partei Deutschlands* (USPD) and remained opposed to the war throughout.

Friedrich Ebert was the SPD co-chairman during the war. He was on the moderate side of the SPD and when he was General Secretary in 1905 had declared 'I hate revolution like mortal sin'. A more radical member was Karl Liebknecht, the only member of the Reichstag to vote against the war in 1914 and the son of one of the 1875 SPD leaders. It was he and others who thought the same way, including Rosa Luxemburg, who founded the USPD.

Their ablest spokesman in the Reichstag, Philip Scheidemann, declared that defending the country from attack was consistent with the party's principles. In effect a party political truce (called the ***Burgfriedenspolitik***) was agreed: political parties agreed not to criticise the government or the war. In addition, the trade unions agreed to the cessation of industrial action: there would be no strikes during the war.

The SPD had more than one reason for agreeing to this arrangement:

- They were patriotic Germans and genuinely felt that they had a responsibility to support the government and the troops in wartime. The party's co-chairman Hugo Haase, who had been organising anti-war demonstrations as recently as June 1914, declared: 'We will not desert our fatherland in its hour of need.'
- Many of them had lived through one period of repression during the Anti-Socialist Laws and no doubt didn't want to take the SPD back to being banned. Ebert's first action on the outbreak of war was to move party funds to Switzerland and lay plans for the SPD to operate from outside Germany in the event of it being made an illegal organisation again.
- The war was often represented in Germany as a struggle between a moderate and liberal Germany with a constitutional monarch and an autocratic Russian Tsar with no constitutional controls on his actions. Clearly, given the choice, the SPD would want to support the kaiser and the democracy of the 1871 Constitution.
- They hoped that having proved themselves responsible, reasonable and patriotic, they would be well placed after the war to take forward their campaign for further reform and greater democratisation.

ACTIVITY 2.1

How important do you think the 1914 split in the SPD was? What consequences did it have *at the time*?

Tackle the second question first by creating a list of consequences. Then add comments to each item on the list, explaining what it was, why it happened and what its significance was. Use the analysis in the comments to tackle the first question.

- They feared that their own natural supporters would regard them as unpatriotic and that they would lose support.

Like their Reichstag representatives, Germans appear to have supported the war when it came in 1914. The German historian Heinrich August Winkler cautions us not to assume universal support, however: there was little evidence of a 'widespread nationalist patriotism amongst social democratic workers.' Nevertheless, Wilhelm II and his government's decisions were barely questioned at this point, let alone challenged. The Social Democrat split in 1914 was an early sign of divided opinion in Germany, but few would have seen that at the time.

Chancellor Bethmann Hollweg was naturally delighted with the attitude of the SPD and as part of the *Burgfriedenspolitik* took the opportunity to bring them closer into the wartime government. He had tried to avert war in 1914 and, as his pre-war foreign policy had been based on being pro-British, was surprised and disappointed when Britain declared war on Germany in defence of Belgian neutrality. The Conservatives, meanwhile, were less than delighted to see the closer ties between the chancellor and their left-wing rivals in the Reichstag.

At the beginning of the war, the imperial government had formulated no war aims. The result was the development of a 'war aims' movement. In widely circulated pamphlets, a campaign was mounted to give the country a rallying point, and the troops at the front a sense of higher purpose. The argument was that the war should bring together all German-speaking peoples and bring major territorial gains to the empire. Unsurprisingly, the campaign was backed by nationalists, especially the **pan-Germanists**.

The movement was supported by a powerful collection of prominent national pressure groups:

- Central Association of German Industrialists
- German Countrymen's Federation
- Farmers' Federation
- Association of the German Middle Classes.

Some had particular reasons for defining war aims. Alfred Hugenberg, for example, the chairman of the Supervisory Board of Krupp of Essen, Germany's leading arms manufacturer and steel producer, was keen on the seizure of Normandy in France because of the deposits of iron ore there. Many wanted security for Germany from Britain by the command of the Channel coasts down to the river Seine, which in 1914 was Belgian territory.

The Conservative Party was cautious about these pan-German war aims but came to accept something similar. So too did the National Liberals under Gustav Stresemann and also the Centre Party.

The Social Democrats did not participate in the war-aims campaign. Scheidemann made clear that, while national self-defence was something the SPD could support, a war of conquest was not. Annexations and offensive war aims were unacceptable. Bethmann Hollweg hovered uneasily between a 'German Peace' as proposed by the war aims party and a compromise, which became known as a 'Scheidemann Peace'.

The chancellor's position was difficult:

- The party political (and matching industrial) truce was intended to draw all sides together but in the end alienated both Left and Right.
- The military became a more powerful voice as the conflict carried on.
- Discontent at home mounted as casualties increased alarmingly.
- Wilhelm II himself was increasingly seen by the public as a marginal figure.
- The most prominent military leaders, Hindenburg and Ludendorff, became household names.

The army chief of staff, General Erich von Falkenhayn, was replaced by General Paul von Hindenburg in August 1916, following the failure of the major assault on the French forces defending Paris at Verdun early that year. The new man demanded change.

In particular, in 1917 Hindenburg and General Erich Ludendorff, Quartermaster General of the army, wanted to remove all restrictions on which ships their submarine commanders could attack. Until then US ships had been safe from attack, but Generals Hindenburg and Ludendorff felt that this restriction damaged the war effort and they argued strongly that all restrictions be removed. Bethmann Hollweg disagreed but he was overruled, a measure of increasing military and declining civilian political influence in Germany during the 1914–18 war. Early 1917, all restrictions on targets were lifted for German submarines. This may have been operationally more efficient but it was a decision with important consequences. American ships were sunk in the North Atlantic and, as Bethmann Hollweg had feared, the USA entered the war in April 1917.

This was a humiliation for Bethmann Hollweg and he resigned as chancellor in July 1917. Hindenburg and Ludendorff suggested first the former chancellor Bernhard von Bülow and then the former naval minister Admiral von Tirpitz but the kaiser refused both. Their third suggestion was a civil servant called Georg Michaelis, so obscure an individual that the kaiser wasn't entirely clear who he was. Michaelis thus became the first person to hold the office of chancellor who was not from the nobility.

This resignation and new appointment point to the political changes brought about by the war. Combined with the fading in political authority of the kaiser in favour of military leaders, they amount to a major shift in the structure of German politics. State governments and even the imperial central government dwindled in the face of the growing power of the military High Command.

For the imperial general staff, a key virtue of Michaelis as chancellor was that he had little real support in the Reichstag, making him dependent on the army. However, this political isolation meant that, as crises mounted, the Reichstag demanded his resignation and after only a few months he was out of office again.

His successor, Georg Friedrich Graf von Hertling, was a Rhineland politician from the Centre Party; indeed, he was the first party politician to hold the job of chancellor. He was therefore the first chancellor to have a political base in the Reichstag (he also held the post of Prussian prime minister, something chancellors

ACTIVITY 2.2

Do you think that the *Burgfriedenspolitik* built on elements already in the Kaiserreich system or was it an innovation?

Draw up a table with two columns. In the left-hand column, write down the ways in which the wartime party-political truce was a natural development of existing German practice; in the right-hand column list the ways in which it was a new departure.

consistently did). This was another indicator of change in the way that government was conducted.

The politics of wartime inevitably meant full employment and the economy accordingly benefited. However, the **blockade** by the British Royal Navy badly disrupted German exports of manufactured goods, on which so much depended. The 18 Dreadnought-class battleships that Admiral von Tirpitz had been so determined to build for the Imperial German Navy stayed in Kiel harbour and only left port to confront the British Navy once, when in 1916 they fought the inconclusive Battle of Jutland (*Skagerrak schlacht*).

Like its military and political leaders, German civilians and soldiers had largely expected a war lasting a matter of weeks or months at most. As the years went by, the stresses on German society became more and more marked. A characteristic of pre-war imperial Germany had been the elevation of the kaiser to the pinnacle of German society. As the war went on, the power of Wilhelm II faded to be replaced by the new military heroes – Hindenburg and Ludendorff – after 1916. Indeed, the army retained and even enhanced its prestige through the war until, perhaps, late 1918.

Political change and breakdown by 1918

By 1918 Germany was a changed country; the flag-waving of 1914 was now a distant memory.

Imperial German society had been consistently trained to be orderly and obedient to authority, and this discipline was largely maintained in the army. The civilian population was another matter. As the war dragged on, people at home became increasingly weary of deprivation, rationing and standing in queues. Civilians were increasingly bitter and more willing to listen to the political radicals who in August 1914 had commanded so little support or attention. In 1917 there were several strikes, supported reluctantly by the trade unions, for better conditions at work. In August 1917, there were mutinies at the naval centre of Wilhelmshaven; the authorities responded by executing the supposed ringleaders. (This had been part of the background to Michaelis's forced resignation.) For the SPD, the political truce of 1914 was ever harder to sustain.

As the military situation deteriorated, von Hertling resigned the chancellorship. Once again, the generals advised the Kaiser on the appointment of a new chancellor. Following the first commoner and the first Reichstag party politician, the new appointment might have looked like a return to Hohenzollern governmental normality. Maximilian von Baden was a prince from the Grand Ducal House of Baden, and related to the Russian tsars and Napoleon's imperial dynasty. He had been considered as a husband for Queen Victoria's granddaughter who went on to marry Tsar Nicholas II. In fact, this time the appointment was that of the first Liberal. Perhaps unsurprisingly, Wilhelm II twice refused to make the appointment and it was only the support of the generals for the candidature that persuaded him.

Not content with the appointment of a prominent Liberal, Ludendorff also urged increased democracy, with a government based on the representation of the political parties in the Reichstag.

Had Ludendorff undergone a conversion to democratic values? On the contrary, his real purpose was all too transparent:

- The German High Command hoped to shift responsibility for the impending defeat onto a civilian government. This would allow them to claim that an undefeated army had been let down by civilian politicians.
- Although a Liberal himself, von Baden was known to have links to the Social Democrats. Ludendorff wanted to see a range of political parties drawn into government in order to spread the blame across all politicians, especially the Liberals and Socialists.
- The intention was also to look as democratic and reformed as possible to make the Americans favourable to a negotiated peace. Ludendorff believed that President Woodrow Wilson of the USA might be more receptive to an approach from a democratically constituted government.

Ludendorff was the driving force behind this attempt to shift any blame for the defeat. In a recent book, the German historian Manfred Nebelin describes him (as others have done) as a military dictator, the most powerful man in Germany in 1917 and 1918.

In 1917 the German High Command had advised that, especially with the arrival of US troops on the Western Front, Germany's military situation had become hopeless. Despite this, they continued with a business-as-usual policy, as though all was still in good order. As late as October 1918 (the very month of the appointment of von Baden) they sent new drafts of conscripted German soldiers to the front, even though they knew that the war was lost.

Meanwhile, the new chancellor accepted his largely thankless task, included Social Democrats in his cabinet and entered negotiations with the USA in an attempt to get the most reasonable peace terms possible. Domestically, he announced an amnesty for political prisoners. Among those released was Karl Liebknecht, who headed for Berlin to lead the revolution.

The 1918 revolution

The top army command had realised as early as the summer of 1918 that the war was lost. Finally, on 29 September 1918, General Ludendorff informed Paul von Hintze, who had been in post as foreign minister for less than three months, that the Western Front might collapse at any time and that any request for the ceasefire should come from the (civilian) government.

Towards the end of October 1918 the German Imperial Navy's High Seas Fleet received an order to put to sea to confront the blockading British Royal Navy fleet. Not since the Battle of Jutland in 1916 had the German fleet left its main base at Wilhelmshaven near Kiel. The order went out to sailors, many of whom already had longstanding grievances about their conditions which had led to mutinies the previous year. The sailors believed that such a naval attack would be:

Figure 2.1: Chancellor Max von Baden (in white coat) leaving the Reichstag, October 1918.

ACTIVITY 2.3

List the main decision-makers of 1917–18 – chancellors, Reichstag politicians, generals and others – and make notes to answer the following questions:

1. What was their power base?
2. How much authority and freedom of action did they really have?
3. Which decisions did they make or affect?

- Pointless: the war was already lost and negotiations to end it were known to be underway
- Counterproductive: it would undermine the credibility of the new more democratic government's peace negotiations and thus risk dragging out the war.

Many sailors mutinied, refusing to obey orders and forming revolutionary committees on the model of events in revolutionary Russia in 1917. These committees were often badly organised and lacked direction but they represented a new form of political action. The delegates to these committees were elected by their fellow sailors.

Germany was still at war at this time and a **mutiny** in an important part of its armed forces was a serious matter. It became even more serious as revolutionary committees combining soldiers, sailors and workers spread from Kiel across Germany. The authorities proved unable to stop this spread. Sometimes the committees concentrated on local issues, sometimes on national ones, but all reflected anger with a leadership that had led Germany into a long and difficult conflict, causing misery and suffering to millions. What was more, Germany was close to losing the war and the prospect of defeat was undermining social cohesion.

Many cities, including Berlin and Munich, became gripped by a revolutionary mood at the end of 1918. Winter was coming, the effective British blockade of the North Sea coast was still in place and an attempt by the German army to launch a successful offensive on the Western Front had failed, despite initial victories. Many felt hungry, bitter and angry. In particular, they blamed the national leadership for their problems. This included even the Kaiser and his top generals. The revolutionary committees would not have spread as they did throughout Germany in the autumn of 1918 unless these grievances had become intolerable for many.

The October 1918 appointment of Prince Maximilian von Baden as chancellor was thus a response to three things:

- The crises in discipline in the army and navy
- The crises in political authority in German society
- The crises in the conduct of the war.

The prince himself had already been critical of the conduct of the war by Ludendorff, Hindenburg and the other generals.

The prince's short-lived government had Social Democrats as cabinet members. On 28 October, the Constitution was changed and political power was moved to the Reichstag. The SPD felt that appropriate constitutional steps had now been taken. But the situation was moving beyond their control.

As the political, social and military situation deteriorated further, on 7 November Ebert decided that the SPD had to have an increased role in the government, and that the reforms at a federal level should also be carried through in the largest state, Prussia. The kaiser and Chancellor von Baden concluded that only a Social Democrat government could prevent Germany from disintegrating as Russia had done the year before amid two revolutions.

In addition, Ebert announced that both the emperor and his oldest son should renounce the throne. The kaiser's cousin Tsar Nicholas II had abdicated (naming first his son and then his brother as the new tsar); yet he and his family had been shot by revolutionaries. The unrest in Germany seemed comparable to events in Russia. Events had also forced the Tsar of Bulgaria (who had family connections to both the kaiser and his new chancellor) to abdicate; he did so in good order and left the country, his son becoming the new tsar. This, too, helped set the tone for the kaiser's **abdication**, as the contrast with Nicholas II was no doubt cautionary.

Reviewing the situation, and despite his own social position, Prince Maximilian von Baden agreed that Wilhelm II had to abdicate as Emperor of Germany and King of Prussia. Tens of thousands were gathering at key points on the streets of Berlin in apparently revolutionary mood. Yet the prince was unable to persuade the kaiser to step down. The emperor's family, the Hohenzollerns, had ruled for four centuries as Dukes and then Kings of Prussia, and then from 1871 as German emperors. Wilhelm was a proud if arrogant and sometimes hasty man. The decisive moment came when he was informed by General Wilhelm Groener of the army High Command that he could no longer rely on the support of the army.

The kaiser accordingly travelled over the border, accompanied by his family and a trainload of possessions into permanent and wealthy exile in the Netherlands on 10 November 1918. The 46 years of the Kaiserrreich had ended.

Although the kaiser's abdication was announced, Wilhelm did not actually sign the formal abdication letter until the end of the month. Indeed, according to the British historian John C.G. Röhl, hours before signing Wilhelm had argued that he should march back into Germany at the head of his troops and with them end the rebellion and mutiny by lynching the ringleaders, whom he characterised as a hundred Jews and a thousand workers. His suggestion was not acted on.

 Voices from the past

Wilhelm II's letter of abdication

These are words extracted from part of Wilhelm II's letter of abdication:

I herewith renounce for all time claims to the throne of Prussia and to the German Imperial throne connected therewith.

At the same time I release all officials of the German Empire and of Prussia, as well as all officers, non-commissioned officers and men of the navy and of the Prussian army, as well as the troops of the federated states of Germany, from the oath of fidelity which they tendered to me as their Emperor, King and Commander-in-Chief.

I expect of them that until the re-establishment of order in the German Empire they shall render assistance to those in actual power in Germany, in protecting the German people from the threatening dangers of anarchy, famine, and foreign rule.

Proclaimed under our own hand and with the imperial seal attached.

Amerongen, 28 November 1918

Signed Wilhelm

Discussion points

1. What do you think are the key things that Wilhelm's letter of abdication intended to achieve?
2. How far do you agree that Wilhelm II was right to abdicate in 1918?

What do you think was the correct thing for Max von Baden to do in November 1918:

1. Remain as chancellor
2. Give his resignation to the emperor immediately before the abdication
3. Hand his resignation to the speaker of the Reichstag
4. Something else?

Draw up a table of advantages and disadvantages for each course of action, taking account of who would be pleased and who displeased in each case.

The chancellor felt that his position was impossible. Faced with the abdication crisis and the naval mutiny in Kiel, he decided to resign. But with the kaiser abdicating, how should the process of resignation properly take place? The emperor had been removed but the imperial structures of power were still in place. Should he hand his resignation to the newly empowered Reichstag? In the end, he clearly decided that he possessed legitimacy and authority himself. On 9 November 1918 his final act as chancellor was to hand over the chancellorship personally to the Social Democrat leader, Friedrich Ebert.

Ebert himself had wanted to retain the monarchy, though he thought that there had to be a change of emperor. He wanted to avoid social and political chaos. He had told von Baden: 'If the Kaiser does not abdicate, revolution is inevitable.'

A ceasefire on the Western Front came into effect at 11 a.m. on 11 November 1918. According to the rules of diplomacy, the war didn't formally end until the signing of the peace treaty the following year and its ratification by national assemblies. On the ground, fighting continued in some sectors for a while afterwards. But to all intents and purposes, the war was over.

The establishment of democratic government in the Weimar Constitution

Germany's soldiers and civilians were witnessing rapid and large changes. On 9 November alone:

*   Kaiser Wilhelm II's abdication was announced
*   Chancellor Prince Max von Baden resigned
*   The Social Democrat Friedrich Ebert became chancellor
*   Philip Scheidemann proclaimed a republic from a balcony in the Reichstag
*   Karl Liebknecht, recently released from prison, proclaimed a Free Socialist republic from a window of the Berlin City Palace
*   Later the same day Ebert asked von Baden if he would stay on as chancellor.

As chancellor, Ebert formed a government of his own Social Democratic Party (SPD) but brought in some of their more radical former colleagues, who were in the Reichstag as deputies from the Independent Social Democrats (USPD).

Ebert was not comfortable working in government with those whose radical and revolutionary politics he did not support. However, he had had to cope with the developing parallel state of workers' councils. He managed to ensure that the declaration of a provisional government met the demands of these committees in a process dominated by SPD supporters. He himself became the head of the new government. The government led by Ebert had thus the revolutionary legitimacy of being voted in following debates by the committees. It would please the revolutionaries by being Socialist and radical.

The government also had the legitimacy of continuity from von Baden. It would, accordingly, be cautious and seek to collaborate with the existing forces of social, economic, political and military power. This was going to be a difficult balancing act.

Then Ebert received a telephone call from General Groener. We are dependent for what we know about this entirely on Groener's account because Ebert never spoke of it. According to Groener, he told the chancellor in a telephone call late on 10

November that, as head of the army's High Command, he was willing to support Ebert's government, but that the army had to be taken care of and that he and Hindenburg wanted to head off any drift to revolution. In what has become known as the Groener–Ebert pact, the two men agreed that:

- The government would back up the officer corps: discipline and order had to be maintained in the army.
- The government would ensure that the army's food supplies would be protected.
- The army would back up the government in the fight against Bolshevism.

Bolshevism was the very kind of revolutionary socialist politics that Ebert was opposed to in any case. He had no objections to discipline in the army, or to law and order in the streets, or to putting an end to revolutionary activities.

Groener was already that rare thing, a soldier whom the SPD felt they could do business with. This dated back to events in 1917 when he interested himself in the welfare of the munitions workers. Realising that their pay and conditions affected their **productivity**, he had put forward the radical proposal that they be given a role in management. Such a proposal was close to SPD's own policies; Groener's name was therefore one that they would have remembered.

The new **republican** government led by Ebert moved swiftly to bring the First World War to an end. Four million weary, angry, defeated and disillusioned soldiers tramped back to Germany from France, Turkey and Russia. They did not understand that they had been defeated in battle. Only a few months earlier, in March and April 1918, Ludendorff's Spring Offensive had achieved the first real advances and victories since the autumn of 1914, and yet it had all ended in retreat.

Many troops came to believe that they had been let down by the politicians and others: this would become known as the *Dolchstoß*, the 'stab in the back'. It left many of the soldiers distrustful of politicians and the entire political process. For a society brought up on respect for authority, patriotism and autocratic rule, this was a challenging development.

By the end of January 1919 the German army of four million had been reduced to just one million. This demobilisation was impressively rapid but chaotic. Many soldiers simply went home without waiting for their demobilisation papers. Many retained their weapons. The arms factories also demobilised as there was no longer a need for weapons, ammunition and so on. Many workers were dismissed. Millions of women who had been recruited during wartime were told that the jobs were needed for the returning men.

Germany was now not just defeated and poor, it was disillusioned and heavily-armed – a challenge to any administration. Early on, Ebert's government issued a flurry of decrees that established:

- freedom of religion
- freedom of speech
- freedom of the press
- a widening of the suffrage, including votes for women
- an amnesty for political prisoners.

Key term

Dolchstoß: German word meaning 'stab in the back'; the view that the German army was not defeated in the First World War but that left-wing civilians surrendered and signed a peace treaty in an act of treason.

Collectively these measures established democratic norms in the new Republic.

All women over 20 now had the right to the vote and this introduced a new element into elections in Germany. In the event, in federal elections held on 19 January 1919, the most female votes were cast for the Catholic Centre Party and for other Conservative parties. However, the SPD won a victory, with nearly 38% of votes cast. Philipp Scheidemann was appointed Chancellor of Germany by President Ebert in February 1919. This time, the SPD allied itself with the Centre Party and the Liberal German Workers' Party (DDP). Their combined share of the vote was 76%, giving the coalition a comfortable majority in the Reichstag. It was known as the Weimar Coalition.

About 220 km south-west of Berlin is the small town of Weimar in a part of Germany called Thuringia. It was here that the Constitutional Convention of the new German Republic started its meetings in January 1919. But why Weimar?

- Berlin was still an unsettled place, with army and *Freikorps* deployed (with the full support of the government) to suppress disorder on the streets. January saw the Spartacist Uprising; this was followed in March 1920 by the Kapp-Lüttwitz Putsch and a general strike.
- Weimar had strong associations with German classical culture, with the great German poet Goethe and other luminaries. It was not Berlin, with its associations with Prussian militarism.

In any event, the unsettled security situation in Berlin meant that Ebert and his government had moved well away to the safety of Weimar.

The Constitutional Convention was dominated by the politicians of the Weimar Coalition. This brought together three parties:

- SPD: centre-left
- German Democratic Party: left-Liberal
- Centre Party: more socially conservative but still supportive of the project of democratic, constitutional republicanism.

Between them, the parties of this coalition had the largest number of representatives in Weimar. A notable absentee and opponent was the *Deutschnationale Volkspartei* (DNVP), a party to which we shall return.

The Weimar Constitution 1919

The Weimar Coalition wanted to create a Republic of Germany that would restore stability and security while remaining true to the principles – Socialist, Social Democratic, Christian, Liberal – that underpinned each of the parties.

The constitution was drafted by the Liberal politician and lawyer Hugo Preuss, with valuable comments from many, notably by the well-known teacher of constitutional law Gerhard Anschütz. It had many provisions, but in brief it declared:

- Germany was to be a democratic parliamentary republic.

Key term

The *Freikorps* (literally 'free corps') was a phenomenon of the newly post-war Germany, as well as a bad sign for the future. Well armed and highly trained, they were paramilitary groups of nationalistic anti-Republicans, usually ex-soldiers, that formed after November 1918. They were used to supplement the army and police.

Figure 2.2: Philipp Scheidemann, November 1918.

- The Reichstag would be elected by all men and women aged 20 or over (it was 21 for men and 30 for women in the UK at the time).
- Voting was to be by proportional representation.
- Citizens would enjoy freedom of speech, freedom of religion and freedom of political activity (unless subversive).
- There would be a free press.
- There were to be fixed-term parliaments with elections every four years.

President Ebert signed the new constitution into law in August 1919. The state itself continued to be known as the *Deutches Reich* (German Empire). However, because of the constitutional conference's location, Germany from 1919 to 1933 is known to history as the 'Weimar Republic'.

Two articles in the 1919 Constitution in particular were to have long-lasting and finally fatal consequences for the republic.

Article 22 stated that the system of voting members to the Reichstag was to be by proportional representation (PR). This voting system is in use today in 80 or so countries around the world (including for regional parliaments and assemblies in Scotland, Wales and Northern Ireland). It is designed to ensure some measure of representation for minority views. Particularly in a divided country, this ensures that a wide range of groups feel that their voice is being heard and that their votes count. It also means that the balance of opinion in the assembly is like that in the electorate itself, something which is clearly good for the democratic process of what is called 'the representation of the people'.

However, critics argue that it is a voting system that usually produces more coalition governments than the 'first-past-the-post' system which is used in the UK for local councils and the national government. Coalition governments tend to move more slowly, be less clear and decisive, and thus appear to offer less leadership. The Weimar Constitution adopted a form of PR that allowed even the smallest political parties the chance to win seats in the Reichstag or state parliaments. While this accurately reflected the divided nature of German politics, it made all political decision-making protracted. It also ensured that those who were used to autocratic imperial and military rule saw politicians endlessly arguing and believed that the country was being inefficiently, weakly and corruptly governed.

By contrast with Article 22, Article 48 gives the head of state certain emergency powers. Under this article, the president could suspend the constitution in case of national crisis and rule by decree rather than through legislation that had passed though the Reichstag.

As with PR, the Weimar Constitution was by no means the only one to embody such a provision. The usefulness or danger of such powers stems from how politicians or a constitutional court might choose to define 'national crisis'. In Germany's case, the problem was the frequency with which presidents decided that there was a national crisis. These powers were frequently used in the Weimar period. President Friedrich Ebert, a Social Democrat and lifelong opponent of autocratic rule, used Article 48 no fewer than 134 times. All other presidents were

Key term

Proportional representation: An electoral system whereby the number of seats that a political party holds in an assembly closely reflects the number of votes cast for that party in an election.

Figure 2.3: The Weimar Constitution

to act similarly. Indeed, the country would have been ungovernable without the activation of Article 48.

If Article 22 was the door through which the National Socialist German Workers' Party was first able to walk into power by democratic means, Article 48 was one of the means by which they then slammed the door on democracy altogether.

Government and opposition to 1924

Post-war political problems

The main political problem facing Ebert, Scheidemann and the new government was order and security:

- The parties of the revolutionary Left now had far more support than before the war; they also had the inspiration of the Russian Revolution to show that overthrowing the state was possible.
- The rapid demobilisation of the defeated German army left behind millions of battle-hardened veterans, many still armed, many yet to adjust to the new political order (and some already members of the *Freikorps*).
- Unsurprisingly, there were also **monarchists** calling for the return of the kaiser.
- The very fact that the constitutional debates had to take place away from the capital tells its own story about the ability of government agencies to enforce the rule of law.

For Ebert and those who thought like him, the Russian Revolution of 1917, far from being an inspiration, was a warning about the breakdown of law and order.

The new government was SPD-led, but it was a coalition with partners from the more left-wing USPD. Social Democrats had never held power before and, despite involvement in von Baden's cabinet, had little experience of government and taking responsibility for basic services or responding to strikes. Although the SPD was the largest party in the Reichstag, it had no absolute majority. Its relationship with its coalition partners the USPD contained both political and personal strains.

Ebert decided that the SPD needed allies from outside the left wing of politics. He set about making deals with three conservative groups in particular who were likely to oppose Social Democratic policies:

- Military officers agreed to help the government suppress any challenges to their authority in exchange for guarantees that the army would remain free of civilian control and that the status of the military would remain high.
- Senior civil servants agreed to work with the government in exchange for similar guarantees about the preservation of their status and privileges.
- Industrialists agreed to work with the government, to recognise trade unions and to introduce an eight-hour working day in exchange for a guarantee about the preservation of private property rights and of private capital.

These powerful conservative elites had not changed their dislike of Social Democracy but they feared worse – Bolshevik chaos – and recognised that the Weimar government was the best bulwark available for now. The Russian Revolution which was such an inspiration to the revolutionary Left was a cause of

Speak like a historian

The Weimar Constitution

Historians continue to debate the strengths and weaknesses of the Weimar Constitution, and whether it contributed to the fall of the Republic. Eric D. Weitz has written:

> … the flaws in the constitution so much debated as the republic entered its death throes in the 1930s and then after 1945, had less to do with the political system it established than with the fact that German society was so fragmented. A less divided society and one with a more expansive commitment to democratic principles, could have made the constitution work.[1]

Discussion point
Given the divisions in German society, was the Weimar Constitution a suitable basis for government?

real fear to the Centre and Right, and Ebert used that fear to bolster, if not support, at least a grudging acceptance.

There was serious unrest in Berlin early in January 1919, with the Spartacist Uprising and a general strike. Street violence from 4 to 15 January was led by a revolutionary group called the Spartacus League after the gladiator Spartacus, who led a revolt in ancient Rome. It was suppressed with great violence by the army and the *Freikorps*. The leaders of the revolt – Rosa Luxemburg and Karl Liebknecht, both of whom had earlier been imprisoned for their anti-war activities – were both captured and killed.

The Spartacist Uprising was a good example of how fragile law and order were in Germany, especially in Berlin. Luxemburg and Liebknecht had disagreed with the SPD leadership over its support for the First World War. They had formed the Spartacist movement in 1915 to oppose the war and the compromises made by the Social Democrats, and to promote their left-wing ideas. They had been expelled from the SPD in 1916 and had formed the USPD with like-minded radicals the following year. Luxemburg wrote from prison in 1915:

> *The modern working class must pay dearly for each realisation of its historical mission. The road to the Golgotha of its class liberation is strewn with awful sacrifices.*[2]

Both Liebknecht and Luxemburg had a deep mistrust of the government of Ebert. In particular, they were alarmed by the close working relationship that Ebert had established with the army and the *Freikorps*. Conventional politics through the USPD did not meet their concerns and they turned to street action. Luxemburg herself was not in favour of an armed uprising by the Spartacists but when it started, led by Karl Liebknecht in January 1919, she joined in.

The uprising began with a general strike in Berlin. Union shop stewards, the German Communist Party (KPD) and the radical USPD met and decided to attempt to overthrow by force the Social Democrat government of the German Republic. The Spartacus League was fully involved.

ACTIVITY 2.5

1. List the different aspects of the Weimar Constitution. What do they tell you about the priorities of those who drew up the document?

2. How far do they contribute to, for example, social justice, economic efficiency, national unity?

3. What do you think needed to be added, changed or removed to improve the 1919 Constitution?

4. Why do you think the steps you would have recommended had you been in Weimar in 1919 weren't taken by the politicians and lawyers themselves?

Key term

A **putsch** is an attempt by a small group to take over control of a state by armed force. The word is originally German but is often used in English.

On 8 January the insurgents had seized some key points in the city. Ebert called in a combination of the German army and the *Freikorps* to suppress the uprising. By 15 January the uprising was over. Karl Liebknecht and Rosa Luxemburg were both captured by the *Freikorps* under Captain Waldemar Pabst and summarily shot while being held as prisoners.

Other similar uprisings took place over the following months in Berlin and were similarly suppressed. Then in May 1919 in Munich, a Bavarian Soviet Republic was declared. Once again, the left-wing uprising was brutally suppressed by a force of 30 000 army and *Freikorps* members, including the group known as the Ehrhardt Brigade after its leader Hermann Ehrhardt. Again, women and men thought to have been involved were summarily executed, usually by *Freikorps* units.

These tests of army and *Freikorps* loyalty were easily passed, since the revolutionary Left were the common enemy. By contrast, an attempted seizure of power and overthrow of the Weimar Republic in March 1920 put the alliance between Social Democrats, the army and veteran irregulars under a more severe test. Like the Spartacist Uprising, it took place in Berlin but this time the coup was attempted by monarchists, nationalists and conservatives. The leaders were:

- Wolfgang Kapp, a Prussian civil servant
- General Walther von Lüttwitz, a serving army officer in charge of a key military group.

The Kapp–Lüttwitz **Putsch** was sparked by the attempt by the defence minister, Gustav Noske, to comply with the Treaty of Versailles. The treaty required Germany to reduce the size of its armed forces. To do this, Noske had ordered two *Freikorps*, those of Ehrhardt and Loewenfeld to disband. Von Lüttwitz had refused to carry out the order. The Ehrhardt Brigade marched into Berlin and seized government buildings. They proclaimed Kapp chancellor and demanded the return of the monarchy. Noske ordered General Hans von Seeckt to intervene and put down the rebellion.

This time the army stood by for several days while the coup leaders attempted to take over Berlin, forcing the government to leave Berlin for their own safety. In doing this, Seeckt had disobeyed a direct order from the minister of defence to suppress the uprising and sat firmly on the fence to await developments. Seeckt's political sympathies were strongly conservative and monarchist. During his time in post (1920–26) he sought to evade the military restrictions imposed on the German armed forces by the Treaty of Versailles, with some success. He had little

Hidden voices

Emotions of defeat

An army lieutenant describes his feelings in November 1918 marching back home defeated:

We sat in our bunkers and heard about the mess behind the lines, about the dry rot setting in back home… We felt that the Frenchmen and the Tommies were no longer our worst enemies, that there was worse to

come, real poison was being brewed in the witches' cauldron at home… The march home was my most bitter experience… I was a broken man… From blood, muck and misery we returned. But when we glimpsed Germany the ground under our feet began to sink.[3]

time for the Weimar government but wanted above all to preserve the reputation and unity of the *Reichswehr*.

The Kapp–Lüttwitz Putsch was supported by conservatives and monarchists, and by army leaders. But it lacked popular support and ordinary members of the government bureaucracy didn't take orders from the putsch leaders. Social Democrats in government called for a general strike to make it impossible for the rebels to govern. They were supported in this by trade unions, the KPD, the USPD and the DDP. Around 12 million workers came out. The strike brought Berlin to a standstill and the putsch fizzled out.

Kapp died in prison in 1922 while awaiting trial. Lüttwitz's resignation was accepted by the vice-chancellor, Eugen Schiffer, of the DDP. Lüttwitz left the country (on a full pension) using a passport that the Berlin police had given him. He returned in 1924 following an amnesty and was never prosecuted.

The call for a general strike brought a strong response in the Ruhr area, which witnessed strikes, marches and demonstrations. This may have begun as support for the Weimar government, but it began to turn into a rebellion itself. Workers' councils such as those of the 1918 revolutionary period formed, often with KPD and USPD leadership. A 'Red Ruhr Army' of 50 000–80 000 was also formed. This quickly overwhelmed the government (army) forces that were in the area and then disarmed the first *Freikorps* sent against them.

The response of the army and *Freikorps* units to events in the Ruhr contrasts tellingly with their calculated inactivity in Berlin in the same period. While the participants and leaders of the Kapp–Lüttwitz Putsch were treated leniently, the Ruhr Uprising was suppressed by the army and *Freikorps* with considerable brutality. The leaders were given death sentences and there were illegal summary executions as well.

The Kapp–Lüttwitz Putsch may have failed, but it was a polarising event that highlighted the deep divisions that still existed in German society.

The issue of what powers and forces were required to defend the new government did not go away. As we will see now, the Munich Putsch of 1923 may not have seemed of major importance at the time, but subsequent events elevated its significance.

At the end of September 1923, the Bavarian prime minister declared a state of emergency following a period of unrest and disorder in Munich and elsewhere in the state. Taking advantage of this unsettled period, the relatively obscure National Socialist German Workers' Party (NSDAP) attempted to seize power by force in Munich on 8 November 1923. Despite their name, they were a nationalist right-wing party that expressed the widespread public indignation at the presence of foreign troops on German soil. Their chairman was an Austrian-born former German soldier called Adolf Hitler.

In the event, the putsch failed and, over a couple of days, police supported by loyal army units easily rounded up the leaders.

ACTIVITY 2.6

1. Why do you think that the Social Democrat Friedrich Ebert was prepared to work with the army and other conservative forces in Germany in November 1918? Create a list of what he stood to gain with the deal and what he stood to lose without it.

2. How important was this deal between Ebert and the conservative elites? To achieve a balanced view, write a first paragraph beginning 'On the one hand', a second paragraph beginning 'On the other hand' and a third beginning 'On balance'.

Although the NSDAP was small and little known outside Bavaria at this point, it had the support of the national war hero and retired general, Erich Ludendorff. It also had powerful friends in Bavaria and in the army, and Ludendorff was still popular among many nationalists. Hitler feared deportation back to his native Austria but the judge at his trial for treason declared that anyone 'who thinks and feels like a German' should remain in the country. Hitler was fined 500 Marks and sentenced to five years in prison. In fact, in addition to some time spent on remand, he had just eight months of rather comfortable imprisonment in the fortress of Landsberg am Lech, receiving visitors and working on his memoirs, titled *Mein Kampf* (*My Struggle*), before his release for good behaviour. This was the first time that Adolf Hitler's name had any national prominence.

The leniency of Hitler's treatment and the sympathy of many in the army underlines the degree of support for nationalist and autocratic government that still existed in Germany in 1923.

The working of the Weimar government: strengths and weaknesses

The first federal elections were held on 19 January 1919 despite the social and political instability of the country. They were held using PR, with revised constituency boundaries, so that urban areas were fairly represented for the first time since the rapid urbanisation of the previous century. It was also the first time that women and men aged 20–24 had voted.

Ebert was elected *Reichspräsident* (president); he in turn appointed Scheidemann chancellor (strictly speaking, the latter initially had a different title and 'chancellor' was held back until the new constitution had been signed into law). The three parties of the Weimar Coalition that had kept the country running since the collapse of imperial government between them received more than three-quarters of the votes cast. Voter turnout was 83%. Altogether the result was a vote of confidence in the government in particular but also in the republic in general.

The Treaty of Versailles

Paramilitaries roamed German streets. Revolutionaries and **reactionaries** tried to overthrow the government from the Left and the Right. There were widespread demonstrations and strikes. At the same time as all this, the government had to be ready for peace negotiations, because the Allies who had won the First World War met in Paris in January 1919. France, Britain, Italy and the USA, the so-called 'Big Four', had the most influence. Their initial meetings did not consult the German government. Then, in April 1919, a German delegation was summoned to Paris.

Germany could now present itself to the world as a reformed country. Ebert and his colleagues hoped that the new liberal, democratic political structures would commend themselves to the victorious Allies. They especially hoped that this would influence the USA, a powerful nation that was likely to be very influential when it came to drawing up peace terms. Ebert knew that he could expect little sympathy from France and Britain. Nevertheless, the German delegation were shocked by their reception when they did at last reach Paris.

They were further shocked by the Allied demands. They had expected to negotiate and knew that the initial terms might be harsh. In fact, the Treaty of Versailles was the settlement presented to Germany, not for negotiations but on a take-it-or-leave-it basis. There were many provisions of the treaty but what especially troubled the delegation, dismayed Ebert and rankled with the majority of Germans for years after was Article 231, known to historians as the 'War Guilt Clause'. This declared that:

- The only cause of the war was German aggression and the country was therefore responsible for all loss and damage caused by the fighting. Almost all Germans rejected this view.
- The Allies demanded reparations of 132 billion Marks or £6.6 billion (about £285 billion in today's terms).

In addition, Germany would:

- lose territory at home and overseas
- have restrictions placed on the size and weaponry of its armed forces.

The German delegation refused to sign. Scheidemann spoke passionately in the Reichstag against the treaty and resigned as chancellor. Ebert asked the retired head of the army, Hindenburg, and also the current head, Groener, for their advice. If the government refused to sign the treaty, if the Allies then attacked, what would the army do? The army would fight and it would be defeated, was the advice. Germany was, in effect, undefended. Ebert went back to the Reichstag and advised that the treaty had to be accepted. The assembly agreed.

The Treaty of Versailles was signed by all parties in June 1919. This was a major political problem because it was so widely regarded by Germans of many political persuasions as being very unfair. It could be argued that, by uniting the great majority of Germans behind outrage at the treaty terms, the divisions in German society in 1919 might have been set aside for a while. However, the sharp divisions that did exist were not to be bridged. Left and Right blamed one another.

However, it was the Conservative parties and groups on the right of German politics who were loudest in their complaints and allegations, and they won the propaganda competition. According to their analysis, the undefeated German army had been betrayed by socialist politicians. Hindenburg himself said as much when brought unwillingly to be questioned by a Reichstag committee investigating how the war had broken out and how it had ended in defeat. The army declared that the old field marshal had been on the verge of winning. It had been betrayed by a stab in the back. This was the *Dolchstoß* myth mentioned earlier. The expression may have been used before, but Hindenburg's testimony gave it greater currency than it had had and the expression, and the myth, became a persistent part of German society and its political life.

The SPD-led coalition government faced a daunting task. The question of how Germany was to pay reparations and when was to become a dominant issue. Opposition in the Reichstag and outside on the streets came from the many Conservative parties and groups on the Right, making reparations and law and order the joint most pressing concern of the government of the Weimar Republic. A crisis was not long in coming.

The occupation of the Ruhr

Belgium and France were both particularly determined that Germany should pay reparations in full. In fact, the reparation payments were not always made on time and in full. As a result, in December 1922 the Reparations Commission, the body given the task of overseeing the reparations process, declared Germany in default.

In January 1923, Germany was found to have defaulted on its reparations, which it was paying through the delivery of goods, as it lacked gold currency. France and Belgium felt that, because they had suffered the most material loss in the war, they were entitled to attempt to ensure that these payments were maintained. Both countries believed that Germany was attempting to use the rapidly devaluing Mark as a way of meeting their repayments without too much difficulty.

The Ruhr river valley near the western border with France and Belgium was the industrial powerhouse of Germany. From Duisburg in the west to Dortmund in the east stretched roughly 30 km of heavily industrialised cities, including Essen, home to the main factory of Krupp. It was an area rich in coal and the centre of iron and steel production in Germany.

In response to the default, on 11 January 1923 French troops invaded and occupied the Ruhr industrial area. They were later joined by Belgian forces. They took control over factories and mines, assuming that these would continue to work as before. They considered that the seizure of the area and a demand that future reparations payments were to be in goods and commodities was a way to achieve their aim.

Up to this point, the victorious Allies had dealt with Germany within the rules and with the agreement of the League of Nations. The occupation of the Ruhr had no League of Nations sanction.

Belgium and France saw the occupation and the forcible seizure of all profits made by the many industrial concerns of the area as justified. To them, it was a drastic but fair way to ensure that reparation payments to repair the extensive war damage were paid on time. In addition, it was in the interest of both countries to keep Germany weak: neither wanted their neighbour to rebuild its pre-war economic and military power. Not only had both been invaded in 1914, but the French had still not forgotten the national humiliation of the 1870–71 Franco-Prussian War – within living memory for some.

However, German public opinion was outraged at this latest national humiliation. Nationalist groups were particularly angered by the presence of foreign troops on German soil. It is no coincidence that the NSDAP chose this year as the one in which they attempted unsuccessfully to seize power in Munich.

The Ruhr area was the main industrial region of Germany and home to many of the country's biggest companies. The occupation could only further disrupt German industrial output, making the economic burden of reparations payments even harder to achieve. In addition, the invasion of part of Germany was resented by many Germans as a national humiliation.

Key term

The League of Nations was an international body created in 1920 to promote disarmament, arbitrate disputes between countries and thus avoid wars. Germany worked to achieve membership in 1926. The **Nazi** government took Germany out of the league in 1933.

The president was still the Social Democrat Ebert, but the government was now led by Wilhelm Cuno. A businessman who had been involved in negotiations regarding reparations, Cuno was not a party member and had been appointed by Ebert by decree, not following a Reichstag vote. His centre-right cabinet drew on several parties, but not the SPD, who had refused to serve under him. He included General Groener, who was not a member of any party, as minister of transport at the president's urging.

The government responded to the invasion of the Ruhr area with a campaign of passive resistance. There was no cooperation with the invaders. The Germans in the area went on strike. Factories shut down and mines closed. Transport came to a halt. The Weimar government supported the strike at first.

The public finances of France and Belgium suffered. However, the resulting loss of production in Germany's most important industrial area seriously damaged the country's fragile economy.

Cuno held the post of chancellor for nine months, resigning after losing an SPD-sponsored vote of confidence in the Reichstag in August 1923. At the end of October 1923 the new chancellor, Gustav Stresemann, announced the ending of resistance to the occupation of the Ruhr, followed by the declaration of a state of emergency. His known political sympathies and in particular his reluctance to deal firmly with the 1923 Munich Putsch were responsible for the Social Democrats leaving the coalition, which collapsed without them.

All in all, the occupation of the Ruhr reminded Germany that it was now a state incapable of the basic task of self-defence.

Government and opposition, 1924–29

The impact of the Ruhr invasion and the leadership of Stresemann

In August 1923 President Ebert replaced Wilhelm Cuno with Gustav Stresemann as chancellor.

Stresemann came from a lower-middle-class background in Berlin. He was the youngest of seven children and his father bottled and distributed beer. He had received an excellent education. He spent time at the University of Berlin and then became active in politics in Saxony, becoming a member of the Reichstag in 1907. Declared unfit for the army in 1914, he became leader of the National Liberal Party in 1917 and went on to become founder and Chairman of the German People's Party (*Deutsche Volkspartei* or DVP) in 1919.

Figure 2.4: Gustav Stresemann c. 1925–29.

Initially, the DVP opposed the Republic and the SPD government. Stresemann himself moved to the Right during and after the war, sharing the popular anger at the Versailles terms and making no secret of his monarchist sympathies. He became prepared to work with the Weimar government for the time being if only to free Germany from foreign occupation. As he put it to the kaiser's oldest son, the exiled former Crown Prince Wilhelm, 'first we must remove the strangler from our throat'. In this spirit he accepted the posts of chancellor and foreign minister of the coalition government in August 1923. He was chancellor only until December the same year, but he remained foreign minister until 1929.

Stresemann worked to end the French and Belgian troops' occupation of the Ruhr area. Their presence only gave additional energy to the development of nationalist politics. Political parties such as the Catholic Centre Party and the DVP drifted to the Right and became divided internally into factions. Further to the Right than Stresemann's DVP, Conservatives had already formed an umbrella group in 1922: a consortium of nationalist associations known as the *Vereinigten Vaterländischen Verbände Deutschlands* (United Patriotic Associations of Germany or VVVD). With over 130 member organisations, the VVVD was intended to coordinate right-wing political activities with the aim of overturning both the Treaty of Versailles and the Weimar Constitution. The events of 1923 boosted its appeal and it continued in existence for another ten years, withering away because of inadequate resources but also because of the NSDAP increasingly becoming the vehicle for right-wing political aspirations.

Stresemann was eager to reverse what he regarded as the unjust and burdensome provisions of the Treaty of Versailles. In particular, he wanted the removal of the War Guilt Clause and the reparations payments demanded by the victorious Allies as a consequence. However, he believed that Germany needed breathing space if the country was to prosper again and that the best way to keep the Allies content was by adopting a policy of meeting the obligations placed on Germany by Versailles. This policy became known as 'Fulfilment'.

As foreign minister in a series of governments, Stresemann became the acceptable face of Germany on the international circuit. His cool intelligence, obvious competence and ability to suppress his indignation at what he regarded as the unfair treatment of Germany in 1919 impressed others at international gatherings.

At one of these in 1925, in the lakeside town of Locarno in Switzerland, a series of peace treaties were signed by all the major European powers. On behalf of Germany, Stresemann gave guarantees against any future aggression against France or Belgium, confirming the country's western borders. At the same time, France and Belgium agreed not to attack Germany. All of these undertakings were to be guaranteed by the USA and Italy. It was a complex series of seven agreements. In recognition of their contribution to peace in Europe, Gustav Stresemann and Aristide Briand were awarded the Nobel Peace Prize in 1926.

In the east, Russia's revolutionary government had pulled Russia out of the war in November 1917, and in March 1918 had signed the Treaty of Brest-Litovsk. Although this was important at the time, it was overtaken by events as Germany surrendered in the west on 11 November 1918. In April 1922, Germany signed a new treaty with Russia at Rapallo, under which each country renounced all financial or territorial claims on the other. Stresemann refused to do the same regarding Germany's frontiers with Poland. Recovery of lands transferred to Poland by the Treaty of Versailles was to remain a high priority of German foreign policy and a matter of significance in internal politicking throughout the Weimar period.

The admission of Germany to the newly formed League of Nations as a permanent member of the Council in September 1926 was a sign of international approval and a remarkable moment for Gustav Stresemann and his country after the humiliations of 1919. It also gave Germany the power to block any League of Nations proposal that might help to stabilise the economy of Poland or guarantee the security of Germany's neighbours to the east.

Even in his short period as chancellor, Stresemann managed, with substantial support from the USA, to stabilise the currency and so to prevent a continuation of the damaging inflation that affected the everyday lives of almost all Germans. This, and the restoration of Germany's international position, were substantial achievements.

Gustav Stresemann died of a stroke in 1929 at the age of 51.

The degree of governmental change

On Stresemann's resignation, the Centre Party politician Wilhelm Marx became Chancellor of Germany and held the post for 13 months (November 1923–January 1925). Although longer than Stresemann's three months (and Stresemann's predecessor Cuno's nine months), this term of office was still short. The frequent changes of chancellor underline the lack of stability in German politics in this period. A major cause of this was that no single political party could command a decisive majority of the electorate; German society was too divided. The result was that no party could win a majority of seats in the Reichstag, and thus no single party could push through its preferred legislation and, if challenged, win confidence debates in the Reichstag without the support of the votes of other parties.

In his year and a month as chancellor, Marx presided over four cabinet meetings of a coalition government of the Centre Party, the DVP (German People's Party) and the DDP (German Democratic Party). In addition to the presence of four different political party representatives in the cabinet, the president was the SPD leader, Ebert.

Marx deserves some part of the credit for the international success of his foreign minister, Gustav Stresemann. In addition, it was during his chancellorship that the economic situation stabilised following the crippling **hyperinflation** of 1923. It was also his government that accepted the Dawes Plan from the USA.

As a lawyer himself, Marx had an interest in legal matters. In January 1924 he declared a state of emergency in the face of the continuing unrest and social disorder and under it issued an emergency decree. Trial by jury in Germany was abolished, to be replaced by a mixture of judges and lay (volunteer) judges. This major legal change is known as the Emminger Reform, after Marx's justice minister. Despite the angry representations of the SPD and the German Bar (lawyers), trial by jury was not restored after the end of the emergency decree in 1925. This change was an unforgivable intrusion into human rights for a few but was of little popular interest. As with rule by decree, it was a further example of a democracy using the methods of an autocracy. It may have been an unavoidable step, but

ACTIVITY 2.7

List Gustav Stresemann's political priorities. Add comments explaining each one and showing how he carried these into political action.

it paved the way for further, and worse, departures from the rule of law and a further, and worse, autocracy.

Having weathered the violent storms of 1923–24, the Weimar Republic enjoyed a few years without attempts to seize power by force, general strikes or new foreign occupations of German territory. This does not, however, mean that the republic was now calm or that its politics had stabilised.

The elections at the end of 1924 left the parties that had made up Marx's cabinet debating whether to draw in people who were to the government's left, the SPD, or to its right, the DNVP. In the event, Ebert invited Hans Luther to form the next government. Not a party man, Luther was a civil servant with legal training, who had served in the Cuno, Stresemann and Marx cabinets as minister for food and agriculture, and then finance. Gathering the support of four parties, his cabinet included one deputy each from the Centre Party, the *Bayerische Volkspartei* (Bavarian People's Party), the DVP and the DNVP. But alongside them were unelected civil servants who were either members of one of those four parties or at least in sympathy with one of them. A further addition was one member of the DDP; the party was not officially part of the coalition but Otto Gessler was an experienced minister of defence having taken over the job when Gustav Noske resigned in the aftermath of the Kapp–Lüttwitz Putsch in March 1920.

Following Ebert's death in February 1925, presidential elections were held in March. There were candidates from the SPD, the Centre Party, the **Communists** and others. General Ludendorff stood for a small right-wing, anti-Semitic party which had been founded in 1922 and merged with the NSDAP in 1924. After the first round, the SPD withdrew and agreed to support the Centre Party candidate. The different right-wing candidates all withdrew and the parties of the right nominated General Paul von Hindenburg, who had not even stood in the first round and had declared his lack of interest in holding a political post. Had the KPD, like the SPD, withdrawn its candidate, the Centre's Wilhelm Marx would have won. In fact, Ernst Thälmann stood for the KPD, but Hindenburg was elected.

In office for 16 months, the Luther government reformed both taxation and social insurance, extending accident insurance to cover 11 occupational diseases. The Locarno Treaties which Stresemann negotiated was more than the DNVP could accept but Luther was able to survive their departure. When a hostile Reichstag forced Luther from office, the task of forming the next government once again went to Wilhelm Marx.

Marx was chancellor from 1926 to 1928, under President von Hindenburg, whose right-wing sympathies were well known. In July 1927, Marx's government steered through a law that established a new system of unemployment insurance. His term ended when the SPD increased their share of seats in the 1928 elections. The Social Democrat Hermann Müller formed a cabinet of SPD, Centre, DDP and DVP members. This coalition was even more divided than usual and Stresemann for once had to use his diplomatic skills to help Müller put the government together. This cabinet saw the return of General Groener to politics as defence minister, a post that he would hold for more than four years as chancellors came and went.

The *Reichswehr* was, as usual in German politics, a crucial element. The days when the Social Democratic chancellor Friedrich Ebert could reach an understanding with General Groener were long gone. At this time, at least until his resignation from the army in October 1926, the *Reichswehr* was commanded by General Hans von Seeckt, a traditionalist whose political sympathies (as we have seen) were not supportive of the Weimar Republic. Nevertheless, the similarity of his views on the Polish Republic created by the Treaty of Versailles to those of Stresemann is worth noting:

With Poland we come now to the core of the Eastern problem. The existence of Poland is intolerable and incompatible with Germany's vital interests. She must disappear and will do so through her own inner weakness and through Russia – with our help. Poland is more intolerable for Russia than for ourselves; Russia can never tolerate Poland. With Poland collapses one of the strongest pillars of the Peace of Versailles, France's advance post of power is lost. The attainment of this objective must be one of the firmest guiding principles of German policy, as it is capable of achievement – but only through Russia or with her help.[4]

In 1926, Seeckt agreed to let Prince Wilhelm, grandson of the exiled former emperor, join *Reichswehr* manoeuvres. This caused a major storm and allowed Marx to engineer the general's retirement from the army later that year. However, the army continued to rearm and to get new weapon systems designed in secret after the departure of Seeckt.

Clearly, Seeckt's downfall was the result of his politics being out of tune with the principles of the Weimar Republic. However, his actions should not be seen in isolation. Gustav Stresemann was another person in public life who held openly monarchist views. Like Seeckt he maintained contact with the exiled royal family himself and it was while he was chancellor that the crown prince, Wilhelm II's son, had returned to Germany in November 1923.

In fact, for most politicians of the Centre or Right there was little emotional or intellectual engagement with democracy. For all the democratic potential of the Weimar Republic, the old traditional elites had retained their power and influence in the major institutions of the state. These included the army, the churches and state bureaucracy. This was an unusual mixture and one that gave the period its particular character, perhaps its nervous energy.

The degree of opposition

German politics flowed through three main channels:

- There was the world of formal politics, which took place not only through the Reichstag but also through the national assemblies of the Länder, the states that made up the federation, and local towns and cities.
- There was the world of the paramilitary groups and their pitched battles in the streets of Berlin and other cities.
- There was also a flourishing world of political action away from these two, but related to both of them.

Let us look at these three in turn.

ACTIVITY 2.8

Create a family tree, showing how the KPD came into existence. It should show the SPD, the USPD, the Spartacist League and the KPD itself. Label each one of these 'family members' with the names of significant members and add some significant dates. Add labels explaining why the splits and mergers occurred.

Political parties of opposition

The Communist Party of Germany (KPD) was the largest and most important in Europe after Russia's governing party. It was also the largest opposition party, never serving in the Weimar government. Where the SPD was now a party committed to reforms achieved through electoral and parliamentary processes, the KPD openly believed in revolution. It had grown out of the people who had left the SPD because of its support for the First World War and who had been involved in the Spartacist Uprising and other revolutionary activity. It had itself suffered splits, not least over its relationship to the USSR, but it had also succeeded in absorbing the USPD.

Like many of the political parties at the time it was learning to become much more organised, with a large and well-defended headquarters in Berlin and an increasingly skilful use of propaganda. In the January 1919 election, the USPD won 22 seats; in the following year's elections they won 82, making them the second largest party. They dropped back to 62 in May 1924 and in December 1924 they were on 45. When the KPD leader Thälmann ran for president in 1925, he received nearly 2 million votes or 6.4%. In a first-past-the-post system, the Communists would have been an irrelevance but under PR they were a significant party of opposition.

Figure 2.5: Election campaign by the KPD in Essen, in the Ruhr valley, 1925.

Fear of Bolshevism had persuaded the traditional elites of Germany to support the Weimar Republic as the lesser evil but that did not mean that they had anything politically in common with Social Democracy. As the likelihood of a Bolshevik uprising on the Russian model began to reduce, so the dislike of conservatives, nationalists and monarchists for political parties such as the SPD came more to the fore.

At the other end of the political spectrum from the KPD was the *Deutschnationale Volkspartei* (DNVP). It had been created as a direct response to the 1918 revolution, when two Conservative parties merged, to be joined by four others. Nationalist and anti-Semitic (and largely Protestant), it was in favour of restoring the Hohenzollern monarchy and retaking those parts of the old Kaiserreich that had been lost through the Treaty of Versailles (against which it voted in the Reichstag).

Like the KPD, the DNVP was by nature a party of opposition, since it was hostile to the very existence of the republic and did not take part in the 1919 Constitutional Convention. Unlike the Communists, it did take part in government: with representation in just 2 of 19 cabinets, it spent nearly 13 of the 15 years of its existence in opposition.

Like the army, the DNVP neither helped nor hindered the 1920 Kapp–Lüttwitz Putsch, being sympathetic but not wanting to be drawn into an armed failure, though one DNVP member did serve in the short-lived Kapp-led 'provisional government'.

Following the 1922 murder of the foreign minister Walter Rathenau, the Centre Party chancellor of the day, Joseph Wirth, accused the DNVP of having blood on its hands. Wirth's government introduced a Law for the Defence of the Republic the same year, increasing the punishment for conspiracy to murder and giving the government the powers to ban both terrorist organisations and those that supported terrorism. The DNVP, the KPD and the small, right-wing Bavarian People's Party voted against the new law; all other parties supported it.

The DNVP found itself voting with the KPD a second time the following year. The response, both official and unofficial, to the Ruhr occupation had been a campaign of passive resistance and strikes. Assessing the economic cost (not to mention the damage to social order and political process) that this response had created, the DVP Chancellor Stresemann ended government support for the campaign. The DNVP found itself on the same side of the argument as the Communists, calling this a treasonable surrender.

By contrast with the DNVP, the National Socialist German Workers' Party (NSDAP) was a far smaller, extremist political party of the Right. Their leader, Adolf Hitler, had spent a relatively comfortable eight months in prison after the shambolic failure of the Munich Putsch of 1923, which had nevertheless given a measure of national coverage to the NSDAP and to Hitler. From then on he was concerned to keep everything legal, to do things by the book. The NSDAP contested elections to the Reichstag from 1924, at first with little success. As a banned party, it was not allowed to put up NSDAP candidates, so in the 1924 elections they stood as 'National Socialist Freedom Movement' candidates instead and received first 6.5% and then 3% of votes cast. They contested the federal elections again in 1928. This time their ban had ended and they were stood as NSDAP candidates. Their vote sank again to 2.6%. In this period their representation in the Reichstag accordingly dropped from 32 to 14 to 12.

Few would have bet on them entering government within five years. That this did nevertheless happen remains one of the most fascinating and instructive stories of modern political history, not to mention one of the most frightening ones.

The party's success was not achieved through its leader's effective organising genius. Hitler was never a good organiser and his focus was on re-establishing himself as party leader after being out of circulation for eight months. Even so, the NSDAP continued to develop as a national party from 1925, though still shunned by the respectable majority of Germans because of its extreme views, its street violence and Hitler's demagogic speaking style.

However, the NSDAP was gradually emerging from the pack of far-right extremist parties. Some others dwindled and some were absorbed. The NSDAP had most electoral support in mainly Catholic Bavaria and in old industrial regions such as Thuringia. It also did well in mainly Protestant rural areas such as Schleswig-Holstein, Pomerania and East Prussia. Working-class areas in Berlin were never very secure for the NSDAP, nor were the Ruhr valley or Hamburg.

Political paramilitaries

Rosenberg writes about how the Nazis built a paramilitary wing to defend its meetings against left-wing attacks. There were in fact a number of paramilitary groups operating on the extreme right of German politics. One of the most prominent was the *Stahlhelm*, named after the steel helmets they wore. This was an association of army veterans from the 1914–18 war. They held rallies of a militaristic sort and acted as security guards for the DNVP. In this period the *Stahlhelm* were outside the formal party system but were nationalistic and monarchist in their views and actively sought physical confrontation with KPD supporters.

Voices from the past

Alfred Rosenberg

Alfred Rosenberg was an early and highly influential member of the NSDAP and did much to formulate their **ideology**, especially their extreme anti-Semitism. His handwritten diary was used in evidence against him at the Nuremberg trials in 1946, where he was found guilty of war crimes and executed. It is now in the Holocaust Museum in Washington.

Nationalist organisations and clubs offered to join forces. Many a member of the Free Corps wanted to know what was going on in Munich … From Westphalia and Saxony came itinerant prophets. One of them, a poor devil carrying a huge knapsack, said: Just give me propaganda material and explain things to me. I'll return home immediately and shall go from village to village to distribute your stuff. Another one produced a filthy manuscript and said: If I could make these things come true, Germany would be saved. Letters containing suggestions, programs, poems, arrived constantly in an endless stream. They probably weren't kept. Occasionally all this turned our offices into a sort of a spiritual torture chamber – and yet, what a wealth of suppressed love was here, that merely could not express

itself! How much need and despair, anxious to find something to cling to! … In the beginning few people I knew called at the editorial offices of the Völkischer Beobachter. I myself contributed only an occasional article. During these years Hitler had gained my respect and loyalty. I saw in him a man continuously wrestling for the soul of a people. I witnessed his maturing, saw how he constantly thought and brooded, only to be ready suddenly with amazingly apt answers to whatever questions arose. Thus, time after time, he gave evidence of sound instincts and natural cleverness.[5]

Discussion point

List the elements in the rise of the NSDAP that Rosenberg focuses on in this extract. Do you find: organisation, planning, debate, campaigning, emotion, study, personality or what? What does your answer tell you about the nature of the NSDAP and its lack of appeal in the period 1924–28? How do you imagine that the same elements will contribute to its later rising popularity between 1929 and 1933?

Campaigns and pressure groups

Extra-parliamentary campaigns were, in their way, a sign of Germany's beginning to develop a healthy democracy. Hundreds of different pressure groups developed in this period, usually to advance special interests. They came from right across the traditional political spectrum, although far more were from the conservative and nationalist side. Their activities resulted in a blizzard of posters, leaflets, petitions and letter-writing campaigns, accompanied by marches, rallies and meetings.

The power of their many and various campaigns is well illustrated by the one to save young people from reading 'Filth and Trash' (*Schund und Schmutz*), even though censorship was explicitly banned under the Weimar Constitution (Article 118). Film was the only exception to this and the target here was pornography and other 'indecent content'. The campaign had started well before 1914 but reached a peak a decade or so later.

A leading role in the campaign was taken by Hermann Popert, a judge of the Hamburg juvenile court. Both Protestant and Catholic churches were prominent in this campaign and so too were a number of pressure groups of teachers, social workers and parents, anxious, as they saw it, to preserve the morals of young people. They believed that this 'filth and trash' distracted the young from reading the classics of German literature.

The Law for the Protection of Youth from Trash and Filth Writings of December 1926 was controversial at the time as it seemed to many to go against an important guarantee of the Weimar Constitution. It took three readings in the Reichstag and a mixed majority before it could become law. Others argued that if film was exempt, why was writing so different? And there was no shortage of popular books widely available of doubtful quality and content. Meanwhile, the lively cabaret scene in Berlin's nightclubs was seen by some as degenerate and the same people found the new freedoms gained by women to go against traditional values.

A governmental board was set up by the minister of the interior in cooperation with the state governments. This board scrutinised newly published books and had the power to ban any that they deemed unsuitable. In the event, the new law was not very successful. By the spring of 1932 only 114 titles had been placed on the banned list. It only applied to book distribution and therefore only took effect after publication. Nothing could be banned for political, social, religious or ethical reasons.

There were many other interest groups, both large and national and small and local. One of the largest was the National Rural League (*Reich Landbund*). Established in 1921, it represented the interests of right-wing farmers and landowners, especially those from east of the River Elbe. As a result it was politically close to the DNVP. It had a strong central administration and a number of affiliated organisations. By 1924 it had some 500 district offices and by 1929 nearly 200 press outlets directly or indirectly controlled. Its membership was around one million.

Speak like a historian

Gary D. Stark

Some historians make a distinction between the traditional 'old Right' and the 'new Right' (or 'neoconservatives') of German politics at this time. Gary D. Stark, in his pioneering history of neoconservative publishers in Weimar Germany published in 1981, distinguishes between an 'old Right' based on the traditional social elites such as landowners and industrialists, and the neoconservatives, who were mostly middle class in origin and not overtly materialistic or politically active but ethically based (as they saw it) and moralising, the 'new Right'.

Both groups were keen to spread their message because they despised political action within the existing political framework of the republic. As a result, Stark found that publishing houses make a good subject for detailed study in this context. The 'old Right', meanwhile, made use of the large media group of newspapers, magazines and journals controlled by Alfred Hugenberg – the Hugenberg–Scherl publishing empire.

Neoconservatives typically organised into small clubs or societies on a local basis and included writers, journalists, philosophers and teachers. They drew on the services of small- to medium-sized, less well-known publishers. Some were in reality only founded to publish one journal (usually their own). For example, Dietrich Eckart founded the Hoheneichen Verlag in Munich in 1916 to publish his own anti-Semitic weekly *Auf gut Deutsch* (On good German) and in 1927 Anna and Ernst Niekisch established Widerstand Verlag in Dresden solely to publish their journal *Die Widerstand* (The Resistance).

Stark observed of German neoconservatives that in some ways they 'broke the ground' for conservative extremists such as the NSDAP.

Neoconservatism was hardly a well-defined, coherent front, much less an organised political force; it was rather, a loose collection of diverse groups and individuals, moving towards roughly similar goals … the German neoconservative movement was eventually overshadowed and skilfully shunted aside in the Weimar Republic by the collateral, but more coherent, organised, and politically active National Socialist movement.[6]

Discussion point

Do you think that the extra-parliamentary activity by pressure groups and special-interest groups in Germany 1924–29 was a sign of a healthy democracy?

Economic developments

The impact of war

The politics of wartime inevitably mean particular requirements. These wartime requirements meant full employment and the economy accordingly benefited. However, the **blockade** by the British Royal Navy badly disrupted German exports of manufactured goods, on which so much depended. The 18 Dreadnought-class battleships that Admiral von Tirpitz had been so determined to build for the Imperial German Navy stayed in Kiel harbour and only left port to confront the British Navy once, when in 1916 they fought the inconclusive Battle of Jutland (*Skagerrakschlacht*).

The response to the British blockade was the use by the German Imperial Navy of submarine warfare. There was great debate about this policy in Germany. Nearly eight million tons of British merchant shipping were sunk by German submarines during the war. The USA, still neutral, suffered the sinking of many ships, including the passenger liner *Lusitania* in 1915. The 1917 decision to remove all target restrictions for U-boats brought the USA into the war in April 1917, just as the opponents of the policy, including Chancellor Bethmann Hollweg, had feared.

The Imperial General Staff had anticipated a fairly short war and consequently the German political leadership had done so as well. Initially, as German troops swept through Belgium and attacked France, the assumptions seemed correct. However, when the conflict became bogged down in static trench warfare on the Western Front, the lack of German planning for a long conflict became apparent. **Total war**, the dominant military idea, required the involvement of the entire population in the war effort, meaning that priority was given to supplying the military even when the civilian population suffered.

Contemporary sources describe the winter of 1916–17 as especially harsh. It was known as 'the turnip winter' because this vegetable, usually reserved as fodder for animals, had to substitute for many for bread and potatoes, after the poor potato harvest. The British blockade of the North Sea ports, through which most food imports had to pass, had been very effective: Germany's heavy reliance on imported food was exposed as a major weakness.

The historian G.J. Meyer notes that: 'according to a report from a prominent Berlin physician, eighty thousand children had died of starvation in 1916' (*A World Undone*, Random House, 2006).

However, Belinda Davis reminds us that it is important not to overestimate the impact of a single winter:

General narratives credit the Turnip Winter of 1916–17 with severely buckling public support for the war, but Berliners' support plummeted even before then as the state appeared increasingly helpless against merchants and farmers. The English blockade, mass conscription, livestock confiscation policies, inefficient transport and storage, poor harvests, and the state's failure to regulate merchant practices all combined to create food crises already by late 1914. The food question dominated public morale and 'played a significant role in transforming relations between state and society' even by 1915. Attempting to forestall unrest that would weaken Germany's warrior image, Prussian and Imperial authorities – in marked contrast to their prewar tendency to repress protests – moved quickly during the war to respond to the demands of poor consumers, who after all could not be prevented from assembling for food. This apparent responsiveness won public approval and extended the state's legitimacy for several years. Berlin's women of little means led a slide in public opinion during

1915–16 from a judgment against the war to one against the government, now seen as jeopardizing the nation itself.[7]

The situation was made even worse by the switching of almost all factory production to the output of military items. This meant that there were shortages of clothes because most garment factories now produced uniforms. Also, many miners had been conscripted into the army, leading to shortages of coal owing to the mines being understaffed. Those food supplies that were available to the civilian population were focused mainly on bread and potatoes, and it became ever harder to buy meat. Dairy products, such as milk, cheese and eggs, dropped to about 20% of peacetime levels.

A few **profiteers** found opportunities to make money by exploiting the situation. **Black-marketeers** profited by illegally supplying goods at high prices. The wealthy used their money to buy scarce items despite shortages. In rural areas the opportunities for growing food and keeping chickens for your own needs meant that the worst of the shortages were kept at bay. But for the majority of Germans these were grim times, with shortages, hunger and endless queuing. As the war dragged on, these miseries became worse. Diseases of malnourishment appeared. It was not so much that malnourishment and hunger killed, but that bodies weakened by an inadequate diet were much more vulnerable to disease. It has been calculated that nearly half a million more civilians died in Germany during the First World War than would have been the case in peacetime.

The conflict was expensive for all participants. Germany's federal structure left its central government with limited means of raising money through taxation, and tax reform was postponed as a potential menace to national unity. The government raised additional funds through the sale of government bonds (effectively promissory notes). These proved quite popular, but were still not enough to bring in money at the rate at which the government was spending it. The government printed extra paper money, which meant that a gap opened between what the paper money suggested people had to spend and what the country's gold reserves said they really had to spend. This set inflation in motion.

Under normal circumstances, this might have been manageable, but neither domestic nor international circumstances were normal. For one thing, Germany had the war reparations to pay.

Post-war economic problems and policies

The economy of the defeated Germany suffered in many ways. Both the war and then the peace had a disturbing effect on the workforce. Millions of Germans were on the move from late November 1918. Some of these were only soldiers returning to Germany from years of fighting. The rapid demobilisation of millions of soldiers was disruptive, as were the continuing exploits of the various *Freikorps* paramilitary bands throughout the country. Others were the women workers in factories who had been summarily dismissed. As manufacturing concerns attempted to return to peacetime production, many members of the workforce, mainly women, were made redundant and replaced by ex-soldiers. In large manufacturing operations such as Krupp of Essen in the Ruhr valley, this change was rapid and not always welcomed by employees. By the end of November 52 000 workers had left Krupp's Essen factory, many of them female.

Krupp had been a main supplier of equipment and munitions for the German army. It took some time for them, and other manufacturers, to switch back from wartime manufacturing demands to peacetime production. At the same time, the unsettled environment, dislocated transport networks and interrupted export trade combined sharply to decrease industrial output.

The British Royal Navy did not lift the blockade of the North Sea coast until the Treaty of Versailles was signed in June 1919 so rationing endured in many areas. Food shortages continued, especially during the grim winter of 1918–19. It is no surprise that, at this stage, industrialists were prepared to give their support to the Social Democratic government in exchange for guarantees on private capital and private property.

Germany lost significant territory in the Treaty of Versailles. To the east, Danzig (in Polish, Gdansk) passed to Poland, together with a wide corridor of land cutting off the remains of East Prussia, while other land was surrendered to Lithuania and Czechoslovakia. To the west, Alsace-Lorraine had gone to France and some land had been taken by Belgium. French troops occupied the Rhineland region for a time. In addition to the diplomatic and security issues (and the question of national pride), these changes had economic consequences because resources and markets had been lost. Germany was also stripped of all its colonies, which had been a valuable source of raw materials and a useful captive market for the country's manufactured goods.

To complete the misery, deaths from the influenza pandemic of 1918–19 climbed throughout September 1918 in Berlin from 2% of the population to peak at the end of the month at 4%, before falling back to 2% by 9 November 1918. As usual, poverty and insanitary living conditions were major factors in the spread of this disease. The appalling living conditions in the wartime trenches may also have been an important factor.

Reparations

Hanging over all of this was the question of reparations: the money that Germany would have to pay the victorious Allies in compensation for the damage they had suffered during the war. The sum demanded was 132 billion Marks, equivalent to £6.6 billion at the time (about 40 times that in modern values). Between 1920 when payments began and 1931 when they were suspended, Germany paid 20 billion Marks. About 60% was paid in money (which had to be borrowed from American bankers). The rest left the country as goods seized or handed over, such as coal or railway rolling stock. According to the American historian Stephen Schuker, the total actually paid (not the total actually demanded) amounted to 'a startling 5.3% of German national income'.

The British economist John Maynard Keynes attended the Versailles Peace Conference as a British Treasury delegate. In 1919 he published *The Economic Consequences of the Peace*; it came out in the USA in 1920 and is said to have been influential on public opinion there. He argued that the reparations demanded by the victorious Allies were unreasonably harsh. He concluded:

But who can say how much is endurable, or in what direction men will seek at last to escape from their misfortunes? [8]

Other economists have since analysed the Treaty of Versailles and have concluded that the reparations demanded were not unreasonable under the circumstances and that the need for payments had only a relatively small effect on the German economy.

The most famous critique of Keynes's argument came from the French economist Etienne Mantoux, who disputed the figures. Mantoux's argument has been praised by both Stephen Schuker and the British historian A.J.P. Taylor, who agreed that the Germans could have afforded to pay the reparations. Other historians have argued that the fact that the reparations were so politically unpopular meant that they were an inherently destabilising force in the economy, whether or not they were fair or affordable. Two economic historians have made the interesting case that because the treaty limited the size of Germany's army, this imposed on it a budget saving that politically it would not otherwise have been able to achieve. They too conclude that the reparations were affordable.

This is clearly a complex and disputed area of history. What is not in doubt, however, is that most Germans believed that reparations payments were a real burden on the German economy and a grossly unfair one.

The first reparations payment was made in full by Germany in June 1921. The default of December 1922 led to the Ruhr occupation, which in turn sparked a general strike. However, the resulting loss of production in Germany's most important industrial area was seriously damaging to the country's fragile economy. Faced with high unemployment and worsening hyperinflation, the newly formed coalition government, now led by Gustav Stresemann, called off the campaign of passive resistance in the Ruhr in September 1923.

Hyperinflation

To obtain the hard currency required, increasingly worthless Marks were used to buy foreign currency with which to pay. In order to start paying off this huge sum and to purchase foreign currency, the Reichsbank, the state's central bank, printed large numbers of banknotes, a policy adopted during the final years of the Kaiserreich to pay for the war. This was followed by severe inflation that proved disastrous for many Germans. The purchasing power of the money they earned or had saved sank to dangerous levels between August 1922 and December 1923. This is known as **hyperinflation** and it proved damaging for the German economy. Stories are often told of the need to carry money in a suitcase or wheelbarrow when shopping.

Germany had already experienced some measure of inflation during the First World War. However, between June 1921 and January 1924 the Weimar Republic experienced severe inflation and then hyperinflation. The Mark had been stable enough before this at about 60 Marks to the US dollar. During the first part of 1922 the exchange rate climbed to 320 Marks per dollar and by November 1923 hyperinflation had driven it to an unsustainable 4,210,500,000,000 Marks per dollar.

Hyperinflation was at its worst in October 1923, when it reached 29 500%. This meant that prices of goods in shops, including food, doubled every four days. Few people understood what was happening or why. As a result, the assumption was partly that some people were to blame and partly that a few were becoming rich while the majority were getting poorer. There were rumours of foreign speculators, profiteers and bankers.

The inflation was disastrous for those on fixed incomes. Although guaranteed by the Reichsbank, the Mark had effectively become worthless. The Weimar economic crisis deepened. A number of the Allies were also in financial difficulties in 1918, a point noted by Keynes at the time:

The inflationism of the currency systems of Europe has proceeded to extraordinary lengths. The various belligerent Governments, unable, or too timid or too short-sighted to secure from loans or taxes the resources they required, have printed notes for the balance.[9]

The Dawes and Young Plans and foreign loans

During the period 1924–29, the economy of the Weimar Republic stabilised and even experienced a modest growth. Briefly as chancellor and then over a longer period as foreign minister in successive Weimar governments, Stresemann was a key figure in this. His first success was the negotiation with the USA of the Dawes Plan of 1924, an attempt to solve Germany's economic difficulties. This was the policy of Fulfilment in action.

Stresemann is credited with setting up a financial stabilisation package with the encouragement and support of the USA. A new currency, the Rentenmark, replaced the now worthless Papiermark on 16 November 1923 and the Reichsbank was ordered to stop issuing paper banknotes. At the same time, twelve zeros were deleted from the prices of goods. Hjalmar Schacht was appointed as Currency Commissioner in November 1923 and later as president of a restructured Reichsbank. The Monetary Law of August 1924 allowed the exchange of each old paper 1 trillion Mark note for one new Reichsmark.

The financial situation stabilised and the alarming period of hyperinflation was over. Nevertheless, the many enemies of the Weimar Republic used the financial crisis of the period as further evidence of the supposed inability of the government to protect German interests and the German way of life.

Meanwhile, the Reparations Commission had turned to a prominent US banker (and US general in the First World War), Charles G. Dawes. A committee was formed consisting of two members each from France, Belgium, Britain, Italy and the USA; one of the US representatives, Dawes, took the chair. The work of this committee was enthusiastically promoted, at least in Britain and the USA. Their task was to find a workable plan that would ensure that Germany resumed

Key term

Hyperinflation is a process by which prices rapidly go up in leaps, making goods and services far more expensive. As this leaves consumers with quickly falling purchasing power, it often leads to demands for higher wages. Need to pay for these puts up the prices of manufactured goods, which further feeds hyperinflation. Hyperinflation is extremely dangerous as it suddenly wipes out the value of savings and wages, and, by destroying economic confidence, undermines social cohesion and political stability.

Figure 2.6: Germany, January 1923. The photograph was intended to illustrate the worthlessness of the currency by showing it being used as wallpaper.

ACTIVITY 2.9

Study the main provisions of the Dawes Plan listed. Write a paragraph about each of them, explaining its importance to the country's economy and how it would affect different groups within German society.

reparations payments and that calmed the disturbed situation in Germany at the time.

The Dawes Committee produced a plan relatively quickly, by August 1924. Its main provisions were:

- a rescheduling of reparations payments, starting with 1 billion Marks in the first year and rising to 2.5 billion Marks by Year Five
- the removal of French and Belgian troops from the Ruhr
- German assurances that rescheduled payments and the other terms of the Treaty of Versailles would be met
- a reorganised Reichsbank under Allied supervision: half of the new 'general council' were foreign.

The Dawes Plan relied heavily on the offer by a consortium of US banks, under the supervision of the US State Department, to loan Germany 800 billion Marks. This huge sum was intended to be enough to allow the country to resume reparations payments and to stabilise the economy.

Germany's Social Democratic governments had limited scope for action, so dependent were they on the decisions and actions of the Allies. Presented with the plan, they had little choice but to agree. Dawes himself went on to be awarded a Nobel Prize and to be elected US vice-president.

The period between 1924 and 1929 was a more settled one economically in Germany. The stabilisation of the currency and massive financial loans from the US, as well as the rescheduling of reparations payments called for by the Dawes Plan, were largely responsible for that. In many fields of economic activity – banking, industry, commerce and farming – the mantra was 'rationalisation'. This was despite quite modest economic growth rates, but at least it was a more optimistic time.

The economy of Weimar Germany was in relatively good shape by 1929. The hyperinflation of 1923 was over, the currency was stabilised and industrial growth resumed, albeit on a modest scale. Many of the state's major assets – the Reichsbank, the National Railways System and many industries – had been used as collateral for these huge US loans but even so, compared to what had gone before, times were good. No wonder this period is known as the Golden Twenties (*Goldene Zwanziger*).

A population of nearly 65 million benefited from the Weimar Republic's liberal reforms, although unemployment remained stubbornly high at about 2 million. There was even a resumption of trade, internal as well as overseas, although, as with industry, the growth was relatively modest. As Currency Commissioner and President of the Reichsbank, Schacht played an important role in the stabilisation of and growing international confidence in the new currency. Meanwhile, the removal of foreign troops from the key Ruhr industrial area negotiated under the Dawes Plan in 1924 was not only of political importance but also provided a significant industrial boost.

However, it became clear to the Allied Reparations Commission after 1924, that Germany was unable or unwilling to make even the rescheduled reparations payments of 132 billion Marks laid out in the Dawes Plan. The US industrialist Owen D. Young, who had been the USA's other member of the Dawes Committee, was asked early in 1929 to form a new committee to consider the problem and to suggest a solution.

The Young Committee met in the first part of 1929 and agreed a package of measures that they thought to be fair and one that would be acceptable to the Allies. Reparations payments were to be reduced by 20% to 112 billion Marks over 59 years. There was little expectation that this sum would be paid in full but the annual payment of 2 billion Marks was, the Young Committee hoped, a feasible sum. To ensure as far as possible that it was achievable, they agreed to split the annual payment into two parts – one-third unconditional and two-thirds that could be postponed until later. This latter part did attract interest but it was to be managed by a consortium of leading US banks.

These were quite generous terms but they were never put to the test. Between their agreement in mid-1929 and formal adoption in January 1930, the Wall Street Crash took place in the USA and the world was plunged into economic crisis which changed everything – economically, socially and politically.

Industrial growth

The Dawes Plan of 1924 had taken the urgency out of the political equation by playing a major part in stabilising the German economy. In the period 1924–29, industrial production increased at an annual rate of 7.9%, while the economy as a whole grew at about 4% annually. This was not a booming economy (Germany lagged behind its industrial competitors), but growth was growth and the government was glad to have it. The Reichsbank succeeded in attracting inward investment, intended to allow business to grow. This was good news, although the fact that so much of this money was on short-term loan was to create problems later, because the debts fell due at the time when Germany was least able to repay them.

A good sign was that housing construction was accelerated and 2 million new homes were built during the Weimar period.

Nevertheless, companies were still under considerable pressure and there was a widespread attempt at rationalisation. This meant that they tried to make changes to the way they worked in order to get the best possible use out of their labour force, machinery, raw materials and the fuel or energy they used. Secondly, there was concentration, or what is called 'cartelisation'. A number of mergers took place, creating fewer, larger companies. This put these companies in a stronger position where they could reduce costs or raise prices or both. These developments (in an economy which was already relatively cartelised) was not necessarily a benign development as it threatened competition and flexibility. The government's suspicion of the process was indicated by the fact that it had already tried to tackle cartelisation in 1923.

There were three further major economic problems, all to do with the workforce. The first was that of wages. After the Mark had stabilised, wages rose quite quickly and then, after a patch of stabilising, rose again. Wage demands were probably driven by the fear of inflation. Higher wages meant higher costs for the companies who employ them.

The second problem was productivity. Economic historians often argue that German workers in this period only achieved relatively low productivity. This means that the average amount that each employee made was lower than in a comparable business in another country.

The final problem was unemployment. This remained high: even in what might be regarded as the economy's best year, unemployment was still higher than in the pre-war period's worst years. The government suffered in two ways. First, more unemployed meant more people to whom it had to pay unemployment benefits. There was a strong tradition of social and industrial welfare in the Weimar Republic, despite its political shift to the Centre-Right. In 1924 a Public Assistance programme was introduced by the Weimar government of the day and the following year the accident insurance programme was reformed, allowing certain occupational disorders to be insurable. The second problem for the government was that fewer employed people meant fewer people paying taxes.

In this context, the fact that central government spending almost doubled between 1924 and 1929 was clearly a matter of concern. Another indicator that all was not entirely well with the German economy was that the state had run budget deficits. This meant that, as a country, Germany had spent more than it had earned. In a mature, stable economy, this need not be a problem. But Germany was far from being stable and its politics were far from mature.

Agriculture

Germany's agriculture had suffered during the war. Hit by poor harvests in 1916 and 1917, production had fallen. As the war ended, the country was only producing 50% of the butter and 60% of the meat compared to pre-war levels.

Agriculture was heavily dependent on manure to fertilise and the drastic wartime reduction in the national livestock herds left farms short of this resource. There was also a shortage of fodder, so increasing the herd size was something that could only be done slowly. Imports of fodder and fertiliser helped, but they only increased slowly and both added to costs. A combination of the use of artificial fertilisers and the slow growth of the numbers of animals meant that production gradually crept up.

Germany's agricultural sector was hit by a severe drop in prices in 1921. Although less affected than industry by hyperinflation, farmers were hit again in 1925–26 when the world had a grain surplus, which meant that prices for grain plummeted. In addition, imports of food at prices lower than the farmers could compete with created a problem.

The obvious solution – to modernise and improve productivity – was easier said than done. Change is usually expensive in the short term even if it pays dividends in the longer term. In agriculture, change meant investing in new technology, buying farm machinery such as tractors. Increasing automation of agriculture did lead to some increases in productivity but it also meant fewer jobs in agriculture, thereby fuelling rural unemployment and an increasing drift of the population towards urban areas. At the same time, investment in machinery often required loans. Farmers who borrowed to invest sometimes ended up defaulting, unable to keep up the interest and repayment: bankruptcy meant that the sales of farms increased.

In 1928 farmers undertook several demonstrations against these foreclosures (farms being seized when farmers did not pay their debts) and the low prices they were receiving for their products. These tilted over into riots.

The tendency of governments to respond to the problems in the countryside by providing subsidies to the agricultural sector was politically and socially understandable. However, it increased government expenditure without increasing productivity. The other policy, of introducing protectionist tariffs, protected farmers but hit consumers, as had been the situation under Bismarck.

By the later 1920s, agriculture production looked as though it was returning to the levels it had achieved before the First World War. But in 1929, German agricultural production was still less than three-quarters of its pre-war levels.

Social developments

The effect of war on German society

The major social effect of the First World War was, of course, the departure of so many men to fight. With husbands and fathers in uniform, wives and sons were relied upon to earn money and fill their places in factories and on farms.

The fact that many women found jobs in factories represented a major social change from pre-war imperial Germany. Before the war, middle- and upper-class women in particular were expected to remain at home, looking after their children and husbands, being tied to house cleaning, attending church and maintaining an unquestioned loyalty to the kaiser. Now many were out and about in the world of work.

Around a million or so German soldiers were killed in the First World War. In addition, many others returned home badly injured. It became a common sight, especially in the cities, to see wounded ex-soldiers begging at street corners. A further consequence of mounting wartime German casualties was the increasing number of widows and of women supporting disabled men.

Large numbers of women now lived in circumstances which left them either less able or less willing to behave as the pre-war society of imperial Germany expected. These things changed assumptions about a society based on the family unit.

A second major effect of the war was the shortage of food. Shortages naturally pushed up prices so that the food that was in the shops was expensive. The resulting poor diet caused a deterioration in people's health. Children and the old were particularly vulnerable.

Social changes in Weimar Germany

The inflation that hit most Germans between 1919 and 1923 itself produced profound social changes. The middle class, the bedrock of society, seemed to

ACTIVITY 2.10

In what ways can we regard the increasing employment of women as a positive development?

Make notes on the positives and negatives. Put these into the context of German society: was it inevitable that some of these changes were short-term?

Figure 2.7: Children queue up at a soup kitchen, Berlin, 1924.

many to be disappearing. Middle-class households sold their silver and porcelain. Teachers and professors had to sell their libraries and many had to take unskilled manual jobs. Unaccustomed to poverty, these genteel families had to learn new survival skills. Inflation hit all those on fixed incomes hardest, but even those with any savings in German banks saw them become worthless.

Some did well enough. Anyone who had access to foreign currency, such as US dollar bills, had an advantage. Farmers who exported items, or even those who sold produce at local markets, did well too. The old rural nobility, such as those with estates in East Prussia, could prosper.

Not far beneath the surface was a deep resentment of what the great majority perceived as the unfairness of the Treaty of Versailles. This was especially true of the reparations payments demanded by the Allies. Economics and politics were never far apart in Weimar Germany and the bitterness over reparations created a fertile field for the more extreme politics of right and left.

Social changes continued to occur but at least Germany was free of the corrosive effects of massive inflation. The proportion of the population working in industry continued to grow. For women and men, the flight from rural areas to jobs in the ever-expanding towns was marked. There was a huge increase in white-collar jobs – in scientific laboratories, on the display floors of department stores and in government. Many observers commented on the appearance of a new middle class.

The Weimar period saw important changes in the role of women in German society. The new constitution gave the vote to women, who now could feel that they had a stake in the political destiny of Germany. This was of enormous potential significance, since women made up well over 50% of the electorate. In the 1919 elections, 49 women were even elected to the Reichstag.

Nevertheless, social historians have drawn attention to two things. The ability of women to vote and the presence of women in the Reichstag did not greatly affect the attitudes of society to women or of women to themselves. Furthermore, although extending the suffrage to include women was clearly a radical political step, it did not result in women voting for radical political parties. The SPD, which might be regarded as the main parent of the 1919 Constitution, did benefit to some degree, but there was no great swing in their favour. Women appear to have voted largely for Conservative parties; indeed, recent decades have seen various studies of the support that women gave to the NSDAP. Commentators have pointed out that the women's suffrage movement had only ever been small in Germany and that most women, including suffragists, had been taken by surprise by the Constitution. However, although voting patterns did not change dramatically, the main political parties did now have to consider the female vote when developing their policies. The Social Democrats, for example, made a direct appeal to women in some of their election posters.

The factory jobs undertaken by women during the war (which were quickly reclaimed by men after 1918) had at least persuaded women that they could match their male colleagues as employees. Despite rationalisation and the return of the demobilised soldiers, women continued to be a significant part of agriculture and domestic service, but were also moving into clerical work. By 1925 they made up more than a quarter of the white-collar and civil service employees; by 1933 they were nearly a third of that group.

It is important to put in perspective the advances made in women's rights in Weimar Germany. The conviction that woman's natural role in society was in marriage and the bearing of children within a secure family framework was a deeply rooted one.

Nevertheless, as the German economy stabilised after 1924, the growth in business and in many aspects of daily life created employment opportunities. The new department stores in many cities created jobs for saleswomen and, sometimes, salesmen. The innovative designs of new affordable housing developments, as well as the department stores, new automobile design and **infrastructure** improvements, all changed the face of urban areas in Germany.

The wartime General Staff, senior ranks and the most fashionable regiments had still been dominated by the Prussian Junker class. Now the military was much reduced in size by the terms of the Treaty of Versailles. The regular army was to be reduced to 100 000 men and the General Staff abolished. This left fewer job opportunities for the younger sons of Junkers.

The social status of the army was reduced and its morale damaged. Nevertheless, the military worked hard in the Weimar Republic to restore their battered reputation. The commander-in-chief of the German army between 1920 and 1926 was General Hans von Seeckt. He sought to fashion an army within the military restrictions imposed by Versailles that was as ready to defend Germany's interests fiercely as any German or Prussian force in the past. He did this in a number of ways:

- He selected only the best officers for his trimmed army, who would be well capable of commanding troops at a higher level.
- He developed an efficient system of army reserves, who could expand the standing army at short notice.
- He trained his diminished forces well, using the latest military techniques.

Seeckt was greatly assisted in his task by the sometimes secret support of major German arms manufacturers such as Krupp, many of whom shared his conservative political views. New weapons were designed in secret and plans were drawn up. Submarines, military aircraft and tanks had all been explicitly banned by Versailles but their development did take place, often outside Germany. At the same time, German military designers were kept active, often working on contract overseas.

Cultural changes in Weimar Germany

The Weimar period, with its freedoms of thought and expression, is notable for the richness and diversity of its cultural life. The lack of restrictions led to a great flourishing of both the sciences and the arts.

In **architecture**, little was designed and built during the first phase of the Weimar Republic, but the best-known buildings were yet to come. The angry, stark artistic school of Expressionism gave way to a new, softer, cleaner style called the 'New Objectivity, a movement through all the arts'. Famous buildings include Erich Mendelsohn's Schocken Department store (built 1929–30). The Bauhaus building in Dessau, designed by Walter Gropius and built 1925–26, is, perhaps, the most famous building of the Weimar period. It was a centre for the study and practice of art and design. The influential German architect Ludwig Mies van der Rohe was Director of the Bauhaus school from 1930 to 1933.

In **music**, the Austrian composer Arnold Schoenberg had settled in Berlin before 1914. His early works were in a rich, highly emotional, late Romantic style, but he moved into an atonal style and developed the 12-tone technique, perhaps the most important influence on 20th-century music. His work divided audiences and critics – then and now.

There are a number of significant contributions to **literature** in this period. Alfred Döblin's 1929 novel *Berlin Alexanderplatz* is set in a working-class area of Berlin in the 1920s. Döblin was a doctor active in working-class Berlin and he knew about the struggle for survival in these areas from personal experience. Thomas Mann had been famous since publishing *Buddenbrooks* in 1901. His novel *The Magic Mountain* (*Der Zauberberg*) was started in 1912 but only published in 1924. It uses the imagery of illness and health to open up questions about the way in which society works and the importance of individuals pursuing a spiritual development. Erich Maria Remarque's novel *All Quiet on the Western Front* (in German the title literally means 'in the west, nothing new') came out in 1929. It sold well but was heavily criticised by those who felt that it demeaned the soldiers it described. A few years after publication, it was being burnt in the street, and the film made of it caused demonstrations that turned into minor riots.

The 1920s were particularly vibrant for German **cinema**. In 1920, the silent expressionist classic film *The Cabinet of Doctor Caligari* was released, directed by Robert Wiene, and 1926 saw the appearance of F.W. Murnau's *Faust*. These are examples of film influenced by developments in late Romantic and Modernist literary ideas. Fritz Lang's silent expressionist science fiction film *Metropolis* was released in 1927. It was an attempt to make a film that genuinely caused audiences to think about the way in which society and the economy worked. Lang went on to direct *M* (1931) telling the story of a notorious child-killer and asking questions about criminality, law and justice. Another famous example of Weimar cinema was *The Blue Angel* (1930). Directed by Josef von Sternberg, it starred Emil Jannings as Professor Unrath and it made a star of Marlene Dietrich, who played the part of Lola Lola, a nightclub singer. The film was freely adapted from a novel by Heinrich Mann called *Professor Unrat* (1905).

The playwright Bertolt Brecht and the composer Kurt Weill collaborated several times, notably on *Der Dreigroschenoper* (The Threepenny Opera). This tells the story of criminals and prostitutes plotting robberies, surely a commentary on capitalism by the Marxist playwright. Weill's score was heavily influenced by jazz and cabaret. By the time that Brecht fled from Germany in 1933, the opera had been translated into 18 other languages and had been performed over 10 000 times.

Figure 2.8: The main Bauhaus building, Dessau.

Figure 2.9: Emil Jannings and Marlene Dietrich in *The Blue Angel* (1930).

Jazz itself took off after 1924, when German radio regularly started playing it and popular German band-leaders such as Eric Borchard and Stefan Weintraub had success. US stars such as Paul Whiteman, a regular visitor to Berlin after 1926, were always popular in Germany. The nightclub scene thrived at this time, although it was regarded by some as degenerate. This was a frenetic, exuberant period when people – both men and women – were given previously unheard-of freedoms of speech, of thought and of religion. Those of a traditional cast of mind, who looked back to the social certainties of imperial Germany, were dismayed.

The history of modern **dance** was strongly influenced by the dancer and choreographer Mary Wigman (born Marie Wiegmann). In 1918 she opened a dance school in Dresden and taught expressionist dance, with an emphasis on free and uninhibited movement. She rejected *pointe* ballet shoes and the style they demand. She was also a pioneer in the use of dance as therapy.

George Grosz belonged to a group of artists known as the New Objectivity movement. His pictures lampooning German institutions and characters are irreverent and show no respect for authority. He was arrested following the 1919 Spartacist Uprising, but was exonerated and later that year joined the KPD. He was fined for insulting the army in 1921. Having visited Bolshevik Russia, he resigned from the KPD in 1922.

Innovation in **science** needs a willingness to rethink established and accepted ideas, and the freedom to experiment without limitations. The spirit of Weimar, its open-mindedness, lack of deference and tolerance of criticism, created the sort of atmosphere in which science could flourish.

Women were given greater civil rights and greater access to education and employment in Germany in this period. Lisa Meitner, an Austrian physicist, set up a laboratory with her colleague Otto Hahn in the Kaiser Wilhelm Institute (KWI) in Berlin-Dahlem in 1912. She worked without a salary until she was given a paid job there in 1913. In 1922, after serving as a nurse in the First World War operating X-ray equipment, she discovered the cause of the emission of electrons with particular amounts of energy from a surface. (This is called the Auger Effect after Pierre Auger, a French scientist who independently discovered the effect the following year.)

She and Hahn jointly discovered the chemical element Protactinium (Pa) in 1917/18. Hahn received the Nobel Prize for Chemistry in 1944; Meitner did not.

Perhaps the most famous scientist at KWI in this or any other period was Albert Einstein, Director of Physics between 1914 and 1932. His revolutionary work on relativity and quantum theory had transformed the subject and in the process undermined the consensus that had existed since the time of Isaac Newton in 17th-century England.

The political, economic and social condition of Germany by 1929

Weimar Germany began 1929 looking relatively settled, despite the presence of extremist parties and a history of frequent changes in the make-up of governments.

The fear of a repeat in Germany of Russia's 1917 revolution had faded and the spectre of Bolshevik chaos had lifted. For many on the right of politics, this removed an important prop from their support of the Weimar Republic. The KPD that had grown out of the Spartacus League never had the support or resources to challenge government or establishment, however much they claimed to be able to do so.

The powerful institutions in Germany – the army, the industrialists and financiers, the Protestant and Catholic churches, landowners and the professions – retained their nostalgia for an autocratic, monarchical form of government. The criticisms of the Weimar Republic by these groups became louder and louder as the decade progressed and the fear of Bolshevik-style revolution faded. Only in the civil service had the Weimar Republic made inroads into this conservative cast of mind and even so the senior ranks had limited commitment to Weimar beliefs and democratic principles.

The arrangement that President Friedrich Ebert had made in 1919 with the military – protection for the new Weimar Republic from insurrection – had been bought at a high price. Many of Germany's traditional elites remained unreformed or with their status unchallenged. The 'stab in the back' (*Dolchstoß*) interpretation of German military defeat in 1918 had become even more embedded for conservative political groups.

By the summer of 1929, the inflation of 1921–24 was over and its worst effects were slowly fading. Unemployment was still high but at least it had gone down, while exports were up. Prices were fairly stable and wages rose slowly. As a whole, the German economy in this middle period of the Weimar Republic (1924–29) grew modestly, although there were no spectacular technological innovations or surges in production.

Socially there had been many changes in Germany since 1918. The position of women in German society, especially in the big cities, had changed markedly. Their actual experience of the freedoms guaranteed by the Weimar Constitution – to vote, to live, to work – may have been different from what was written on paper, but these freedoms were nevertheless available as they had not been before.

The traditional view of historians since the end of the Second World War in 1945 has been to see the period 1919–33 in Germany as one of cultural experiment, during which the country underwent a series of political and economic crises. However, in the last decade, historical analysis of the Weimar Republic by Eric D. Weitz and other predominantly cultural and social historians has revealed a dynamic, democratic period in German history that may be seen in its own right rather than as an experiment doomed to political disaster because it 'failed' to prevent the rise of National Socialism and with a fragile economy unable to withstand a series of crises in 1919, 1923 and 1929.

The very title of Anthony McElligott's 2013 book, *Rethinking the Weimar Republic: Authority and Authoritarianism 1916–1936*, is challenging. Beginning in 1916 and ending in 1936 (rather than the more conventional 1919 and 1933) reflects the argument that the defining issue of the period was one of political authority. McElligott's analysis is that the issue arose during the First World War and continued during Nazi rule. Some have even extended it to the end of the Second World War in 1945.

There has been no questioning of the cultural dynamism of Weimar Germany. Its products are there for all to see and hear, but questions still remain. Was all this cultural activity appreciated by just a handful of the social elite, while the great majority carried on with the daily struggle regardless? Were many of the artists as busy criticising and mocking the republic as the extreme political parties of right and left? What does seem common ground, however, is that the rich cultural life of Weimar Germany was in some way related to the creation of a supportive atmosphere, a period of remarkable freedoms.

Timeline

1914	August: outbreak of First World War; SPD vote in the Reichstag to approve military expenditure – Liebknecht is the only member to vote against; War Raw Materials Department (*Kriegsrohstuffabteilung*) established under the industrialist Walter Rathenau
1915	Sinking of the *Lusitania*
1916	May–June: Battle of Jutland (*Skagerrakschlacht*) August: General Paul von Hindenburg becomes Army Chief of Staff Turnip Winter
1917	January: all restrictions on targets removed for German submarines April: USA enters the war; formation of the USPD July: Bethmann Hollweg resigns as chancellor, replaced by Georg Michaelis August: mutinies at the naval centre of Wilhelmshaven October: Michaelis resigns as chancellor, replaced by von Hertling

1918	March: Germany signs Treaty of Brest-Litovsk with defeated Russia
	September: General Ludendorff informs Paul von Hintze, foreign minister, that the Western Front might collapse at any time; von Hertling resigns the chancellorship
	October: German Imperial Navy's High Seas Fleet ordered to put to sea to confront the blockading Royal Navy fleet; appointment of Prince Maximilian von Baden as chancellor; SPD joins cabinet; constitution changed; political power moved to the Reichstag
	7 November: Ebert demands increased role in the government for SPD and further reform; he calls for emperor and crown prince to renounce throne
	9 November: Kaiser Wilhelm II's abdication is announced; Chancellor Prince Max von Baden resigns; Ebert becomes chancellor
	9 November: Scheidemann proclaims a republic
	9 November: Liebknecht proclaims a Free Socialist Republic
	10 November: Ebert forms government of his SPD and the USPD
	10 November: imperial family goes into exile
	10 November: Ebert–Groener telephone call
	11 November: ceasefire on Western Front
1918–19	influenza pandemic
1919	January: victorious Allies meet at Versailles
	4–15 January: Spartacist Uprising in Berlin
	19 January: federal elections; SPD win nearly 38% of votes cast
	January: Constitutional Convention begins in Weimar
	February: Ebert resigns as chancellor and as president appoints Scheidemann
	April: German delegation summoned to Paris
	May: Scheidemann opposes draft Treaty of Versailles in the Reichstag; Bavarian Soviet Republic declared in Munich
	June: Treaty of Versailles signed by all parties; British Royal Navy lifts blockade of the North Sea; Scheidemann resigns as chancellor, replaced by Gustav Bauer
	August: President Ebert signs Weimar Constitution into law

1920	March: Kapp–Lüttwitz Putsch in Berlin; Ruhr Uprising; Bauer resigns as chancellor, replaced by Hermann Müller
	June: federal elections; Müller resigns as chancellor, replaced by Constantin Fehrenbach
1921	April: Germany signs Treaty of Rapallo with Russia
	May: Fehrenbach resigns as chancellor, replaced by Joseph Wirth
	June: inflation becomes severe
1922	June: assassination of Foreign Minister Walter Rathenau
	November: Wirth resigns as chancellor, replaced by Wilhelm Cuno
	December: Reparations Commission declare Germany in default
1923	January: French troops invade and occupy the Ruhr industrial area
	August: Wilhelm Cuno replaced as chancellor by Gustav Stresemann
	September: Bavarian Prime Minister declares state of emergency
	October: Chancellor Stresemann announces ending of resistance to the occupation of the Ruhr and state of emergency; hyperinflation reaches 29 500%
	November: Munich Putsch; Crown Prince Wilhelm visits Germany at Stresemann's invitation; Stresemann resigns as chancellor, replaced by Wilhelm Marx; Hjalmar Schacht appointed Currency Commissioner (and later president of restructured Reichsbank)
1924	January: Marx declares state of emergency, issues emergency decree replacing trial by jury by trained and lay judges (Emminger Reform); end of hyperinflation
	March: Reichstag seeks to discuss abolition of decrees; Ebert dismisses parliament to avoid discussion
	May: federal elections
	August: Dawes Committee produces proposals; Monetary Law allows the exchange of each 1 trillion Mark note for one new Reichsmark
	December: federal elections; Hans Luther forms government
1925	January: Marx replaced as chancellor of Germany by Luther
	February: Ebert dies
	March: General Paul von Hindenburg wins presidential elections
	December: Locarno Treaties signed

1926	May: Luther resigns as chancellor, replaced by Marx
	September: Germany joins League of Nations
	October: Hans von Seeckt allows Prince Wilhelm to join *Reichswehr* manoeuvres; later Seeckt resigns as head of army
	December: Law for the Protection of Youth from Trash and Filth Writings
1928	May: federal elections
	June: Marx resigns as chancellor, replaced by Müller
	Farmers' demonstrations
1929	Young Committee meet and agree a package of measures
	October: Wall Street Crash in New York, USA
	October: Gustav Stresemann dies

 Practice essay questions

1. To what extent do you think that Weimar Germany was characterised by a cult of militarism that it had inherited from the Kaiserreich?
2. 'The governments of the Weimar Republic were no more successful in creating an alliance of different social groups than had been Wilhelm II.' Assess the validity of this view.
3. 'The traditional elites continued to dominate German politics between 1900 and 1929.' Assess the validity of this view.
4. With reference to these extracts and your understanding of the historical context, which of these two extracts provides the more convincing interpretation of the impact of the Ebert–Groenerpact on Weimar Germany in the 1920s?

Extract A

The Ebert–Groener pact was an ambivalent achievement. It secured for the socialist republic authority the means to enforce order and protect itself against further upheavals. This was a major step forward for an executive structure that had no meaningful armed force of its own and no constitutional foundation for its authority, save the right of usurpation bestowed by the revolution itself. Seen in this light, the Ebert–Groener pact was shrewd, pragmatic and in any case necessary, since there was no plausible alternative. Yet there was also something ominous in the army's setting of political conditions even for the fulfilment of urgent tasks within its own remit, such as demobilisation. What mattered here was not the substance of Groener's demands, which were reasonable enough, but the army's formal arrogation of the right to treat with the civilian authority on an equal footing.

Source: Clark, C. *Iron Kingdom: The Rise and Downfall of Prussia, 1600–1947,* Penguin, 2007

Extract B

Although the full implications of the Ebert–Groener pact could not be guessed by Ebert's colleagues, the Independents were uneasy about it, and Haase's son afterwards wrote of his father at this time, that he 'very soon suspected that Ebert was intriguing behind the backs of the other People's Commissars and was in very close contact with the army. But he could not realise to what extent that was in fact the case.' Dittmann later denounced Ebert's policy as one of sabotage and claims to have noticed at the time the effect of Ebert's nocturnal talks with Groener in his attitude at the cabinet next morning. Ebert's relationship with the supreme command has been described as 'bordering on treason towards his own party'.

Source: Lutz, Ralph Haswell, *The German Revolution, 1918–1919,* Ulan Press, 2012

Chapter summary

You should now have a good understanding of how the German republic was founded, and the way in which the politics of the republic were shaped by the events of 1918, the work of the Constitutional Convention in 1919 and the terms of the Treaty of Versailles. In particular, you should remember that:

- The First World War began amid an atmosphere of apparent national unity. It ended in defeat, recrimination, mutinies and revolutions.
- Following the war there was a major reshaping of the political landscape, with parties merging, splitting, being founded and being closed down.
- The terms of the Treaty of Versailles were even worse than expected. Economic historians still debate how fair or unfair, possible or impossible the reparations were. The loss of territory was an offence to national pride and the invasion of the Ruhr by foreign troops only added to this. Jews, foreigners and left-wing politicians were among the people blamed by those who did not understand how the country had been defeated or did not believe it had been.
- The 1919 Constitution introduced a number of social reforms, but the republic never commanded the support of enough of the population: nationalist and monarchist parties continually attracted large numbers of voters.
- The framework of democracy was in place, with elections, parties, lobby groups and campaigns, but political life was also marked by a profusion of armed groups who fought one another in the streets.
- Hyperinflation became a major problem but it was brought under control. Yet unemployment remained high and productivity remained low even during the more prosperous years.

End notes

1   Weitz, Eric D. *Weimar Germany*, Princeton University Press, 2007

2   Luxemburg, Rosa, *The Crisis in German Democracy*, 1915

3   Merkel P. *Political Violence under the Swastika*, Princeton University Press, 1975

4   Seeckt, Hans von, quoted in Wheeler-Bennett J, *The Nemesis of Power*, Macmillan, 1967

5   From *The Diary of Alfred Rosenberg*

6   Stark, Gary D. *Entrepreneurs of Ideology: Neoconservative Publishers in Germany, 1890–1933*, University of North Carolina Press, 1981

7   Davis, Belinda J. *Home Fires Burning*, University of North Carolina Press, 2000

8   Keynes, John M. *The Economic Consequences of the Peace*, Macmillan, 1919

9   Keynes, *Economic Consequences*

3 The Nazi experiment, 1929–49

In this section, we will be studying how Germany's democracy did not survive a dramatic economic crisis. An authoritarian party came to power, established a persecuting tyranny and took the country into a war that it ultimately lost, leaving a ruined nation to be invaded, occupied and partitioned. We will look into:

- Political authority, 1929–45: the collapse of Weimar democracy and the establishment of the one-party authoritarian Nazi state; the roles of Hindenburg and Hitler

- Government and opposition to 1945: Nazism as an ideology and in practice; Hitler's style of government; the terror state; opposition and resistance; key Nazi leaders; the effect of war

- Political authority and government 1945–49: post-war occupation and division; the issue of Berlin and the blockade; the division of Germany

- Economic developments: the impact of the Depression; recovery and development under the Nazis in peace and war; post-war economy

- Social developments and tensions; Nazi social policies, including *Volksgemeinschaft* and the racial state; Nazi culture; post-war German society and the legacy of Nazism

- The political, economic and social condition of Germany by 1949.

Political authority, 1929–45

The collapse of Weimar democracy

There were clear signs of political instability in the last years of the Weimar Republic:

- There were four national elections between 1928 and 1933 – two of them in 1932 alone.
- In 1932, President Hindenburg appointed no fewer than four chancellors.
- Voters began to abandon the parties of the political centre ground and to move their support to the extreme parties of both Right and Left.

In the two and a half years between the 1928 and 1930 elections, politics in the Weimar Republic had become more and more unstable as successive governments struggled to cope with the economic crisis of the Depression.

The Social Democrats had founded the republic in 1919 on democratic principles. Historically the strongest party in the Weimar Republic, they remained so in 1928 with 153 seats in the Reichstag, but their support declined from then on.

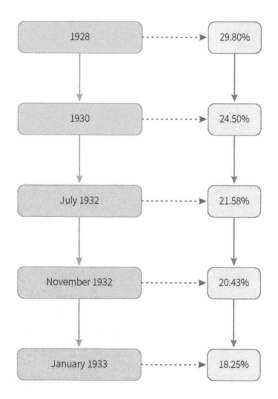

Figure 3.1: Flow diagram showing SPD electoral support, 1928–33.

Only the Catholic Centre Party kept a steady vote in federal elections between 1928 and 1932 with around 15%. However, even it showed the way in which the political climate was changing, as it had drifted to the right and was in alliance with the conservative *Bayerische Volkspartei* (BVP).

It was to the political parties of the extreme Right and extreme Left that many voters turned for a solution to Germany's problems.

The political parties of the extreme Right, especially the NSDAP, had enjoyed a close relationship with the Army High Command for many years. The Army Purge of January–February 1938 saw the removal of Generals Werner von Blomberg and Werner von Fritsch from their senior positions in the Army High Command and also the creation of a new military command structure, the OKW (*Oberkommando der Wehrmacht*). Chancellor Adolf Hitler regarded the two generals as lacking the enthusiasm needed for his preparations for war. Hitler also purged the Army of other senior generals, replacing them with those guaranteed to be more loyal. The German Army were now firmly under Nazi control.

This control was strengthened in December 1941 after the German military defeat in Russia and their failure to capture Moscow. Hitler now assumed personal command of the armed forces through the elevation of the OKW under Field Marshall Wilhelm Keitel. The OKW was now in overall charge of the German Armed Forces, replacing the existing Army High Command. Keitel was put in charge because he was known to be loyal to Adolf Hitler, who increasingly took the decisive military decisions. (See section 'Government and opposition to 1945: Hitler's style of government' for an assessment of Hitler as a strong or weak leader.)

A major part of the background to these developments in politics lies in a rapid economic change which had begun outside the country.

The Wall Street Crash and its initial impact on Germany

The 'Wall Street Crash' of late October 1929 was a sudden fall in the prices of shares on the New York stock exchange. It led to soaring bankruptcies and unemployment in the longest, deepest and most widespread economic depression of the 20th century. How did such an economic disaster happen so suddenly?

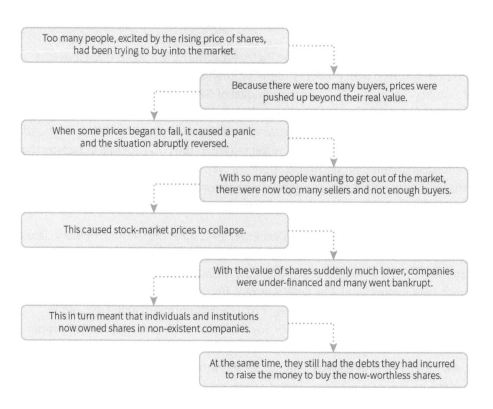

Too many people, excited by the rising price of shares, had been trying to buy into the market.

Because there were too many buyers, prices were pushed up beyond their real value.

When some prices began to fall, it caused a panic and the situation abruptly reversed.

With so many people wanting to get out of the market, there were now too many sellers and not enough buyers.

This caused stock-market prices to collapse.

With the value of shares suddenly much lower, companies were under-financed and many went bankrupt.

This in turn meant that individuals and institutions now owned shares in non-existent companies.

At the same time, they still had the debts they had incurred to raise the money to buy the now-worthless shares.

Figure 3.2: Flow diagram showing the reasons for the Wall Street Crash.

The economy of the USA plunged into depression and, such was its economic power, it dragged the rest of the world with it into an economic depression that lasted ten years. Indeed, it was 25 years before the prices of shares returned to where they had been in the boom of 1929.

Under economic pressure, the US government and banks recalled their overseas loans. This was disastrous for many foreign institutions and governments, but it was a particular catastrophe for the fragile economy of Germany. The huge US loan negotiated under the Dawes Plan in 1924 was withdrawn. The decline in world prices hit Germany's export of manufactured goods hard and the modest economic growth of Weimar Germany since 1924 collapsed. Unemployment rates in Germany rose to 6 million. For the historian William Carr, the existence of large-scale unemployment was a test not just of governments but of political parties and democracy itself, a test that the voters increasingly decided they had all failed:

Because parliamentary institutions seemed incapable of dealing boldly with mass unemployment, critics on the right and left called into question the basic liberal concepts of freedom and the rule of law even in the well-established democratic countries. Authoritarianism in the 1930s was generally accompanied by a resurgence in nationalism.

The Young Plan of 1929 was agreed before the Crash, but formally adopted after it. It effectively reduced Germany's indebtedness by 90% and the US agreed not to press for any immediate resumption of reparation payments. US President Hoover proposed a one-year moratorium on such payments, well aware that right-wing parties in Germany would see the weakness of the Social Democratic government of the Weimar Republic as an opportunity to attack it.

Governments come and go

The SPD was the largest party after the May 1928 elections so Hermann Müller became chancellor, leading a **coalition** of SPD, DDP, DVP and the Centre Party. Agreeing the 1929 budget and the external liabilities of the Reich was problematic and the partners pinned their hopes on renegotiating the conditions set by the Allies. As the Depression began to take effect in Germany, all issues to do with the budget became of ever greater importance and disagreements within the coalition were fatal to its survival. Hindenburg refused to support Müller's government by using the Article 48 emergency powers, so Müller resigned.

The Centre Party's Heinrich Brüning was appointed as the new chancellor. In his cabinet were representatives of the Centre itself, but also the DDP and DVP as before, but the SPD were dropped in favour of right-wing parties: the BVP from Bavaria, the DNVP and a DNVP breakaway, the small, Conservative KVP (*Konservative Volkspartei*).

Brüning saw tackling inflation as his government's priority. He made cuts to government spending and tightened control over money supply. The army and industrialists were initially in favour of his appointment as chancellor, believing him to be a Conservative who would take the Weimar government to the right. His appointment of Groener as interior minister (he was already defence minister) was calculated to retain the army's support.

But as company profits declined and bankruptcies increased Brüning became less popular with these powerful groups. Lacking a majority in the Reichstag, he relied on President von Hindenburg to push his economic policies through by decree. Brüning's policy of distributing land to unemployed workers unsurprisingly earned the anger of landowners, including the wealthy Junkers. Hindenburg, a Junker himself, ceased to sign emergency decrees. Brüning resigned in April 1932.

He was replaced in June 1932 by Franz von Papen, a Catholic **aristocrat** and Centre Party politician who came to be one of Hindenburg's closest advisers. Like Brüning, von Papen had little support in the Reichstag (he left the Centre Party shortly after accepting the post of chancellor), which left him reliant on the president. Even among the right-wing parties, only the conservative DNVP was willing to back him.

Von Papen called the July 1932 election hoping to win a Reichstag majority. Seeing the results, he asked Hindenburg to decree its dissolution. Before he could read this to the assembly, however, the Communists tabled a vote of no confidence in his government. Unexpectedly, the NSDAP blocked his move to dissolution and supported the Communist motion; von Papen's government lost the vote and another election was automatically triggered.

This time the NSDAP dropped their number of seats for the first time, but they remained the largest party. Hindenburg tried to appoint von Papen chancellor, but when he could not put together a government, the president turned to von Papen's former defence minister, General von Schleicher. Von Schleicher

ACTIVITY 3.1

- What do you think were the causes of the economic and political crisis in Germany?
- Was the Wall Street Crash of 1929 solely responsible for triggering it?
- Was the economic condition of Germany such that disaster was bound to happen?
- Was it only caused by economic problems or did politics play a role?

Using your knowledge of Germany in the 1920s and earlier, list the short-term and longer-term causes of the crisis and put them into what you think their order of importance was.

Make notes on the different governments in the period 1929–33. In each case note down:

- which parties were in the government
- which parties had also been in the previous government
- which parties from the previous government had been excluded
- which parties had been introduced who weren't in the previous government
- their key policies
- how the new government differed from the previous one.

was a military man but active in civilian politics as well, serving as minister of defence under von Papen from June to November 1932, when he himself became chancellor. He resented the Treaty of Versailles of 1919, and believed in authoritarian government. For him, only an authoritarian government could run a 'total war' involving the entire population in the war effort, with mass conscription, mobilisation of the civilian population, strategic bombing, blockade, unrestricted submarine warfare and the use of civilians and prisoners of war as forced labour. This led him to be relatively favourable towards the NSDAP.

Like von Papen, von Schleicher did not have support in the Reichstag. He tried to draw the NSDAP into his cabinet, as von Papen had done. Some Nazis were in favour of joining, but Hitler was not and Hitler won the argument.

Von Schleicher reversed Brüning's austerity policies. He replaced cuts in government spending with a public works programme. This policy contributed to a fall in unemployment but he was not in office long enough to see the results. Like Brüning, he offended landowners: he had promised to introduce protectionist tariffs on food imports and had not done so. The agricultural lobby complained bitterly to Hindenburg.

The president was running out of options. The NSDAP were the largest party in the Reichstag, so the president decided that he had to turn to Hitler.

The 'Liberty Law' (*Freiheitsgesetz*) campaign

The political mood in Germany became increasingly tense after 1929. The legitimacy of the Weimar Republic had been based initially on its ability to prevent Bolshevik unrest, and since 1924 on a measure of economic recovery. Fear of revolution and civil war had been fading for some time as Russia's 1917 and Germany's 1918 moved gradually into the past. With the abrupt end of relative prosperity, more people were prepared to listen to the views of the extreme parties. The various right-wing groups in Germany increased the vigour of their agitation against the liberal democracy of Weimar. They were influential in many of Germany's most powerful institutions and began to gather increasing popular support. Some of this support was channelled into special-issue campaigns.

An early example was the campaign for a 'Liberty Law' (*Freiheitsgesetz*). In response to the Young Plan, a coalition was formed to lobby for the implementation of this law, which had three aims:

- To put an end to reparations payments and make it a criminal offence for any civil servant to collect any
- To repudiate the presence of foreign troops on German soil
- To reject absolutely the War Guilt Clause (Clause 231) of the Treaty of Versailles.

The coalition was formed by the nationalist politician and media baron Alfred Hugenberg and comprised a number of Conservative groups including his own DNVP, the NSDAP and the *Stahlhelm*. Under the terms of the Weimar Constitution, if 10% of the electorate signed a petition on an issue, it then had to be put to a vote in the Reichstag. The coalition held mass rallies and set about gathering signatures. In this they succeeded and the measure was accordingly put to a vote in the Reichstag, where 18% voted for it, not enough for it to become law. In

December 1929 the campaign moved, under the constitution, to a referendum, where it again failed to garner enough votes. Even so, this was the sort of political activity that Hitler's Nazi Party relished, and the fact that the campaign got as far as it did was a measure of the weakness of Weimar democracy and of the growing strength of the Right in German politics.

Hugenberg went on to be the driving force behind the founding of the **Harzburg Front** in October 1931. This brought together a number of political and paramilitary parties and groups of the Right, once again including the DNVP, the NSDAP and the *Stahlhelm*. The Nazi faction was already reluctant to be led in any sense by established, elderly politicians such as Hugenberg, but they were prepared to play along. In any event, by this stage matters were moving out of the control of people like Hugenberg. Adolf Hitler had already met President Hindenburg to discuss the future.

It was typical of the politics of the unsettled years 1928–33 that the parties of the Left reacted to the establishment of the Harzburg Front in October 1931 with the formation of the **Iron Front** a few months later. This included the *Reichsbanner*, the SPD and other groups on the democratic left of Weimar politics, but excluded what they regarded as the extremist KPD. It was also typical of the period that both Fronts were ineffective and quickly fell apart, mainly owing to internal rivalries.

The *Reichsbanner* itself was a paramilitary organisation consisting mostly of former soldiers, who were dedicated to the protection of the Weimar Republic and parliamentary democracy from extremist Conservative groups on the right and Communists on the left. Their banner was the black, red and gold of the Republic. The organisation was formed in 1924 from members of the SPD, the Catholic Centre Party and the liberal German Democratic Party (DDP) but came increasingly to be seen as the militant arm of the first of these. It protected SPD meetings, marches and rallies and fought Red Front Communist and Nazi *Sturmabteilung* members in the streets and in halls. This was street politics; it was also gang war.

Rule by decree

Rule by presidential decree had been undermining Germany's democratic process for years. Under the Weimar Constitution, a president could rule in this way but only under conditions of a national emergency. As soon as the president declared a state of emergency, rule by presidential decree became possible, bypassing the normal democratic procedure. This avoided the need for approval by the elected Reichstag. Of course, for the governments, this meant that they could run the country and avoid being bogged down in endless arguments between political parties that refused to compromise or back down. But it also meant that Germany was continually being denied the experience of living in the liberal democracy described by the 1919 Constitution. Government had effectively become a dictatorship.

Those who designed the Weimar Constitution in 1919 included this provision (Article 48) assuming that it would be a very unusual situation, but it is worth noting that all four of the Weimar Republic's chancellors between 1930 and 1933 (Brüning, von Papen, von Schleicher and Hitler) ruled in this way. Presidents also had the power under the Constitution to appoint and dismiss any chancellor, regardless of their support or otherwise in the Reichstag.

The growth in support for extreme parties

In times of increasing desperation, voters tend to turn to political parties on the extremes. The federal election to the Reichstag of May 1928 had seen the NSDAP gaining just 2.6% of the votes cast, getting them 12 seats. However, in the election of September 1930 they gained 18.3% of the vote and 107 seats. It was a breakthrough election for them.

The Nazis owed some of their electoral success after 1928 to the strength of their national and local organisation, including mastery in the use of propaganda, and a great deal to the financial support of the vehemently anti-Semitic Hugenberg. He had been chairman of the board of Krupp before 1914 and had supervised their financial operations with great success. After 1918 he bought up many local newspapers and controlling shares in a number of national media outlets. He used these to keep up a relentless attack on the Weimar Republic. He also took over the UFA film studios near Berlin.

A long-time monarchist and ultra-conservative, Hugenberg's political activity in the late 1920s was concentrated on his leadership of the DNVP, a Conservative and nationalist party, but he also made donations to the NSDAP in order to increase his influence in the Reichstag.

There were two federal elections in 1932, in July and November. In the first of these the NSDAP gained 37.3% of the vote and 230 seats in the Reichstag. This was easily the largest vote, well over 10% greater than the second-placed Social Democrats. In November the Nazi vote slipped back a little to 33.1% and 196 seats but they were still by far the largest party in the Reichstag. Even so, as the total number of Reichstag deputies was 584, the Nazis and other right-wing extremist parties had no absolute majority without the removal of the Social Democrats and Communists.

Ever since the founding of the NSDAP in 1921, they had, in common with other nationalist and monarchist political parties or groups, been loudly critical of the Weimar Republic and all it stood for. The German army had not been defeated in 1918, they declared, but had been 'stabbed in the back' (*Dolchstoß*) by the cowardly civilian politicians, socialists, Bolsheviks and especially Jews back home. These were 'the November criminals', who had gone on to sign the humiliating and unjust Treaty of Versailles. Reparations payments arising from 'war guilt' put an intolerable burden on Germany and the restrictions imposed on her armed forces were unacceptable to a warlike nation.

This deceitful allegation had been repeated so often by the Nazis and others since their foundation in 1921 that by 1932 it had acquired wide public acceptance. It was a message received ever more readily as the Weimar Republic struggled to cope with the third major economic crisis in the 15 years of its life.

With the failure of the Munich Putsch in 1923, Hitler had concluded that most Germans had too much respect for orderly behaviour to accept direct, extra-parliamentary political action. Voters would only support a political party that appeared to work within the Constitution and its democratic structures. He made sure after 1923 that the Nazis did just that until 1933.

Nevertheless, he was determined to exploit any weakness in the Weimar Constitution to further the ends of the Nazi Party with himself at its head. Weimar democracy was just not strong enough after 1929 to resist the growing political power of the Right in German politics. Many right-wing groups began to coalesce around the Nazi Party, which had proved itself to be well organised, ruthless, equally effective in the Reichstag and on the streets, and possessed of an effective propaganda machine.

The most spectacular gains in votes between 1928 and 1932 were made by the Nazis but the Communists (KPD) also added votes. They rose from 10.6% in the federal election of 1928 to 13.1% in 1930 and 16.9% in November 1932. Led by Ernst Thalmann, they could rely on the paramilitary Red Front (RFB) for protection at meetings and rallies and had solid support in working class areas such as Wedding in Berlin.

However, even strong party organisation and effective use of propaganda or adequate funding is not enough for electoral success. The political message has to be one that appeals to voters. Under the Weimar Constitution, all women and men over the age of 20 could vote, so the Nazis managed to persuade 37% of those who voted in July 1932 that their leadership was best for the future of Germany.

The roles of Hindenburg and Hitler

Figure 3.3: Campaigning (Franz von Papen, centre) in front of a polling station in Berlin, July 1932.

ACTIVITY 3.3

Why was it that the Nazi Party was able to come to power when other extreme right-wing groups in Weimar Germany after 1929 failed to do so? Were their ideas different? Were their methods different? Were the times different?

- Make a mind map showing the ways in which the NSDAP was similar to and different from other groups. Remember to include both political parties and pressure groups.
- When you have completed the mind map, consider whether they would have seemed similar to or different from one another to the electorate. Write a short paragraph drawing attention to key similarities and differences.

1. What options did President Hindenburg have in January 1933 and what should he have done? For example, should he have:
    - ruled directly himself?
    - asked the leader of the second largest party, Otto Wels of the SPD, to form a coalition?
    - appointed a soldier with political experience such as Hans von Seeckt or Wilhelm Groener?
    - something else?

2. Make notes on Hindenburg's options, taking account of the constitutional situation, the electoral arithmetic of the Reichstag, and the different powerbrokers in society such as industrialists, landowners and the army.

Figure 3.4: President Hindenburg appoints Adolf Hitler as chancellor, January 1933.

As President, Hindenburg had two key roles in the government under the 1919 Constitution:

- He could appoint and dismiss any chancellor, regardless of their support or otherwise in the Reichstag.
- He could govern by decree, regardless of the support or otherwise in the Reichstag.

In the crisis that followed the Wall Street Crash, both of these powers were central and Hindenburg used both, in consultation with a circle of advisers known as the **camarilla**. This was a small group around the president, comprising Franz von Papen, Kurt von Schleicher, Otto Meissner and the president's son Oskar von Hindenburg. It was an informal but powerful group whose advice the president listened to carefully. Of these, Otto Meissner, who, as long-serving presidential secretary, ran the Presidential Office throughout the Weimar Republic, from Ebert in 1918 to Hitler in 1934, was regarded as Hindenburg's right-hand man. He certainly knew how things worked from a civil service point of view. No records were kept of the discussions within the *camarilla*.

In January 1933, President Hindenburg was again facing the question of who to appoint as Chancellor of Germany. Hitler was the leader of the single largest party in the Reichstag and Hindenburg was bound to consider him for the post of chancellor. Apart from that, at least two members of the President's inner circle of advisers (von Papen and von Schleicher – one past and one present chancellor) urged him to appoint the man with whom Hindenburg had much in common politically but whom he despised as a lowly rabble-rouser.

The Weimar Constitution was clear on the nature of the appointment by the Reich president of the Reich chancellor (Article 54):

The Reich Chancellor and the Reich ministers, in order to exercise their mandates, require the confidence of the Reichstag. Any one of them has to resign, if the Reichstag votes by explicit decision to withdraw its confidence.[2]

This meant that the president's job was to appoint someone whose party had a majority in the Reichstag or who could put together a coalition which would create a majority in the Reichstag. The point, of course, was that the chancellor and his government needed a majority in order to get proposals accepted and laws passed. Hindenburg was no enthusiast for the Weimar Republic but he had taken a solemn oath (Article 42):

I swear to devote my energy to the welfare of the German people, to increase its prosperity, to prevent damage, to uphold the Reich constitution …and, as a soldier, he knew about duty.[3]

Since 1930 Hindenburg had appointed three different chancellors (Brüning and von Papen from the Centre Party and von Schleicher) who did not meet the constitutional test of having 'the confidence of the Reichstag'. Von Papen had been chancellor for less than six months and resigned after failed negotiations with Hitler. His successor, von Schleicher, was in post for just two months and was dismissed. All three ruled by presidential decree under Article 48 of the Weimar Constitution, but all knew that this could not continue indefinitely.

Both von Papen and von Schleicher were ambitious politicians, close politically but not on good personal terms latterly. Both seemed effective at political intrigue, perhaps von Papen more so, as he died aged 89 in 1969 while von Schleicher was assassinated aged 52 in 1934.

Von Papen is usually credited with persuading President Hindenburg to choose Hitler as Chancellor of Germany. Von Schleicher was also a member of the *camarilla* but was out of favour over agricultural tariffs and his failure to achieve a majority in the Reichstag. Senior officers of the *Reichswehr* (the army) were also lobbying for Hitler and the Nazis. Von Papen seems to have argued that it was better to have Hitler inside government than outside. He believed that a coalition cabinet in which the Nazis did not have a majority, and with himself as effective deputy chancellor, should be enough to control Hitler. Thus in January 1933 President Paul von Hindenburg appointed Adolf Hitler as Chancellor of Germany.

The establishment of the one-party, authoritarian Nazi state

Upon his appointment as chancellor, Hitler immediately set about the establishment of the Nazi state, based on the sort of authoritarian principles that motivated him and his supporters.

The Reichstag fire

On 27 February 1933, just six days before polling day for the March 1933 elections, there was a serious arson attack on the Reichstag building in Berlin. A young Dutch communist, Marinus van der Lubbe, was caught at the scene and later confessed to starting the fire. The Nazis used this event as evidence of a communist conspiracy against the government of Germany. Hitler urged President Hindenburg to declare a state of emergency, suspending a number of civil liberties and allowing him, through his chancellor, to govern by presidential decree as provided for in the Weimar Constitution.

The emergency decree was approved by Hindenburg and in the next few weeks there were mass arrests of communists, including Reichstag deputies. Without KPD delegates in the Reichstag, the Nazis had an absolute majority and could force through any measure they chose. During repairs to the Reichstag building, the parliament met for several months in the Kroll Opera House nearby.

Three leading communists were also arrested in connection with the fire. All were Bulgarians and one (Georgi Dimitrov) was a senior Comintern official responsible for all international activities of the Soviet Union in western Europe. At the trial, which was held in Leipzig in July 1933, van der Lubbe was found guilty but the others acquitted because evidence of their involvement in a criminal conspiracy was lacking. Van der Lubbe, who always maintained that he had acted alone, was executed in January 1934.

Conspiracy theories about the Reichstag fire abound. The issue of who set fire to the building is still hotly debated but at the very least the event was convenient

ACTIVITY 3.5

List the people involved in Adolf Hitler's appointment as Chancellor of Germany in January 1933. Make notes on their politics, their titles, jobs or roles in public affairs, and their part in the process by which Hitler was appointed.

How important was the Reichstag fire of February 1933 in the collapse of the Weimar Republic?

- Use a spider diagram to show the political consequences of the fire. Does this make it look like a key event? What other contributing factors to the collapse of democracy can you think of? Choose two and create similar spider diagrams.

- Now compare the three: what aspects would you focus on if writing an essay answering the question?

timing for the Nazis, just a few days before the election, because it allowed them to discredit and eliminate the communist KPD.

By election day on 5 March 1933, all KPD delegates to the Reichstag had been arrested and their party offices attacked. The Communists had been discredited by association with a violent conspiracy. President Hindenburg had issued an emergency decree. The Social Democrats and the Centre Party had also been harassed and some issues of the newspapers they controlled had been banned. Moreover, three members of the January 1933 cabinet were leading Nazis: Hitler himself, Frick and Göring. The last was appointed Interior Minister of Prussia, giving him control of the largest police force in Germany.

Von Papen and his Conservative allies in the cabinet made no protest about President Hindenburg's emergency decree, with its suspension of certain civil rights. Von Papen was deputy chancellor, and a majority of the January 1933 cabinet were not Nazis, in theory allowing Hitler to be outvoted. In the event, however, von Papen was marginalised even before the March 1933 election.

Table 3.1: Election results for the March 1933 federal election. Figures for votes and percentages have been rounded up.

Party	Votes	%	Reichstag seats
NSDAP	17 million	44	288
SPD	7 million	18	120
KPD	4.8 million	12	81
Centre	4.4 million	11	74
DNVP	3 million	8	52
DDP	0.3 million	1	5
BVP	1 million	2.5	18
Other parties etc.	2.1 million	3.5	9
Total	**39.6 million**	**100**	**647**

The result of the election was that the Nazis took nearly 44% of the vote and were by far the largest single party, even though they did not have a majority.

The Enabling Act

By its decision to carry out the political and moral cleansing of our public life, the Government is creating and securing the conditions for a really deep and inner religious life …[4]

This was how Chancellor Hitler presented his amendment to the Weimar Constitution to the Reichstag on 23 March 1933. Better known as the Enabling Act, it was officially a 'Law to Remedy the Distress of the People and the Reich'. Far from being presented as a piece of law that would allow Hitler dictatorial powers in ruling Germany, it was proposed in moral terms as an act of 'cleansing' and as a remedy for the 'distress of the German people and Reich'. In his speech presenting the Enabling Act, Hitler also said:

The Government will treat all other denominations with objective and impartial justice. It cannot, however, tolerate allowing membership of a certain denomination or of a certain race being used as a release from all common legal obligations or as a blank cheque for unpunishable behaviour, or for the toleration of crimes.[5]

Hitler went on to reassure the main Christian churches, both Protestant and Catholic, that he wanted full and cordial relations with them. However, the warning to 'a certain denomination or of a certain race' would have been well understood by his audience as a reference to Judaism and Jewish people.

The Enabling Act made the Reichstag almost irrelevant because Adolf Hitler could now propose and pass new laws without reference to parliament. The Act did guarantee the continuing existence of the Reichstag but it met infrequently after 1933 and passed only a few new laws. In a deviation from his own Act, Hitler abolished the *Reichsrat*, the upper house that represented the individual states of Germany. Hitler ruled by decree, these being issued in theory by the ageing President Hindenburg. This will have surprised or shocked no-one: it was a process familiar from the preceding three chancellors, and had been used throughout the history of the republic.

Within a few months of the passing of the Enabling Act, political parties other than the Nazis were banned or forced to dissolve themselves. On 15 July 1933 a law was announced that made the Nazis the only legal political party in Germany. It had become a one-party state.

The Night of the Long Knives

By the summer of 1934, the activities of the SA, led by Ernst Röhm, had become a barrier to Adolf Hitler's consolidation of power in Germany. Since the founding of the Nazi Party in 1921 the SA had provided security at meetings and rallies, and had fought the party's enemies in the gangland-style street politics of the times. Now that the Nazis were in government, the SA were an embarrassment. Hitler did not want to offend the innate dislike of Germans for street disorder. The increasing street violence of the SA, especially against Jewish-owned shops, no longer served Nazi purposes. Röhm's talk of a 'second revolution' to redistribute wealth and to fulfil the Socialist goals of the NSDAP was not what Hitler wanted.

The army was also getting increasingly unhappy about the activities of the SA. When Röhm started demanding that the *Reichswehr* be absorbed into the SA, the generals made it clear to Hitler that the SA had to be curbed. Hitler very much wanted the full support of the *Reichswehr* in order to consolidate his position.

Between 30 June and 2 July 1934, many SA leaders, including Ernst Röhm, were murdered, mostly by SS and **Gestapo** units. Hitler also took the opportunity to eliminate the more Socialist faction of the NSDAP, including its leading figure, Gregor Strasser. Strasser was a former soldier and *Freikorps* volunteer, a participant in the Munich Putsch and a leading Nazi organiser. In January 1928 he had been put in charge of the NSDAP national organisation. He became a

ACTIVITY 3.7

List the key provisions of the Enabling Act. Make notes in each case on what they were intended to achieve.

ACTIVITY 3.8

Was the 'Night of the Long Knives' carefully planned or was it improvised? You should consider what it was intended to achieve:

- What did the victims of the 'Night of the Long Knives' have in common?
- Was the destruction of the SA the main point?
- Was reassuring the army the decisive factor?
- Was removing specific individuals the underlying motive?

Make notes towards answers for each of these questions.

prominent figure in the hierarchy. In 1932 he had been offered the post of vice chancellor by von Schleicher, who was plotting to split the NSDAP leadership.

Hitler didn't brook rivals. Von Schleicher himself was gunned down, along with his wife. The fact that von Schleicher and another murdered victim, Gustav Ritter von Kahr, had, as *Reichswehr* generals, suppressed the Munich Putsch in 1923 grimly demonstrates how Hitler used the action against the SA as an opportunity to tidy up and to settle old scores.

Usually known in English as the 'Night of the Long Knives', in German these events are known as the *Röhm-Putsch*. Some German historians argue that the SA itself was not the main target and that both Röhm and Strasser were murdered as much for their Socialist views as anything else. This remains an area of debate.

Whatever the truth of the matter, it was certainly significant that the courts in Germany took no action about these extra-judicial killings, choosing instead to support Hitler's drive for absolute power in Germany. The police were firmly under Nazi control by this time and they took no action either. With Hitler assuming the post of president on the death of Hindenburg on 2 August 1934, and with the marginalisation of the Reichstag and the establishment of the Nazis as the only legal political party in Germany, his drive to consolidate his personal position was complete.

The Nazis and the military

From the outset, governments of the Weimar Republic had been careful to keep the army supportive. The military High Command wanted an authoritarian government which would rebuild the armed forces and reverse the Treaty of Versailles. Many senior officers in the army had been junior officers under Wilhelm II and were used to an autocratic form of government. In the 1920s and early 1930s many former soldiers had joined paramilitary groups such as the *Freikorps* or *Stahlhelm*. These fought in the streets and the *Reichswehr* were reluctant, as were the courts, to take firm action against them.

The NSDAP quickly moved to defy the restrictions imposed by the Treaty of Versailles in 1919 on the size and nature of the armed forces of Germany. They introduced conscription to raise another 100 000 soldiers, and developed a navy (*Kriegsmarine*) and an air force (**Luftwaffe**). Banned weapons – submarines, tanks and artillery – were now openly manufactured.

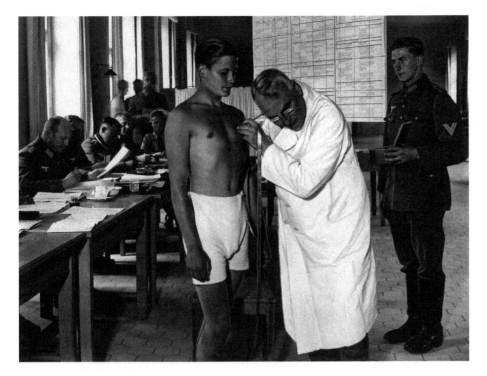

Figure 3.5: Conscripts for the Wehrmacht (army), 1935.

ACTIVITY 3.9

For each of the following questions, write a one-paragraph response:

- Did the Nazis need the support of the German High Command?
- What do you think led the leaders of the army to support the Nazis?
- Do you think the army was enthusiastic in its support?
- What reservations might the army have had about the Nazis?

In each case, present an argument which has some evidence to support your ideas.

The **remilitarization** of the Rhineland in March 1936 and the union (*Anschluss*) with Austria in March 1938 were both reversals of the Treaty of Versailles. Taken with the elimination of the *Sturmabteilung* (**SA**) in 1933, this programme of rearmament and expansion pleased the armed forces and its leaders were broadly supportive of Nazi rule.

Government and opposition to 1945

Under Nazi rule, the German state largely continued to refer to itself simply as the *Deutsches Reich* (German Empire), as before. Sometimes this was expanded into the *Großdeutsches Reich* (great German Empire), to indicate it had grown in size. Sometimes the expression *National Sozialistischer Staat* (National Socialist State) was used. For a while, the regime used *Dritte Reich* (Third Empire).

This new empire was authoritarian and oppressive. It sought to control every aspect of everyday life. The Nazi Party, now the largest in the Reichstag, was well organised at national, regional and local levels. The *Schutzstaffel* (**SS**) built up its control over the police. Communists, Social Democrats and ethnic minorities, particularly Jews, were subject to increasing intimidation, persecution and discriminatory legislation.

Nazism as an ideology and in practice

According to the historian David Crewe, it has been common to view Nazism as the practices of a 'criminal clique'. However, in studying the period, we need to be aware that the NSDAP was more than a gang bent on violent crime. The membership of the NSDAP shared an ideology and believed that the Nazis in power would bring about sweeping social, economic and political reforms.

 Key term

Dritte Reich: The expression 'the **Third Reich**' is a curious partial translation of **Dritte Reich** (Third Empire), an expression coined to show Nazi rule as coming third, following the Holy Roman Empire (which began in the early Middle Ages and ran until the beginning of the 19th century) and the Kaiserreich (1871–1918).

Key terms

Social Darwinism: Late 19th- and early 20th-century pseudo-science based on the scientific ideas and discoveries of Charles Darwin, especially the idea that human beings were animals and that as such the strongest would and should succeed and thrive where the weakest would fail and die.

Volksgemeinschaft: German word meaning 'nation community'; an ideal community of Germans regardless of social status and based on race.

Führer: The German word *Führer* simply means 'leader' or 'guide'. It was not unusual at the time for members of a political party to refer to the party leader in this way. However, it became closely associated with Hitler and was intended to make clear that he was not limited by the Constitution, as previous chancellors and presidents had been.

A key element in the ideology was the ending of democracy. It was thus not surprising that, soon after coming into office, Hitler moved to put an end to opposition, close down political parties and political debate, and reduce the role of the Reichstag to little more than a debating society. This formed part of the restoration of central authority, something for which right-wing parties had been calling since the abdication of the emperor and the foundation of the republic.

The Nazis also developed the *Führerprinzip* (leader principle), according to which gifted individuals possessed certain inherent privileges and responsibilities: some were natural leaders. This was an aspect of the pseudo-science of social Darwinism. It also resembled the workings of the military, where officers gave commands and did not expect to have to discuss them with those of lower ranks before they were carried out. For a society in which many men had military experience, and where there was a longstanding cult of militarism, this was clearly an appealing concept. The result was supposed to be social and economic order and thus peace and prosperity. For everyone who had been adversely affected by unemployment or hyperinflation, the promises of order, peace and prosperity were compelling.

The ruled were not merely slaves, however. So long as they were Germans (and that was a non-negotiable qualification), they were members of an organic nation in which relationships were not unlike those within a family. This was the *Volksgemeinschaft*, a community of Germans regardless of social status and based on race. We shall return to this topic later. The message communicated was that the Nazi government was on the side of the ordinary law-abiding person.

This suggested an approach to the economic problems of the country which contrasted strongly with that of the government. In practice the Nazis were as keen to have the support of big business as any other political party had been in government. Thus, the NSDAP programme of public works was a continuation of what had been begun by von Schleicher.

Finally, the Nazis believed in the use of propaganda to communicate their plans and in the use of terror to enforce them. We shall look further at both of these.

The gap between theory and practice in the Nazi state was even wider than is usual in government, mainly because of the difference in culture and experience between the Nazi Party and the German civil service. However, the gap narrowed as the years went by from 1933 and more officials joined the party for career reasons, more non-Nazi civil servants were dismissed and even Nazi sympathisers had to demonstrate their loyalty to Führer and party.

Hitler's style of government

As chancellor, president and Führer, Adolf Hitler possessed absolute power. His authority was called 'Führer power' (*Führergewalt*) by Ernst Huber, the leading constitutional theorist of the Nazi state.

Hans Frank, the head of the Nazi Association of Lawyers and of the Academy of German Law, and from 1934 a member of the cabinet as minister without portfolio, put it this way in 1938:

At the head of the Reich stands the leader of the NSDAP as leader of the German Reich for life.

He is Head of State and chief of the Government in one person. He is Commander-in-Chief of all the armed forces of the Reich.

The Führer and Reich Chancellor is the delegate of the German people.

The Führer is the supreme judge of the nation …[6]

This was the theory, but in practice, as one individual, Hitler could only properly consider or even take note of a tiny fraction of the huge number of issues arising every day from this form of personal rule. Furthermore, he didn't like paperwork and he had never liked Berlin, preferring to spend time at Berchtesgaden, his mountain retreat in Bavaria in southern Germany. It was those in his immediate circle, regardless of their official rank within the party, who selected the papers he actually looked at and who delivered the Führer's judgments.

For example, Wilhelm Frick served in Hitler's cabinet from 1933 to 1943 as minister of the interior but seldom even saw the Führer and had little influence. By contrast, Hitler's personal car drivers were given a rank equivalent to that of a general and had many opportunities to influence decisions. For this reason, the armed forces all made sure that they had representatives permanently living at Berchtesgaden.

Because Hitler avoided paperwork and committee meetings (especially discussions), many of his decisions were given in one-to-one interviews where no official records were taken of what was said. This makes it more than usually difficult to track or validate pronouncements coming from the Reich Chancellery (*Reichskanzlei*), meaning the Führer and his officials. Unsurprisingly, given this situation, there were often tensions between the Nazi Party and the civil service. Many Nazis had been used to the pre-1933 struggle, a sort of crusade to combat what they regarded as corrupting influences that might pollute the German **Volk**. These Nazis were often intolerant when not openly contemptuous of any civil service concern for legal restrictions and bureaucratic rules.

Prominent Nazis such as Robert Ley, leader of the German Labour Front from 1933 to 1945, often assumed responsibilities that properly belonged to civil servants. So Ley took over affairs from the Reich Ministry of Labour. As commander of the *Schutzstaffel* (*Reichsführer SS*), Heinrich Himmler was another example, taking command of police powers away from the Ministry of the Interior.

Hitler himself took little notice of the fight between the party and the civil service. He considered himself above such things. He shared the priority of building the *Volksgemeinschaft* and his lack of action was interpreted by leading Nazis such as Ley and Himmler as silent encouragement. This encroachment of the Nazi Party into the established system of government became more and more marked as the years went by. When the Gestapo (short for *Geheime Staatspolizei,* the secret police) sent people to **concentration camps** without any right of appeal, even though they had been found not guilty by the courts, this was an example of the party taking over processes normally left in the hands of the police, the judiciary and the civil service bureaucracy of the Justice Department.

ACTIVITY 3.10

In what ways would you assess Adolf Hitler as a powerful autocrat? Why do you think that some historians have described him as a 'dictator'?

Make notes of evidence for the two sides of this debate.

In his memoirs written after 1945, *The Hitler I Knew*, Otto Dietrich, SS *Obergruppenführer,* Nazi Party press secretary and a member of Hitler's inner circle, wrote:

> *In the twelve years of his rule in Germany Hitler produced the biggest confusion in government that has ever existed in a civilised state. During his period of government, he removed from the organisation of the state all clarity of leadership and produced a completely opaque network of competencies.*[7]

Dietrich went on to say that he believed that Hitler had done so as a means of strengthening his personal authority.

The German historian Hans Mommsen has argued that Hitler had little effect on the day-to-day running of Germany and little input into detail. His case is thus that the working of the state generated continual conflicts between different officials and departments. His most famous phrase is that Hitler was a 'weak dictator' with little sense of direction and a habit of reacting to events and pressures. Mommsen's specific example is that Hitler expressed his anti-Semitic views both in public speeches and privately, but had no worked-out plan for expressing this hostility; it was his subordinates who planned and implemented the Holocaust.

The British historian, and biographer of Hitler, Ian Kershaw disagrees with this thesis but he does agree that Hitler was incapable of bureaucracy and so played only a minor role in government and administration. Kershaw's own most famous phrase is 'working towards the Führer', which he took from a Prussian civil servant's speech in 1934. This civil servant explained that with too much responsibility, Hitler could not attend to detail. Waiting for orders was the wrong approach; it was essential to anticipate the Führer's wishes and to act as though he had given orders.

A key figure in the administration of the Nazi state was Dr Hans Lammers, Head of the Reich Chancellery from 1933 to 1945. Hitler disliked getting involved in disputes between departments of state and insisted that only Lammers could present any issues relating to the making of new laws to him. This gave him great power and influence over the Führer.

The tension between party and state was a marked feature of the administration of Germany between 1933 and 1945. Hitler himself was a passionate leader and an extremely effective speaker. He also seems to have understood about the value and use of propaganda. However, he was not a good administrator and, given the nature of his personal rule, this meant weaknesses in the Nazi state.

Much the same might be said of other members of the NSDAP, but they were not the Führer and their weaknesses were not of such great importance. Some were good administrators – Goebbels at the Propaganda Ministry, Himmler with the SS and police, Bormann at the Chancellery.

Key Nazi leaders

At the top of the Nazi state, with absolute power, was **Adolf Hitler.** On the death of President Hindenburg early in August 1934, Hitler had himself proclaimed as president as well as being Reich Chancellor and leader of the Nazi Party.

The next most powerful figure in the NSDAP after Adolf Hitler was **Hermann Göring.** He had joined the Nazi party early, in 1922, and by 1923 had been put in charge of the SA. He had been a war hero in the First World War as a fighter pilot. As Hitler said of him:

> *I liked him. I made him the head of my SA. He is the only one of its heads that ran the SA properly. I gave him a dishevelled rabble. In a very short time he had organised a division of 11000 men.*[8]

Göring was President of the Reichstag from August 1932 and became Minister President of Prussia from April 1933. His social connections were of particular value to Hitler as he sought to gain the support of German elites, and Göring's first wife, Carin, often hosted parties for the Führer. He was jovial in manner, but pompous and vain. He became a trusted colleague of Hitler and was put in charge of rearmament by being given responsibility for the Four-Year Plan in October 1936. Because of his distinguished aviation background, he also led the Luftwaffe for most of the war. Later, as the Luftwaffe proved unable to prevent Allied bombing raids, Göring's political fortunes waned.

When Hitler was appointed chancellor, he in turn appointed **Rudolph Hess** as deputy Führer, and later as a member of the cabinet as Reich minister without portfolio. Hess had oversight of several departments and all prospective legislation had to be approved by him, except matters concerning security. Entirely loyal to Hitler, he made no attempt to build a personal power base in either the party or the country. At the outbreak of war in September 1939, Hitler made him second in line to succeed him, after Göring.

Joseph Goebbels was intelligent, well educated and capable. After conducting academic research in German literature, he became aware of the NSDAP in 1923 as a result of the nationalist campaigns against the occupation of the Ruhr that year by French and Belgian troops. He joined the Nazi Party in 1924 and rose swiftly in their ranks to become **Gauleiter** (District Leader) of Berlin just two years later, in 1926.

Much of the success of the Nazi Party in the national elections between 1930 and 1933 has been attributed to their mastery of propaganda. Goebbels – an academic, an excellent organiser and devoted to Hitler – was the ideal choice to oversee this area. Hitler and the Nazis believed that they were embarking on a social revolution in 1933, one that would embed the idea of *Volksgemeinschaft* deep in German minds. Effective propaganda was therefore vital to this task. Goebbels increased his power over the years, proving himself adept at exploiting the rivalries within Hitler's inner circle. In 1945, unlike many Nazi leaders who fled the oncoming Red Army in Berlin, he chose to remain with his leader. He died with his wife and family in the Berlin bunker by taking poison.

Heinrich Himmler joined the Nazi Party on 1 August 1923. He was a Catholic from a middle-class Bavarian background and had studied agronomy at the Technical University in Munich. Following his enrolment in the party he rejected Christianity and became passionately anti-Semitic. He held various posts under Gregor Strasser, organising the Nazi Party in Lower Bavaria. He joined the SS (then a unit of the SA) in 1925, becoming SS Gauleiter in Lower Bavaria in 1926. He so impressed Hitler with his idea of turning the SS into a totally loyal, racially pure, elite unit that he was appointed to lead the unit as *Reichsführer* SS in 1929. Under his leadership the SS grew in size tenfold. Albert Speer later declared that he was a good decision-maker.

Himmler became the effective chief of security in Nazi Germany after 1933, having control of all the police forces in Germany, including that of Prussia, as well as of the SS. He also controlled the Gestapo (the secret police). He set up the first concentration camp in Germany at Dachau near Munich as early as March 1933. Initially this camp housed political opponents of the Nazis but this was later extended to include all those considered by the Nazis as 'socially undesirable'.

Martin Bormann became the Secretary of the Nazi Party Chancellery in July 1933, in theory working under Deputy Führer Hess. He was responsible for settling disputes within the NSDAP and was its bridge to the state bureaucracy. As the party infiltrated the state, his position became even stronger. He was highly competent, as well as being very ambitious. His was a position of considerable power, even more so as he was appointed a *Reichsleiter* (the highest Nazi Party rank, excluding that of the Führer, of course) and became Head of the Party Chancellery in October 1933. The following year he became one of Hitler's inner circle and went with him everywhere.

The terror state

The organised persecution of those the Nazis regarded as their enemies, required the active participation of several groups. Some of these were Nazi creations, others were already in existence.

The police

The Weimar and Imperial police were run by the Länder. From April 1934 Hitler put Himmler in charge of all the police forces outside Göring's Prussia. Then in 1936, he ordered that all the separate Länder police should be merged into a nationwide force under Himmler's command. Although many of the people and responsibilities continued to be broadly the same as before, they also supported the Nazis in enforcing the racial and political laws, thus becoming part of the terror state.

The lawyers

The Nazis created a National Socialist Lawyers Association which all lawyers, including judges, had to join. Lawyers and legal staff who were Jews or of suspect politics were dismissed. Nazi flags were hung in all courts of law and police stations. The normal processes of police work and law courts did continue, but alongside this there quickly grew up special courts, the *Volksgerichtshof* (People's Court). Trials were quick. Defendants were barely allowed to speak. Little defence was offered. The judge sided with the prosecution and shouted at the accused. Most trials ended in convictions. These courts issued frequent death sentences.

The SS

Heinrich Himmler joined the *Schutzstaffel* (Defence Squad, SS) in 1925. This was a unit of the SA with responsibilities for defending Nazi meetings and officials, and developed into Hitler's bodyguard. Commanded by Himmler, it was turned into a totally loyal, racially pure, elite unit, dedicated to carrying out Hitler's orders. As such it acted as a supplement both to the army and to the police.

Despite beginning as a branch of the SA, the SS played a central role in the Night of the Long Knives.

When the German army invaded Poland in 1939 and the USSR in 1941, the troops were followed by SS death squads called *Einsatzgruppen*. These worked alongside the police to kill Jews and Communists.

The Gestapo

As Minister President of Prussia, Göring created the *Geheime Staatspolizei* (Secret State Police, Gestapo) out of two existing police departments and introduced into it a number of Nazis. Control was passed to Himmler two years later in 1936.

The Gestapo investigated treason, spying and sabotage, including all opposition to Nazi rule. This meant that they monitored individuals and networks from which opposition might come. They operated without reference to any other authority – police, courts or the law. They sent people to concentration camps without any right of appeal even though they had been found not guilty by the courts.

Ghettos

In occupied Poland Jews were deported to **ghettos** by the Germans in hundreds of locations, many in cities such as Warsaw or Lvov. These were areas of towns and cities in which only Jews were allowed to live, and they were not allowed to live anywhere else. This policy of deportation was made easier by the fact that ghettos had been established in earlier centuries. They had been abolished long since, but the areas had often continued to exist as 'Jewish quarters', places where most of the inhabitants were Jews.

The camps

In addition to existing prisons, the Nazis built a network of concentration camps:

- In labour camps, people were forced to work and held in harsh conditions.
- In transit camps, people were held while waiting to be moved to somewhere else.
- Internment camps held anyone considered an enemy or threat of any kind.

These initial camps were not a secret. The first were announced in a press release which listed Communist party, *Reichsbanner* and SPD members as its intended inmates.

Later came the death camps, whose purpose was to kill the prisoners. Their existence was not a secret but their activities very likely were.

Anti-Semitic legislation

The consequence of the idea of a superior race and of building unity out of exclusion is that there are inferior races who have to be excluded. The Nazis were firmly in the *volkisch* (national, or belonging to the people) nationalist tradition, which saw the Germans as tall, fair and heroic, while the excluded remainder were their opposites: swarthy, devious and cowardly. After 1933 they required schools to teach racial biology and population studies. Just as the *Volk* (nation or people) would expel those deviants who did not conform to the moral code of the *Gemeinshaft* (community), the Nazis once in power persecuted and discriminated against ethnic minorities, notably Jews and Roma people (gypsies), but also against other groups whom they found undesirable, including the physically and mentally disabled, and homosexual men.

Anti-Semitic legislation in Nazi Germany was extensive, but two laws stand out. In 1933 the new Nazi state lost no time in promulgating a Law for the Restoration of the Professional Civil Service that barred entry to 'non-Aryans'. The 1935 Nuremberg Laws were even more obnoxious. They classified Jews in terms of the proportion of non-Jewish blood they had in their veins, deprived them of German citizenship and prohibited marriage between Jews and '**Aryans**', supposedly pure-blooded Germans.

Kristallnacht

During the night of 7 November 1938 and in the days that followed, several hundred Jews were killed, about 30 000 were arrested and sent to concentration camps, and a vast amount of Jewish-owned property was damaged or destroyed throughout Germany and Austria. This was **Kristallnacht**, 'the Night of Broken Glass', because of all the shattered windows.

The immediate cause was the shooting of Legation Secretary Ernst vom Rath in the German Embassy in Paris by Herschel Grynszpan, a seventeen-year-old from a Polish-Jewish family. He was driven to this action by his parents' situation.

Poland had become anxious that the 70 000 Polish Jews based in Germany would return to Poland because of the increasing anti-Semitism in German society and law. In March 1938 they announced that Polish citizens living abroad who failed to renew their passports by the end of October that year would lose their citizenship, thus making them stateless. Suspecting that this would leave Polish Jews stuck in Germany, on the night of 28 October 1938 the SS were instructed to arrest 17 000 such Jews in Germany with a view to deportation. Poland closed its borders a few days later. Many of the 17 000 Polish Jews were stranded between the two countries for several harsh weeks.

Thus Grynszpan took his desperate step. Hitler, on hearing the news, authorised Goebbels to organise a series of supposedly spontaneous attacks on synagogues and Jewish-owned shops, offices, factories, hospitals and homes.

Opposition and resistance to Nazi rule

Citizens in opposition

It was both difficult and dangerous to oppose the Nazi state. Opposition politicians had either been arrested or were in hiding. The efficiency of the Nazi network of spies and informers at a local level, the ruthless suppression of dissent by the Gestapo and the obedience of the great majority of Germans, especially in the earlier years, together made this the case. It has been calculated that 77 000 German citizens were executed for one or another form of resistance during Nazi rule.

However, there was little or no coordinated resistance to the Nazi state of the kind that was to be found elsewhere in occupied countries. In Germany itself, opposition came more from individuals or isolated groups.

Most Germans remained loyal to the Nazi state until the end, in 1945, but the research of Detlev Peukert and others has shown a degree of 'everyday resistance' to the Nazi regime. Dissatisfaction was mostly triggered by corruption among high Nazi officials and the state of the economy.

There was just one public show of opposition to the vicious Nazi persecution of German Jews. In February 1943, the *Rosenstrasse Protest* gathered a large crowd outside the Berlin building where 1800 Jewish men married to non-Jewish women were being held prior to shipment to the extermination camps in Poland. Their wives rallied and protested outside for over a week. The Nazis eventually relented and the men were released – an unusual success and a unique event.

Communists in opposition

The Nazis invaded the Soviet Union in 1941. The German Communist Party (KPD) was ordered by Moscow to form resistance cells. A group, dubbed the 'Red Orchestra' by the Gestapo, carried out espionage and tried to inform the Allies about Nazi atrocities. They were betrayed to the Gestapo in 1942 and their leaders secretly executed.

There were individual attacks and acts of sabotage. Seeking to persuade the army to stage a coup against the Nazi state did not bear fruit until late in the war, by which time it had become obvious that Germany would lose. The 1944 assassination attempt by army staff officers was intended to spark a general uprising but it too failed.

Churches in opposition

One area of determined opposition was from the churches. Hitler often used the language of religious morality in his speeches, as when he introduced the Enabling Laws in 1933 in the Reichstag, partly reflecting his recognition of the significance of the churches in German politics.

Of about 60 million Germans, perhaps 40 million belonged to Protestant churches, of which the German Evangelical Church was by far the largest. Within it there was a long-running debate between those who wished to maintain the Church's traditional loyalty to the state and who argued for the idea of German Christians (*Deutsche Christen*) and those of the Confessing Church (**Bekennende Kirche**), who opposed the Nazi state and argued that the allegiance of the Church should be to God and scripture, not to a worldly Führer.

A leading figure in the latter movement was the Protestant Pastor Martin Niemöller, who spent seven years in concentration camps for his temerity. Another leading member was the theologian Dietrich Bonhöffer, who was executed for his part in a conspiracy to overthrow the Nazi regime.

The leaders of Germany's 20 million or so Roman Catholics were initially more suspicious of the Nazis. This was especially the case as the Catholic Centre Party had been one of the main political props of the Weimar Republic. Before 1933 some Catholic bishops prohibited members of their flock from joining the Nazi Party but this ban was dropped after 1933.

Young people in opposition

Another form of opposition came from the Edelweiss Pirates (*Edelweisspiraten*). This protest movement was started in the Rhineland in 1937. It was a youth movement; while Nazi propaganda liked to claim that all young male Germans were members of the Hitler Youth Movement, this was not universally the case. The Pirates were mainly working-class youths and their activities were fairly harmless: wearing Bohemian clothes, playing prohibited music such as jazz and blues, and fighting the Nazi youth movement. There were similar, more middle-class Swing Kids who acted in a similar fashion. Although they were initially regarded by the authorities as merely an irritant, after the outbreak of war in 1939 the Nazi state took a dimmer view of such youth groups and members were sometimes arrested, sent for short periods to prison camps and even executed.

The White Rose (**Weisse Rose**) movement was a very different affair. During several months in 1942–43, students at the University of Munich distributed leaflets and wrote graffiti calling for opposition to the Nazi state. A number of members were executed for treason in 1942, including sister and brother Sophie and Hans Scholl.

Military in opposition

Some members of the army had been opposed to Hitler and to Nazi rule from the beginning. The popularity of the initial successes against Czechoslovakia, Poland and France meant that they were reluctant to speak out. However, there were several planned assassinations hatched by army officers.

The most famous, because it was the one which came closest to success, was led by Colonel Claus von Stauffenberg and took place at Hitler's military command centre for the Eastern Front, the Wolf's Lair (*Wolfsschanze*) in July 1944. Stauffenberg was due to attend a meeting there in his capacity as chief of staff to the Commander of the Reserve Army. His intention was to place a bomb in a conference room where Hitler would be sitting and then slip away. With Hitler dead, the conspirators would then seize control of Germany and aim to negotiate an end both to Nazi rule and to the war. The bomb went off but it seems that the suitcase containing the bomb was moved to underneath the large, heavy conference table and that the table took the force of the blast. Four people were killed and two were seriously injured; Hitler himself had over 200 wooden splinters removed from his legs, his hair was singed and his uniform shredded, but he survived. After the failure of the plot, Stauffenberg and other ringleaders were executed. The Gestapo arrested some 7000 in all, nearly 5000 of whom were also killed, few if any of them connected with the plot.

Conservatives in opposition

One group of opponents to the Nazi regime was known as the **Kreisau Circle** after the estate in Kreisau where they met. The estate belonged to Helmuth James Graf von Moltke, the great-great-nephew of the Prussian field marshal commanding in the Franco-Prussian War. The others in the group were largely from army and aristocratic backgrounds, and tended to be social conservatives, monarchists, liberals and Christians. They shared a vision of a Christian Germany under a restored monarchy with the restoration of the idea of federalism, so that the individual states that made up Germany would have much of their individual character and authority restored. However, this was a debating society rather than a conspiracy: they made little attempt to plan the overthrow of Nazi rule, though even before the war broke out, they agreed that Hitler's rule was a disaster for Germany.

Von Moltke was arrested in January 1944 and tried by one of the NSDAP's so-called 'People's Courts'. Other members of the Kreisau Circle were connected to the July 1944 Bomb Plot; when suspects were arrested following that plot's failure, Peter Graf Yorck von Wartenburg, a member of an aristocratic army family, and others were picked up by the security services, quickly tried, found guilty and executed in August 1944. Von Moltke was found guilty of treason and executed in January 1945.

The effect of war

The early period of the Second World War saw the German military conquer and occupy much of Europe. This vast war had a correspondingly vast impact on German's society, economy, culture and political life.

The initial successes created a mood of intense optimism and excitement. Germany was prosperous and well equipped. It was able to seize goods from the occupied countries and to employ people from those countries as slave labourers to make up for the men who had been sent on military service.

With memories of the First World War, the government worked to ensure that there was enough food to go round. Germany was still a country that depended on imports for some foodstuffs, but there was a scientific programme in place to create artificial substitutes for those goods that were in short supply. Fuel and clothing were also rationed from early in the war. As in any country where there is rationing, there was a black market, so to that extent Nazi rule contributed to an increase in criminality. The control of food and other supplies to consumers worked fairly well, but as the war went on there were more shortages.

When the Allied bombing campaign began (something Göring had promised would not happen), there was an attempt to evacuate children from the main cities, but it only had a minor impact.

In the summer of 1941 Hitler sent a vast army to invade the Soviet Union. His reasons had been set out long before in *Mein Kampf*: Slavs were an inferior race, the USSR was a communist state (and communist parties were believed to be dominated by Jews), Germany needed **Lebensraum** (living space) and the campaign would lead to Ukraine's wheat, Donets's coal and Baku's oil.

A propaganda campaign was kept up to reassure people and urge them to adopt certain courses of action, such as saving fuel and collecting warm clothes for the soldiers in cold places such as the Russian front. Continual use of propaganda meant that, even when the armed forces began to suffer defeats, including the major defeats of the Eastern Front such as that at Stalingrad in 1942, many people continued to assume that Germany would win. In a famous 1943 speech, Goebbels asked an audience if they were ready for total war. The shouted reply – from the well-prepared and carefully chosen audience – that they were was carried to homes across Germany by radio.

'Total war' meant that every part of the economy would prioritise the war effort. For the first time, professional sports fixtures were cancelled, consumer magazines were not published and sweets were not manufactured. Meanwhile, despite the pre-war Nazi campaigns emphasising women's domestic role, the government now struggled to persuade women to go out to work in, for example, factories.

As the bombing campaign increased, those who could left the cities to stay with friends and family in rural areas. The urban population dropped and that of villages climbed, a temporary reverse of what had been a demographic fact of German life for a century.

Late in the war, a civilian defence force, the **Volkssturm**, was created. Inadequately trained, inadequately armed and including old men and boys as well as men who had not been called up, it did in fact fight alongside the army in the final, street-by-street, stages of the conflict.

Although this was the general experience of life during the war, there will have been major variations. Those high in the party hierarchy will have continued to enjoy a wealthy lifestyle throughout. For those in persecuted minorities, food shortages will have been the least of their problems as the terror state set about a campaign of mass persecution that turned, during the war, into one of mass murder.

Political authority and government, 1945–49

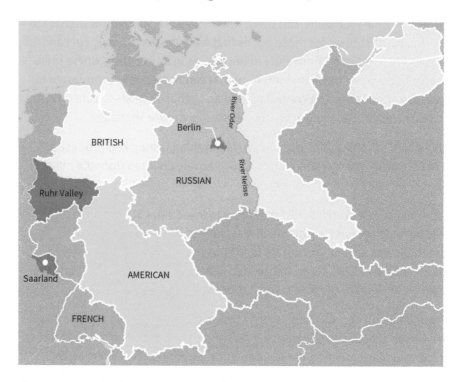

Figure 3.6: Occupied Germany, split into four zones of occupation. Eastern territories were ceded to Poland.

Post-war occupation and division

The wartime Alliance had been forced on a group of countries by the fact of a common enemy and shared danger. However, France, the UK and the USA were democratic, capitalist countries who had regarded the totalitarian, statist, communist USSR with fear and hostility. During the Second World War, cooperation was close. The common enemy defeated and the shared danger ended, pre-war fears and suspicions were not long in reviving.

It was no longer clear what or where Germany was. Created in 1871 in victory, the country had been redefined in defeat in 1919 by the Treaty of Versailles, then redrawn in victory by Hitler's 1930s expansionism. But the 1938 Anschluss had been rejected by the victorious Allies and all the conquests had by 1945 been lost.

During July and August 1945, the UK, US and USSR leaders met in Potsdam to discuss Germany's future size, shape and nature.

The Allies initially expected to run Germany jointly as an occupied country. In the event, relations between them were not good enough and there was not sufficient agreement about what policies to adopt for this to be possible. Key points of difference were:

- France believed that Germany should be broken up into a number of separate countries, thus undoing the work of 1871.
- The USSR began enacting Soviet-style policies, such as land seizure and nationalisation.
- France refused to house and feed refugees arriving in the part of the country that its troops occupied, as it had not been party to the decision that each of the Allies would do this (France had not been invited to the Potsdam Conference).

The 5 June *Declaration Regarding the Defeat of Germany* divided Germany into four zones of occupation:

- The Soviet Union controlled the centre
- The USA controlled the south
- The French controlled the west
- The British controlled the north.

These divisions followed the borders of the existing *Länder*, with the exception of Prussia, which was split up. The division of Germany was initially an administrative convenience. It turned into a reflection of the political divisions among the Allies.

Most books call the Soviet sector the 'east' of the country. In fact, most of the east (including East Prussia and Silesia) was put into the hands of Poland in 1945, and, following a settlement of borders in 1949, became part of that country. Still further east, North-East Prussia and Memel were passed to the USSR and became part of that country. (The former is now part of Russia and the latter is in Lithuania.)

In addition, there was a small sector within the British zone which was administered by Belgium, and a further small area within the French zone which was administered by Luxembourg.

Berlin itself, although in the middle of the Russian zone, was treated as a special case since it was the country's capital city, and was itself split into four zones of occupation.

The zones of occupation thus became areas of semi-independent administrative decisions, run by the military under the oversight of their own national politicians.

The effect of war and defeat

Occupied Germany was ruined, occupied and shattered economically. The country's problems were now the problems of the occupying Allies. On the agenda were:

- Security
- Refugees
- Former soldiers
- War criminals
- Food.

Let's take those in turn.

Security

Initially, there was a high state of alert because of the belief that there were plans for Nazi German resistance, sometimes from a supposed hidden fortress in the Alps in southern Germany, sometimes so-called 'werewolf' units who were hidden in the civilian population but were on standby to begin a terrorist campaign against the occupiers. None of this proved true. Had it ever been true? Some historians argue that all this kind of talk had been nothing but Nazi propaganda to boost German morale and undermine Allied confidence, to make them believe that it would be impossible to occupy and control Germany. Certainly Himmler's belief that he could negotiate with the Allies in the last weeks of the war had been based on the assumption that the Allies would need his services because he could provide policing through the SS, the Gestapo and the regular police forces.

Refugees

The Allies faced an enormous refugee problem. Officially, decisions about the future of Germany were begun at the Potsdam Conference of 1945. This included the plans for moving Germans out of the regions which would fall outside the new German borders. On the ground, Germans had already begun fleeing from these areas and those who were left were being driven out of Poland, Czechoslovakia, Hungary and the USSR.

The refugees also included former concentration-camp inmates, former political prisoners, death-camp survivors and many others. In addition, there were former members of the German army, plus a few who had been camp guards or members of the *Einsatzgruppen* (death squads). Many were simply German-speaking civilians who had fled the advancing Red Army.

Former soldiers

Former members of the armed forces were disarmed and held in camps. Gradually soldiers straggled home from prisoner-of-war camps or internment. The

Key terms

Einsatzgruppen: German word meaning 'task forces'; specialist SS and SD units with the responsibility for arresting and executing Communist leaders and Jews in land taken by the German army on the Eastern Front during the Second World War; death squads.

unfortunate ones who had been captured on the Eastern Front by the Red Army often disappeared into Soviet gulags, never to return.

War criminals

Numerous decisions had to be made about which leaders of the Nazi Party and the country to prosecute. By December 1945, there were more than 100 000 civilians held in internment either because they were seen as a possible threat or because it was believed that they were likely to face trial.

The main Nazi leadership was put on trial for war crimes at Nuremberg in a series of military tribunals held between late November 1945 and early October 1946. The 23 most important surviving Nazi leaders, including those from the armed forces, appeared before the tribunal. Martin Bormann was tried in his absence and sentenced to death; unknown to the Allies he was already dead, killed while trying to escape from Berlin in May 1945. Robert Ley committed suicide in his cell before he could appear. Adolf Hitler, Josef Goebbels and Heinrich Himmler had all committed suicide shortly before or shortly after the end of the war.

The tribunal adjourned on 1 September and sentences were announced at the end of the month. Of the accused, 12 were sentenced to death by hanging, 7 received prison sentences, 3 were acquitted and 2 were not charged. Hermann Göring committed suicide the day before he was due to be hanged.

Food

The food-supply situation was a further critical difficulty. Germany had been a net importer of food; during the war, trade had been replaced with requisitioning: food was seized and sent to Germany. With neither trade nor requisitioning in place, Germany was dependent on the occupiers to bring in food. Each zone decided on the quota it felt it could allow the civilian population. Rations were meagre: Germans were given only about a third to a half of the calories they needed to be healthy and able to work. Even the officially announced ration allowances were often illusory. Inevitably, there were instances of hoarding and black market trading.

Despite the strict rules against occupying forces fraternising with the locals, there were illicit relationships, some of which resulted in children. As after the First World War, these children and their mothers had a difficult time.

The issue of Berlin and the blockade

The Soviet Union plotted to reunite Germany under communist rule and within the Soviet sphere of influence. The Western Allies wanted to see at least the west of the country back on its feet, joining them as an ally in the developing Cold War.

Berlin lay deep inside territory occupied by the Soviet Union. The presence of the western Allies in the city undermined the development of Soviet control over its Zone of Occupation and especially over its sector of the former capital city. Soviet leader Stalin took the decision to force French, British and American forces out of Berlin. It was a city dependent on one rail, one road and three air links to the West for its daily supply. This vulnerability did not go unnoticed in Moscow, and between June 1948 and May 1949 the Soviet Union blockaded Berlin, closing all rail and road links to the West. The Allies responded by undertaking the supply by air of all the food and essential goods needed by the people of West Berlin. In addition to the official 'Operation Vittles', pilots began bringing in confectionery for children in an unofficial 'Operation Little Vittles'. This was the first serious crisis of the Cold War. Allied pilots flew some 200 000 missions in one year, delivering food and other essentials to West Berlin, amounting to over 7000 tons each day. This was the Berlin Airlift.

Figure 3.7: Berlin occupation zones, 1945.

By May 1949 it was obvious to all parties that the Airlift had been a success. More food than had ever arrived by rail and road now reached West Berlin. The blockade was lifted the same month. However the conflict between the Western Allies and the USSR only worsened. The consequence was the splitting up of Germany into two parts: the Soviet Zone of Occupation became the **German Democratic Republic** in the east and French, UK and US Zones of Occupation became the ***Bundesrepublik*** *Deutschland* or **Federal Republic of Germany** in the west. Berlin remained a special case, divided into four zones of occupation.

The crossing points between Berlin's zones of occupation – Russian, British, American and French – were heavily guarded, the best known being 'Checkpoint Charlie' between the Russian and American zones. This was a complicated arrangement, with control within the zones exercised by the military of the respective countries. Civilian political activity was suspended, although the formation of what were called 'anti-fascist parties' was allowed in the Soviet zone. There was much to do. The repair of war damage, the distribution of food to the civilian population, the denazification programme, and the many administrative tasks took a great deal of time and effort. For the civilian population, life was grim and there were many shortages of both food and fuel.

The same applied to all of Germany. Some Allied occupation troops donated part of their food rations to help alleviate the worst of the hunger but the sheer scale of the task was enormous, especially for those cities such as Hamburg, Cologne and the industrial towns of the Ruhr in the west of Germany, and Leipzig and Dresden in the east, all of which had been heavily bombed during the fighting.

The division of Germany

It quickly became clear that each of the occupying powers was administering its own zone of occupation, with minimal reference to the others. Then, on 1 January 1947, the UK and US zones merged to form the '**Bizone**'; following the later absorption of the French zone, this became the '**Trizone**'. The developing Cold War meant that, instead of either a unitary country or break-up into several small nations, an east–west division between the 'Trizone' and the Soviet zone was the beginning of two Germanies.

The Berlin Blockade was the catalyst:

- The 'Trizone' was turned into the Federal Republic of Germany (FRG) or *Bundesrepublik Deutschland* (BRD) in May 1949. It took Bonn as its temporary capital.
- Within months, the Soviets responded, declaring the foundation of the German Democratic Republic (GDR) or *Deutsche Demokratische Republik* (DDR), with the Soviet sector of Berlin as its capital, in October 1949.

In addition to these two states, the Saarland remained under French control until the population voted in 1955 to join the emerging West Germany, something it had to wait until 1 January 1957 to do.

Allied troops remained in both Germanies for several years. Occupation as such ended in the west in 1955, but authority was moved first from the military to civilian administrators known as 'high commissioners', with the foundation of the FRG in May 1949.

Economic developments

The impact of the Depression

The Depression that followed the Wall Street Crash of 1929 plunged first the economy of the USA and then that of the world into a long period of economic slump characterised by high unemployment and low prices. It is still a matter of debate as to whether the Crash on Wall Street was symptom as much as cause, masking deep structural problems in the world economy. The slump in world trade, while harmful to Germany because of the export price of its manufactured goods, was lower than before.

In Germany from 1930 there were strikes, demonstrations and widespread unrest. Unemployment in German industry rose sharply, to over 30%. Industrial

ACTIVITY 3.11

Make notes on the problems faced by the Allied forces occupying Germany between 1945 and 1949. Draw attention to the ways in which the different problems affected one another.

ACTIVITY 3.12

Could the Nazis have come to power without the Wall Street Crash and the subsequent depression? Write out the question and draw up two columns, one marked 'Yes' and the other 'No'. Put down ideas in each column and back each idea with a reference to something specific.

production slumped but had more than recovered by 1936. The Nazi policies of rearmament and militarisation helped to boost industrial output in Germany to exceed 1929 levels.

After the loss of the large US loans and investments in 1929, Germany found it difficult to obtain good credit terms. However, the country was not without supporters in the world and the Weimar Republic had restored a measure of international acceptance after the Locarno treaties of 1925. The currency, the new Reichsmark, appeared to have brought a measure of stability to the Weimar economy. While industrial output rates grew only slowly and there were no major innovations in industry or commerce, the economy seemed to have come back from the brink of the catastrophic inflation of 1923.

The Nazis' initial economic policies

The economy of Nazi Germany from 1933 was above all based on the need to prepare for war (*Wehrwirtschaft*). Hitler and the Nazi leadership always regarded economic policy as secondary to a political programme. The party had been slow to develop an economic policy but by the early 1930s it had found a group of economists ('The Reformers'), such as Heinrich Dräger, whose radical economic ideas seemed a good fit with Nazi political and military aims.

The 'Reformers' helped shape the main Nazi domestic economic policy, which was for the launching of a major programme of public works. This was the (then new) economic policy of John Maynard Keynes. It meant a much higher level of government intervention in the management of the economy and what was called 'deficit spending', which means spending money you don't have at the moment. The argument for this was that a major public works programme – building roads, railways, dams and flood defences – would help directly by bringing down unemployment and indirectly by stimulating manufacturing and the spending power of those in work, and so encouraging economic growth.

Not least of the appeal of these ideas to the Nazis was that they represented a sharp break with what they saw as the failed economic policies of the Weimar Republic, and that they would keep the German population content. The risk was a return of the desperate inflation that had devastated German society in 1923.

 Voices from the past

Gregor Strasser

In January 1928 Gregor Strasser had been put in charge of the Nazi Party national organisation. In May 1932 he made a major speech in the Reichstag. This was later published as a pamphlet titled *Work and Bread*. It was firmly based on many of the 'Reformers' economic ideas:

The necessities of life come from work: food, accommodation, clothing, light, and heat. The wealth of a nation lies in labour not capital and that is the point. And so when it is dealing with the question of wealth creation the State must never ask 'Have I got the money for it?' But rather there is only one question: 'What should I use the money for?'[9]

The Nazis and industry

The general attitude of big business towards the Nazi state, especially outside the coal and steel sector, was mixed. The steel manufacturer Fritz Thyssen was a Nazi enthusiast but many large firms were not, especially those that were dependent on exports. They disliked the greater degree of state intervention, the **autarky** (self-sufficiency) and deficit spending that were built in to Nazi economic plans. The main national pressure group in this field, the Reich Association of German Industry (RDI), attempted to frustrate these plans and was swiftly brought to heel by the Nazi government. The Law for the Preparation of the Organic Construction of the German Economy followed at the end of November 1934.

The steelmaker Gustav Krupp was unusual among industrialists, such as his fellow Ruhr steelmaker Thyssen, in opposing Hitler and the Nazi Party. But as soon as Hitler was appointed chancellor, Krupp became an enthusiastic Nazi supporter, helping to finance the NSDAP campaign for the March 1933 election and later becoming President of the *Reichsverbandder Deutschen Industrie* (German Chamber of Commerce).

The Nazis promised to bring the trade unions to heel and were committed to a massive programme of rearmament. Both of these appealed strongly to a major arms manufacturer such as Krupp, who could see great profits for the company. Many industrialists had never liked the Weimar Republic. They much preferred an authoritarian form of government that prioritised order and stability.

The huge chemicals conglomerate IG Farben, founded in 1925, was a major contributor of funds to the Nazi Party from 1933. In this year, Hermann Schmitz was elected as a Nazi member of the Reichstag, becoming CEO of IG Farben two years later, in 1935. Money to support the Nazi campaign for the March 1933 election was channelled through Ford Germany. Its American owner, Henry Ford, was well known for his great success as a businessman but also for his very strongly held anti-Semitic views. He was awarded a medal by the Nazi government.

Recovery and development under the Nazis in peacetime

Hitler himself did not consider economic matters to be very important. Mainly for this reason, Nazi economic policies remained rather vague. Nevertheless, there were various priorities, which were tied to social cohesion and total war.

A central Nazi economic policy lay in the international sphere. It was the policy of autarky (self-sufficiency). This meant both protecting German production from cheaper foreign imports by the raising of tariffs (import duties) on overseas goods and boosting production within Germany, especially agricultural output. Germany was not self-sufficient in a number of essentials and raw materials. That this made the nation vulnerable in time of war had been shown during the First World War.

Germany lacked oil. The need for fuel for the planned invasion of Poland and the gaining of *Lebensraum* in eastern Europe was paramount. Tanks, planes, armoured cars, military transport and so on all needed to be kept running. In March 1939 Germany signed a bilateral Treaty for the Development of Economic Relations between the Two Countries with Romania. This established German control over

ACTIVITY 3.13

Why do you think some industrialists supported the Nazi party in 1933 and others opposed it? List the reasons and put them into context.

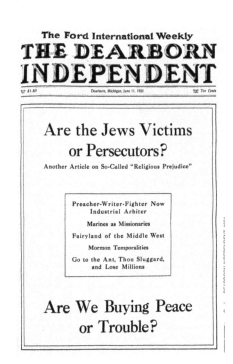

Figure 3.8: *The International Jew*, a collection of Henry Ford's articles reprinted from the *Dearborn Independent*, his own newspaper, 1920.

most aspects of the Romanian economy, in particular over the production of the extensive oil fields there.

The degree of government control over industry and business involved in autarky had a mixed reception from German business leaders, especially those whose businesses were dependent on exports. Against this it was argued that world trade had already been affected by the putting up of protective tariffs by many countries, notably the USA, since the Wall Street Crash.

There were limits, however, to how far a government could impose a war economy in peacetime. The population had to be kept adequately supplied with goods and foodstuffs or the government would lose support. Smaller businesses could not be alienated by the inevitable distortions of their operations. Lastly, pending the projected conquests, Germany was dependent on international supply of many industrial raw materials and foodstuffs. The economic developments of the peacetime Nazi rule reflect these conflicting priorities.

The appointment of Hjalmar Schacht (a former DDP member) as President of the Reichsbank on 16 March 1933 was one of the most important decisions made by Hitler after the elections that month had greatly strengthened his position. For businessmen, economists and the general public who might otherwise have been alarmed by deficit spending, Schacht was a reassuring presence at the head of the Reichsbank, Germany's central bank. By reputation a cool and competent central banker, he was best known for his steady monetary management in the difficult inflationary days of 1923 and 1929.

As soon as he was appointed, Schacht began to develop methods of deficit financing. One of his innovations was the '**mefo**' bill (short for *Mefo-Wechsel*). These were effectively promises by the government to pay tomorrow for work being done today. They ran initially for six months but could be extended and even discounted. Some ran on for four years. They were accepted by a consortium of four major armaments manufacturers (the *Metallurgische Forschungsgesellschaft*) and enabled Schacht to finance the massive rearmament programme called for by the Nazi government.

In recognition of his success, Hitler appointed Schacht minister of economics in August 1934, a post he held until November 1937. Until 1938 German rearmament was still secret, being a flagrant breach of the Treaty of Versailles, but after this time it was in the open and the use of 'mefo bills' was discontinued, by which time a total of 12 billion Marks was outstanding. This gives some idea of the massive scale of these financial operations.

Figure 3.9: Hjalmar Schacht in 1931.

The apparent success of Schacht's economic policy was remarkable:

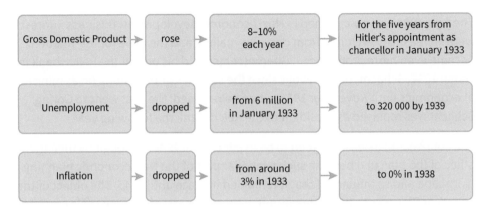

Figure 3.10: Flow diagrams showing improvements in the Germany economy from 1933.

On the other hand, although many more Germans were now in work and inflation was small (partly because of the determined imposition of price controls), at the same time there was the introduction of rationing on many everyday items such as foodstuffs, as the economy geared up for war.

Schacht was bold in the sense that he adopted Keynesian economic principles at a time when they were not common. This involved a much greater degree of government intervention in the control of the economy than had existed in the recent German past. It also shifted the main focus of the economy from the supply side (producers) to the demand side (consumers). Schacht was also quite lucky, as the German economy was entering a recovery phase in 1933 from the depths of 1930.

During the economic crisis of 1936–37 Schacht helped to lead a 'free market' faction in the Nazi government. Supported by his deputy at the Reichsbank, the Reich Commissioner for Prices, Carl Goerdeler, he argued against protectionist measures for German goods and the inflationary effect of the huge increases in the rearmament budget. He wanted to see the economy move away from huge military expenditure. This view was supported by many smaller businessmen, whose commercial operations depended on exports. Goerdeler's leadership of this group was significant, as his task was to control inflation.

Military spending in Germany reached 10% of GDP in 1936 and was higher than spending on civilian matters for many years after. The distortions to the civilian economy in terms of the availability of non-military goods became severe. Such was the control of the Nazis over many aspects of the economy that entrepreneurship was severely reduced in Germany. Under this 'command capitalism', exports declined and imports rose, which is bad for any economy.

Schacht's was not a message that Hitler wished to hear from his top economic advisers. His priority was rearmament and preparing for war. Sometime in August 1936, Hitler took the decision to launch the Four-Year Plan for the development of the German economy. He put his trusted lieutenant Göring in charge of it in October 1936. He felt that it was needed because he did not think that Schacht's 'New Plan' would ever solve the problem of providing sufficient raw materials to sustain the rearmament drive at the same time as providing the population with adequate levels of consumption.

The year 1936 was a watershed in Nazi economic development. Business interests were increasingly excluded from decision-making and the drive for rearmament became even more pronounced. Goerdeler resigned his post at the Reichsbank in March 1937. Schacht, out of favour since the summer of 1936, hung on as minister of economics until November 1937, when he resigned; the post went to Göring. Schacht was replaced as President of the Reichsbank the following year.

The Four-Year Plan was designed to be in effect until 1940, although by then the office of the plan had become such a familiar part of the Nazi economic planning landscape and so influential that it remained in place until 1945. The object of the Four-Year Plan was to boost the output within Germany of raw materials crucial to any war effort. For example, the intention was to produce vastly more mineral oil, including synthetic petrol, between 1936 and 1940. In fact, this was one major area of failure: output did increase but fell well short of the plan's projections.

Many items fell short of Four-Year Plan targets by 1940, with the exception of brown coal and explosives. This general failure to achieve autarky left a continuing dependence on the import of crucial raw materials from other countries for the military effort. The need to bring the sources of these materials and supplies of foodstuffs within the German sphere by act of conquest sometimes determined military priorities when war came in 1939.

The Four-Year Plan also sought to give a boost to the public works programme. It succeeded to some extent and the German economy was much better prepared for war in 1939 than it had been in 1914. However, the Nazis had taken on a task beyond the economic capacity of Germany in trying at one and the same time to:

- achieve autarky quickly
- rearm quickly
- construct Autobahns and massive prestige buildings quickly
- keep a mass population supplied with foodstuffs and consumer goods.

The fact that the Nazis prevented a wage explosion or rapid increase in prices was a testament to their social control through terror and their mastery of propaganda.

Clearly much of NSDAP economic policy was to do with militarism. Recent historical scholarship has examined the economic factors behind the outbreak of war in 1939, including the role of the Four-Year Plan. Some historians, echoing the fears of J.M. Keynes in 1920, have highlighted what they see as the onerous terms of the Treaty of Versailles in putting an impossible burden on the German economy.

The British historian Timothy Mason focused on domestic factors within Germany as the trigger for war, specifically the economic crisis of 1936. He argued that the working class in Germany did not support the Nazis, and their demands for higher wages and their ability to move to other employers to obtain them amounted to mass political resistance. The economic tension between the rearmament programme of the later 1930s and the health of the civilian domestic economy remained unresolved. The Nazi leadership was aware that the Russian Revolution of 1917 was caused in part by shortages of food and manufactured goods and a decline in living standards.

The British economic historian Richard Overy responded that the nature of the economic crisis in Germany had been exaggerated by Mason and that there was no evidence to suggest that Hitler was even aware of it when he took the decision to launch an attack on Poland in 1939.

Recovery and development under the Nazis in wartime

After six years preparing for war, much of Germany's economy was already engaged in military production. Accordingly, the outbreak of the Second World War did not immediately cause great changes. The German economy simply moved further to prioritise the supply of military forces. This rebalancing was taken still further following the German invasion of the Soviet Union in 1941.

The peacetime economic regime, directed in large part by Schacht, had been focused on restoring Germany's leading trading and industrial position in the world. Now, apart from military expenditure, the civilian economy suffered. The war has been credited with reducing unemployment to zero but if the effects of rearmament and conscription are removed, German economic growth rates from 1939 to 1945 were sluggish at best. The government did not initially seek vigorously to draw women into the workforce (as the UK did and as the USA was to do on joining the war). Nor did they substantially increase direct and personal taxes to raise funds.

As in the First World War, the British initiated a blockade to try to limit the country's ability to import. Petroleum, sugar, coffee, chocolate and cotton grew scarce. Germany was an importer of many key raw materials: oil from Romania, iron ore from Sweden, tungsten from Spain and Portugal and grain from the USSR (until Operation Barbarossa in 1941).

Military operations brought new sources of materials under German rule. An eye to the rich grain-producing areas of Poland and Ukraine had a significant influence on strategic military thinking during the war. The invasions of Poland in 1939 and the Soviet Union in 1941 were both in part designed to secure for Germany the grain supplies it needed. In addition, manufactured goods were requisitioned. Occupied countries were also taxed to help pay for Germany's war effort.

Slave labour drawn from 'social undesirables' had been policy even before the war. As large numbers of foreign workers came under German rule, this programme was greatly expanded. IG Farben, Krupp, Ford and Thyssen all had slave labour in their wartime factories. By 1944, forced labourers were a quarter of the workforce.

With total war, more factories were converted to military purposes. This greatly increased the supply of, for example, military vehicles. However, as the war went on, Allied bombing raids gradually destroyed factories and infrastructure.

ACTIVITY 3.14

Make notes on:

- Why the Nazis adopted the policy of autarky
- How they pursued it
- What level of success they achieved.

129

The post-war economy

Initial thinking about the post-war German economy was influenced by the US Treasury Secretary, Henry Morgenthau. The '**Morgenthau Plan**' was to destroy Germany's military strength. This would be done not merely by disarming but also by destroying the entire industrial support for the armed forces. Germany would be split into two states. The main industrial areas of the Ruhr, the Saarland and Silesia would be incorporated into neighbour states. Germany would shoulder a heavy burden of reparations. The country would be left poor and largely agrarian. Nor was agriculture immune: there was even a plan for deforestation to be achieved by heavy felling and export.

As a result of this kind of thinking, the Allies began the period of occupation in much the same spirit as had prevailed in 1918. The German armed forces ceased to exist. The munitions industry was shut down. Civilian factories deemed capable of supporting the military or even with military potential were scheduled for destruction.

It was decreed that German heavy industry could only operate at half its pre-war level; factories would be demolished to ensure this. Car manufacture could only reach a tenth of pre-war levels. German steel production capacity could only operate at a quarter of pre-war levels; any spare-capacity steel plants would be demolished. The German steel industry was banned from importing high-grade Swedish iron ore and limited to lower-grade German ore. This doubled the amount of coal required, with obvious consequences for costs. In addition, coal and steel had to be sold at fixed prices, and those prices guaranteed losses.

In an echo of the settlement that followed the First World War, the Saarland, a coalmining area, was separated from the rest of Germany and placed under French direction.

The restrictions placed on iron and steel had a knock-on effect for other business, to the extent that industry had no difficulty remaining below the levels set.

The Soviets seized German factories, took them apart and packed them onto trains bound for the USSR. They were supposed to be paid for with raw materials, but when the latter did not arrive, the US blocked further shipments. The other Allies did not engage in large-scale seizures of goods as reparations, but there was seizure of copyrights, patents and trademarks. This naturally undermined research and entrepreneurship.

The Allies gradually realised that the campaign of keeping Germany weak was counterproductive: other European countries needed to recover from the war and having so major an economy as Germany held back was harming all of them. They now cautiously encouraged German economic expansion. The levels of industrial capacity that Germany was permitted to achieve were doubled, from 25% of pre-war levels to 50%.

Unlike the First World War, Germany had not surrendered until almost the entire country had been occupied and its army was only defending a few streets. This led to occupation by Allied troops. Although this should have been a national humiliation, the presence of hundreds of thousands of well-paid people made a contribution to economic recovery.

The European Recovery Plan (known as the '**Marshall Plan**' after the US Secretary of State) had been set up to help to rebuild the economy of European countries damaged by war. Whereas Morgenthau had advised that countries should get the funding for recovery from Germany, Marshall scrapped his colleague's proposals and headed up a move for the US to support the recovery process. The Marshall Plan began sending funds in 1947 and Germany was included from 1948; the country had been lent $1.4 billion (about £4 billion at today's values) by the time that the plan ended in 1952.

Social developments and tensions

Nazi social policies

The Nazis sought to control many aspects of life, but what is striking is the speed with which they moved after January 1933. Many key agencies were established that very year. By the mid 1930s the Nazi state was firmly established in Germany.

One of the most far-reaching pieces of Nazi legislation is known in English as the Enabling Act but in German as the Law to Remedy the Distress of People and Reich (*Gesetzzur Behebung der Not von Volk und Reich*). It was passed by an intimidating Nazi majority in the Reichstag on 23 March 1933. Considering its importance it is also very short, with just four Articles. It was an amendment to the Weimar Constitution and gave the right to Chancellor Adolf Hitler to decide what laws were needed and then to issue and announce them without reference to the Reichstag. It effectively made the Reichstag redundant. As we saw earlier, Hitler spoke before the Act was passed in religious terms.

In the early years of the Nazi state, a policy of 'coordination' (*Gleichschaltung*) was pursued by the Nazi Party. This involved the active collaboration of various professional and cultural organisations, political parties and state governments. All this took to a new level the tradition handed down from imperial Germany of state involvement in many aspects of everyday life.

Education

Education was an area of national life over which the Nazis exercised close control. The anti-Semitic legislation of 1933 led to the removal from schools and universities of all Jewish teachers, professors and administrators. Indoctrination in Nazi ideas was made compulsory in January 1934. The primary and secondary educational curriculum focused on racial biology, population policy, geography and physical fitness. Military education became the major component of the last of these. There were even exam questions that pushed Nazi ideas about society, such as:

To keep a mentally ill person costs approximately 4 Marks a day. There are 300 000 mentally ill people in care. How much do these people cost to keep in total? How many marriage loans* of 1000 Marks could be granted with this money?[10]

(*Marriage loans existed to encourage marriage, of which the Nazis strongly approved.)

ACTIVITY 3.15

List what you think were the central purposes of the youth organisations the HJ and the BDM. In each case, comment on what the NSDAP government wanted to achieve.

Bernhard Rust was appointed minister of education in June 1934. He had already been active in Prussia, insisting that all students and teachers should greet each other in schools using the Nazi salute.

The *Hitlerjugend* and the *Bund Deutscher Mädel*

The Hitler Youth (**Hitlerjugend** or HJ) was paramilitary in character and was used before 1933 to break up the meetings of church youth groups. It grew out of the youth wing of the NSDAP, which had been set up in 1922. Under Nazi rule, other youth organisations – those linked to churches or political parties, and also the Scout Association, which was British-founded and international and so inherently suspect – were shut down. Membership of the Hitler Youth was voluntary at first but from 1936 it became compulsory for all boys aged 10 to 21; membership was over 2 million by the end of 1933 and 5 million by the end of 1936.

The HJ had strong links with the army and the German Labour Organisation. It held regular meetings where Nazi doctrine was taught, and semi-military rallies and field exercises. Parents who refused to allow their child to join were warned that the state could take their child into care.

The Nazi youth organisation for girls, the *Bund Deutscher Mädel* (BDM), was put under the Hitler Youth in 1933. They were not paramilitary and did not engage in competitive sport in the same way. They did use meetings for indoctrination, including the importance of preparing for marriage and motherhood. Although the indoctrination seems restricting to us, for many members it was actually liberating as it was an opportunity to be out of doors and away from their parents. This caused some Nazi leaders, including Himmler, to regard the BDM with distaste and distrust.

In wartime, the BDM were drafted to help by collecting money for the war effort and clothes for the troops, as well as in paramilitary roles such as nursing, office work and searchlight management. HJ members worked alongside the adult troops, manning anti-aircraft batteries but latterly also fighting as soldiers. It was through this route that the German novelist Günter Grass was drafted to the Waffen SS aged 16, having tried to be a submariner aged 15. The future chancellor Helmut Kohl was also a HJ member and was drafted for military training aged 15, though the war ended without his seeing action.

Women

The National Socialist Women's League (**National sozialistische Frauenschaft** or *NS-Frauenschaft*) was founded in October 1931. Its leader from 1934 to 1945 was Gertrud Scholtz-Klink. By 1938 its membership topped 2 million or 40% of the Nazi Party membership. This was a tribute to the importance placed by the Nazis on the role of women in society. Feminist groups were closed down in 1933. Women were to look after their husbands, give birth and keep a clean and tidy home.

On the surface, the Nazis believed in a return to patriarchal values and traditional gender roles in society. They had gained much political and electoral support from those Germans who deplored the social and cultural changes that had taken place since 1919. However, even progressive Weimar governments had been troubled by such things as the declining birth rate and rising rates of divorce. The

Figure 3.11: Gertrud Scholtz-Klink, leader of the *NS-Frauenschaft*, 1934–45.

NS-Frauenschaft was intended to reverse these developments by encouraging domesticity and teaching traditional, socially conservative values.

The campaign was sufficiently successful that when in wartime the Nazi message to women changed and they sought to persuade women to go out to work in factories and other industries to support the war effort by taking over the jobs left by men, the response was, from their point of view, disappointing.

Volksgemeinschaft

Volksgemeinschaft is one of those German words that are difficult to translate into English because they are so laden with meaning. It is necessary to understand the concept, however, because it was at the heart of Nazi thinking about society.

The German sociologist Ferdinand Tönnies offered a definition of *Gemeinschaft* as a 'community', rather than merely a 'society'. Implicit shared values and moral code bind the *Gemeinschaft* together. Tönnies thought that the family was the prime case of this.

Even the first part of the word – *Volk* – is a German word that is loaded with meaning and association. The English word 'folk' doesn't do it justice. A better translation would be 'the people'. When demonstrators in the last days of East Germany in 1989 chanted *Wir sind das Volk* ('we are the people'), they were telling the government that they were the electorate, the nation; when the chant changed to *Wir sind ein Volk* ('we are one people'), they were demanding reunification with West Germany.

The word *Volk* is deeply embedded in German culture. Ever since the early 18th century at least one brand of German nationalism had emphasised *völkish* aspects. English translations of German words based on *Volk* give us the not very satisfactory 'folk music' (*Volksmusik*), 'folk song' (*Volkslied*) and 'folk dance' (*Volkstanz*). *Volksmärchen* has ended up as the even less happy 'fairy stories'. That the German word is intended to mean the nation and people is made clear by its frequent use in naming during the Nazi period: most famously the *Volkswagen,* the 'people's car'. But it also has associations with Germany's supposed tribal past, her prehistoric ancestry. It was thus used to promote the supposed 'Aryan' type: the tall, blond-haired, blue-eyed, lean, active warrior.

'Aryan' is another word with a complicated history. It is strictly used to mean a south-central Asian tribe which in prehistory is believed by some historians to have invaded both northern India and Europe. Nazi propagandists adopted this theory and promoted the idea that Germans were their pure descendants, also a conquering nation. This supposed link with northern India was the reason why the Nazis adopted the Hindu symbol of the swastika.

The racial state

The *Volksgemeinschaft* was the Nazi idea of the German nation: a classless society based on ethnic purity, with all foreigners and traitors excluded. The logic of this was that outsiders were, in effect, outlaws. Nazi policies on racial minorities, notably Jews, in Germany and then in the occupied lands, went through several stages.

ACTIVITY 3.16

The Nazi pre-war policy of sending women home to look after their children and husbands proved more successful than the wartime attempt to bring them back into the labour force. Why do you think that was? Draw a mind map showing the different issues, people, traditions and organisations that formed part of this. Show causal connections with arrows.

As soon as the Nazis were in control of Germany after March 1933, they initiated a boycott of Jewish shops. Local SA groups were the first to take the initiative in an unplanned and unofficial way in the same month as the election, standing outside Jewish-owned shops with intimidating placards designed to intimidate prospective shoppers. The boycott had only limited effects and seems to have irritated the German shopping public more than the Nazis expected.

In April 1933 the Nazi leadership published the *Gesetz zur Wiederherstellung des Berufsbeamtentums*. This is usually translated as the Law for the Restoration of the Professional Civil Service. It prevented 'non-Aryans' – which in practice meant Jews – from working for the state, and allowed state employees to be dismissed for reasons of race or politics. This is why the law is also known as the *Berufsverbot* (profession ban) law.

Then, in September 1935, during the huge Nazi party rally of that year (the seventh) held, as usual, in the city of Nuremberg, two new laws were passed that are usually known as the Nuremberg Laws. These laws provided the legal basis for all anti-Semitic action in Nazi Germany. The Law for the Protection of German Blood and German Honour (sometimes called the Blood Protection Law) aimed to isolate Jewish people socially by prohibiting marriage or any sexual relations between Jews and non-Jews. The Reich Citizenship Law that followed within a couple of months deprived Jews of all political rights.

In occupied Poland Jews were relocated in ghettos by the Germans in hundreds of locations, many in cities such as Warsaw and Lvov. Many people died in these places from disease, hunger or thirst. Concentrating Polish-Jewish people in this way made it easier for the German authorities to control them and later to move them out to the extermination camps.

Jews were not the only ethnic group to which the Nazis were hostile. Roma and Sinti peoples (whom we commonly call 'gypsies') were also actively persecuted. They couldn't be isolated on the basis of faith, as almost all were Christian. Instead there was an attempt to define their ethnicity through physical appearance. The science of the process (eugenics) has since been discredited, but it was taken seriously at the time and was useful for the Nazis.

When Himmler took centralised control of all police forces throughout Germany in 1936, he established the Reich Central Office for the Suppression of the Gypsy Nuisance. They too were subject to the racial, eugenicist and criminal laws. Between 1935 and 1938, *Zigeunerlager* (internment camps for gypsies) were set up all over Germany. These camps were just a preliminary stage on the road to genocide.

The logic of supposed science led from concentration camps to death camps. In the wake of the German armies' victories, the Jewish populations of countries under Nazi rule, including Poland, Ukraine and France, all suffered terribly. Germany's allies, and the puppet regimes in occupied countries, adopted matching policies of persecuting Jews.

The German soldiers entering Poland and the Soviet Union had been followed by the death squads called *Einsatzgruppen* (the name just means 'task forces').

These were paramilitary SS and SD (*Sicherheitsdienst* or Security Service) units, who executed anybody suspected of hostility to the invasion. The Polish-Jewish community suffered especially badly and was almost wiped out.

The full list of all Nazi concentration camps includes 70 locations. Seven, including the notorious extermination camps such as Auschwitz-Birkenau, were in Poland. There were others in Ukraine, Croatia, Belarus and Serbia. There were no extermination camps in Germany itself.

Nazi culture

Political opponents were either in jail or in hiding. The Nazis controlled all police services. But the government looked for still further ways to cement their total control over the population.

Social control was an important way of keeping any opposition to Nazi rule intimidated or invisible. One tool in this context that was wielded expertly was the use of propaganda. The constant barrage of images of Nazi power and triumphalism was everywhere. The appointment to the Ministry of Propaganda of Joseph Goebbels came just six weeks after Hitler became chancellor. Goebbels swiftly gained controlling supervision of news media, the arts and information.

The control over culture was close to Hitler's heart. He felt strongly that some of the art of the Weimar period had been 'degenerate' and he wanted what he saw as a more wholesome, more German style. The concept of *Volksgemeinschaft* was fundamental to him and deeply embedded in Nazi culture. A *Reichskulturkammer* (Reich Chamber of Culture) was set up in September 1933 under the control of Goebbels's Ministry of Propaganda.

The composer Richard Strauss was appointed president of the *Reichsmusikkammer* (Reich Music Chamber) in November 1933. Hitler disliked jazz because of its origins, exponents and anarchic style, and disapproved of Modernist and avant-garde, including atonal, music. He preferred Romantic music, particularly espousing that of Richard Wagner. He attended the annual Wagner Festival at Bayreuth in Bavaria every year from 1933.

Many books by authors of Jewish descent, by pacifists or by those suspected of having communist sympathies were publicly burnt in May and June 1933. Radio and the press were controlled through the Ministry of Propaganda. Many museum art directors lost their posts in 1933 to Nazi Party members.

The Nazi state had moved quickly to exercise control over many different aspects of cultural policy. An important and relatively new medium was radio. This was an important tool for the nation-state to influence a mass audience. The Ministry of Propaganda was responsible for the regulation of radio. American jazz was banned but popular music was acceptable provided that it reiterated nationalist themes and did not seek to undermine Nazi cultural values.

The Office of Radio Technology even made a cheap radio widely available. The 'people's receiver' (*Volksempfänger*) was launched in August 1933 at an affordable 76 Marks. Jewish and other non-Aryan composers and performers were removed from the airwaves and a diet of nationalistic, Aryan music replaced it.

In the visual arts, Hitler's personal preference was for Greek and Roman styles. As he saw it, this was art 'untainted' by Jewish influence, an art that was clean, heroic and idealised. There were only a few prominent Jewish artists popular in Weimar Germany in fact, including Marc Chagall. However, an exhibition of 'Degenerate art' was organised by the Nazis and held in Munich in 1937. 'Degenerate art' was defined as any work that 'insults German feeling or destroys or confuses natural form or simply reveals an absence of adequate manual or artistic skill'. Art seized from museums all over Germany was displayed, some 650 paintings. More than a million visitors in the first six weeks may testify to a public appetite. At the same time the *Grosse deutsche Kunstausstellung* (Great German art exhibition) was held to mark the contrast by showing what the Nazis believed to be healthy art. By the time the two exhibitions closed, the 'degenerate' display had attracted three and a half times as many visitors as its 'healthy' rival.

One of the most enduring images of Nazi pomp and power is to be seen in *The Triumph of the Will* (*Triumph des Willens*), a film made by Leni Riefenstahl about the 1934 Nazi Nuremberg Rally. Her innovative use of tracking shots and slow motion caused *The Economist* to call her 'the greatest female filmmaker of the 20th century'. She also went on to make a film about the 1936 Berlin Olympics.

Post-war German society and the legacy of Nazism

From January 1946 the victorious Allies embarked on a widespread programme of 'denazification'. The remaining physical symbols of Nazism that had decorated towns and cities were quickly removed. The most prominent Nazi leaders were brought to trial and sentenced.

The investigation of those who had been members of Nazi-related organisations was a slower and more complex task. About 8.5 million people had been members of the Nazi Party, roughly 10.5% of the adult German population. Nazi-related organisations involved still vaster numbers: 25 million belonged to the German Labour Front, 17 million to the National Socialist Welfare Organisation. How many members of the Hitler Youth or the League of German Women should be judged culpable in some way? What about all the civil servants and bureaucrats? By the end of the winter of 1945/46, nearly half of all German officials had been dismissed.

Industrialists who had been ardent Nazi supporters looked like obvious candidates for investigation and prosecution. Some businesses had benefited from the slave labour and drawn on the inmates of labour camps. IG Farben, the chemicals giant, had manufactured Zyklon B, a cyanide-based pesticide widely used in gas form in the death camps. Other companies had built the machinery of death in the camps or on the battlefield. Who was guilty and of what? However, the same managers and directors also possessed the leadership, skills, economic knowhow and entrepreneurship vital to rebuilding a country whose infrastructure had been destroyed and economy shattered.

With malnutrition rife and war debris to be cleared, the dilemma for the Allies was clear. If every member of a Nazi-related organisation was arrested, investigated and, if found culpable, tried and, if found guilty, imprisoned, who was to run the country after the Occupation forces had left? As a result of criticisms, the Law for

Liberation from National Socialism and Militarism was promulgated by the Allies in March 1946. The following month, over 500 civil tribunals were set up with a staff of 22 000. Even this was not nearly enough, with a caseload of 900 000.

There was inevitably some corruption in the system, with talk of an active black market in denazification certificates. In some areas, hostility to the tribunals and indignation at what many had mockingly called 'victor's justice', resulted in high levels of reinstatement. By early 1947, the Allies had some 90 000 former Nazis in detention; by the following year, Cold War fears meant that the Eastern Bloc was of much greater concern than effective denazification, particularly for the USA.

The political, economic and social condition of Germany by 1949

In 1949 Germany was ruined, defeated and divided. The achievement of 1871 and the years leading up to unification had been undone.

There was a major refugee problem in the north-east. Radically different ideologies prevailed in the east and west. For most Germans, the priority was just on the grim struggle to survive. Germany's cities had been badly bombed, especially in industrial areas. Rail and road infrastructure was extensively damaged. Bridges and docks had often been Allied targets in the war.

Old certainties had proved illusory and for the time being confidence was at an all-time low. However, for a minority even the grimmest of circumstances offer opportunities to those brave or lucky enough to take them. Germany was now the front line of the Cold War. The USA in particular was determined to support the three western occupied zones that in 1949 became West Germany against a perceived threat from the Soviet Bloc. The USSR was equally determined to retain control of the Soviet zone, which was developing as East Germany. On 7 March 1946, at Fulton, Missouri, USA, the wartime British Prime Minister Winston Churchill was guest speaker at a meeting at Westminster College. He used the term 'iron curtain' to describe the division of Europe at that time. Some date the start of the Cold War from this speech.

Figure 3.12: US Secretary of State General George Marshall, 1947.

The Marshall Plan operated for four years from April 1948. By 1949 the economic support had just begun to take effect, in Germany as in other devastated countries in western Europe. The plan was in itself a strong signal that the USA – just about the only country to have increased its power and influence during the war – was supportive. This was an important psychological boost for western Germany after 1945. However, the USSR's rejection of US aid meant that East Germany had to rely on its own resources and on the military and economic support of the Soviet Union.

The US public demanded rapid demobilisation after May 1945 and the repatriation of US forces happened quickly. By 1946 this process had been taken as far as the US wanted. There was also major and rapid demobilisation by the Soviet army and repatriation from Germany. However, substantial ground forces were retained on both sides, each viewing the other's presence as a threat.

The sheer scale of the problem of displaced persons (DPs) was a major one for the Allied Occupation Forces in Germany after 1945. They came from everywhere that German forces had occupied in the war. Many could not be repatriated to their original homes because of fear of persecution. It has been calculated that between 11 and 20 million DPs found themselves living in DP camps or just moving about Europe after 1945.

Figure 3.13: Class portrait of schoolchildren at Schauenstein Displaced Persons camp, Bavaria, c. 1946.

The US forces in western Germany were initially instructed to take no steps to revive the economy. The output of oil, rubber, merchant ships and aircraft was prohibited and German steel production was substantially reduced. When it became apparent by the summer of 1947 that economic recovery in western Europe would not happen without a strong West German industrial base, this policy was reversed. It had become even more important to ensure that a strong West could face the Soviet Union and its satellite states.

In the East, the formation of 'antifascist' political parties had been allowed as early as June 1945. In May 1949, elections were held in the Soviet zone for the German People's Congress, resulting in a victory for the ***Sozialistische Einheitspartei Deutschlands*** (the Socialist Unity Party of Germany), a party formed from a forced merger between Social Democrats and Communists. August 1949 brought elections to the West German **Bundestag**. Taken together these elections mark a tentative revival of party politics.

Until 1949 the occupation forces had administered Germany under the terms of an Occupation Statute but in May 1949 the Basic Law for the Federal Republic of Germany (***Grundgesetz*** *für die Bundesrepublik Deutschland*) came into effect in the west. In practice, this became the constitution of West Germany. Prominent in the election were one new political party and one familiar one:

- The centre-right Christian Democratic Union (CDU) was led by Konrad Adenauer, the 73-year-old former mayor of Cologne.
- The centre-left Social Democrats (SPD) were led by Kurt Schumacher.

The CDU won narrowly and Adenauer became the first chancellor of the Federal German Republic.

This political activity was in itself a sign of life returning to something like normal although it was a very different 'normal' from the one that many Germans had known.

The misery of 1945's defeat and the terror of occupation was followed by the dreadful winter of 1945/46. The clearing of war rubble and the repair of transport infrastructure was the work of years. Gradually some sort of economic revival started to take place. Germans tried to look to the future – albeit in a divided country, each part allied to a superpower that had recently been an enemy.

Timeline

1929	Young Plan
	October: Wall Street Crash in New York, USA
	'Liberty Law' (*Freiheitgesetz*) campaign
1931	October: Founding of the Harzburg Front
	December: Founding of the Iron Front
1932	President Hindenburg appoints Heinrich Brüning, Kurt von Schleicher and Franz von Papen in turn as chancellor
1933	January: Hindenburg appoints Adolf Hitler as chancellor
	27 February: Reichstag fire
	March: federal election
	16 March: Hjalmar Schacht appointed President of the Reichsbank
	23 March: Hitler presents Enabling Act to the Reichstag
	April: *Gesetzzur Wiederherstellung des Berufsbeamtentums* (Law for the Restoration of the Professional Civil Service)
	15 July: Nazis become only legal political party in Germany
	September: foundation of the *Reichskulturkammer* (Reich Chamber of Culture)

1934	30 June–2 July: 'Night of the Long Knives' (*Röhm Putsch*)
	2 August: Hindenburg dies; Hitler assumes the office of president
	August: Schacht appointed minister of economics
1935	September: Nuremberg Laws passed: Law for the Protection of German Blood and German Honour; Reich Citizenship Law
1936	March: remilitarisation of the Rhineland
	October: Four-Year Plan launched; Göring put in charge
	Himmler establishes the Reich Central Office for the Suppression of the Gypsy Nuisance
1937	March: Goerdeler resigns his post at the Reichsbank
	November: Schacht resigns as minister of economics; the post goes to Göring
	Exhibition of 'Degenerate art' and *Grosse deutsche Kunstausstellung* (Great German art exhibition) in Munich
1938	March: union (*Anschluss*) with Austria
	7 November: *Kristallnacht*
	Schacht replaced as President of the Reichsbank
1939	The invasion of Poland by the Germany army
1941	German invasion of the Soviet Union
1942	Defeat of German army at Stalingrad
1942–43	White Rose distributes leaflets; Sophie and Hans Scholl executed for treason
1943	February: *Rosenstrasse Protest*; Goebbels's 'total war' speech
1944	July: Bomb Plot
1945	Potsdam Conference
	Germany split into four zones of occupation
	East Prussia and Silesia put into the hands of Poland
	North-East Prussia and Memel passed to the USSR
1945–46	Nuremberg trials
1946	January: Allies launch 'denazification'
1948	European Recovery Plan ('Marshall Plan') begins in Germany
1948–49	June 1948–May 1949: Soviet Union blockades Berlin

1949	May: Basic Law for the Federal Republic of Germany (*Grundgesetzfür die Bundesrepublik Deutschland*) passed; Federal Republic of Germany (*Bundesrepublik Deutschland*) established
	August: elections to the West German Bundestag
	October: German Democratic Republic (*Deutsche Demokratische Republik*) established

Practice essay questions

1. To what extent do you think anti-Semitism was central to Nazi ideology and its implementation, 1920–45?
2. 'Despite the changes of government, the theme of social reform was central to German politics throughout the Weimar and Nazi periods.' Do you agree?
3. Would you agree that the key thing the German people wanted from Hitler, following the experience of Weimar's hyperinflation and unemployment, was economic stability?
4. Using your understanding of the historical context, assess how convincing the arguments in these three extracts are in relation to economic policy under the Nazis.

Extract A

The Third Reich was the first modern state to face the many new problems raised by permanent full employment, and was totally unfitted to solve them: [first] the Nazi Party had been brought to power to end unemployment, and in the later 1930s the government proved unable to make the great reappraisal and reorganisation necessary to cope with its success; second the labour shortage could not be met by economic contraction since this would have slowed down rearmament; third, the built-in need of the totalitarian regime to obtain the constant loyalty and continuous adulation of those classes of society which had most reason to hate it, disabled it from effective intervention in the labour market until internal crisis had made such intervention essential…

Source: Timothy Mason, Nazism, Fascism, and the Working Class: Essays by Tim Mason, edited by Jane Caplan, Cambridge University Press 1995, pp 49-50.

Extract B

The new regime aimed at complete control of the economic, social, political and cultural life of the nation. In economics, it interpreted the depression as evidence of the failure of the private market economy and of the necessity of state intervention. Although already earlier in the Weimar Republic there had been a great deal of government intervention, for instance in the housing market and in wage policy, the depression brought a call for new controls and regulation; the German government imposed controls and international capital movement and a partial debt moratorium for agriculture. The depression, with its enormous human suffering, the almost seven million unemployed, bankrupt farmers, and closed banks, seemed unambiguous evidence that the unplanned individualistic market economy and also 'finance capitalism' did not work. Banks had called in many loans in order to protect their severely endangered liquidity [cash balances], and earned the hatred of many small and medium-sized enterprises. At the same time, in order to remain in business, banks had demanded, and received, and become dependent on, state subsidies.

Source: Harold James, Banks and Business Politics in Nazi Germany, in Business and Industry in Nazi Germany, edited by Francis R. Nicosia and Jonathan Huene, Berghahn Books, 2004, pages 45-46.

Extract C

Most of the leaders of the business community were never tempted to become Nazis. The NSDAP's promise to destroy the existing elite and impose a new one in its place held little allure for men already at the top of their society. Its plebeian [Working class or commonplace] tone offended their taste. So did its anti-Semitism, for whatever other prejudices the leading men of German big business harboured, that form of bigotry was rare in their ranks. Most also found disturbing Nazism's demand for total power and its voluble strain of anti-capitalism, which focused predominantly on large-scale enterprise. Almost as alarming were the unorthodox fiscal and monetary schemes put forward by prominent Nazis as remedies for the depression. Still, most men of big business viewed Nazism myopically [short-sightedly] and opportunistically. Like many other Germans whose national pride had been wounded by the unexpected loss of the war and by a humiliating peace treaty, they admired Nazism's defiant nationalism and hoped it could be used to help reassert what they regarded as their country's rightful place among the great powers.

Source: Henry Ashby Turner, German Big Business and the Rise of Hitler, Oxford: Oxford University Press, 1985, p. 348.

Chapter summary

You have been studying what forces brought Hitler to power, and the changes that his NSDAP regime made to Germany's politics, economy and society. Unlike the First World War, Hitler's war ended with the whole country being fought across and finally occupied by foreign armies who divided the country into four. In particular, you should remember that:

- The Wall Street Crash affected Germany's economy, society and politics; as it became ever more difficult to form coalitions that could agree programmes of action and carry them out, so rule by decree became the norm.

- Voters increasingly started supporting extreme parties of Left and Right; after appointing chancellors without Reichstag majorities, Hindenburg was advised to appoint Adolf Hitler, now the leader of the largest party.

- The Reichstag fire gave the Nazis an additional excuse to establish a one-party state quickly, harassing, arresting and executing critics and opponents both inside and outside the party. The Enabling Act was a key piece of legislation in achieving this.

- Nazism was an ideology which demanded the restructuring of society; this involved the persecution of several groups. Hitler's style of government reflected his personal strengths and weaknesses: some historians have called him a weak dictator. Like previous governments, Hitler's took steps to obtain the support of the military, but also of other key groups including industry. The Nazis did have opponents but these were never allowed to become resistance movements.

- After Germany's defeat in 1945, the country was occupied and divided into four administrative zones; Berlin was also divided up. After wartime collaboration, the western Allies fell out with the Soviets.

- The Depression had contributed to destabilising not just the economy but also politics in Germany. Under Nazi rule, the economy was steadied, but the NSDAP government's policy was to prepare the country for war. After the war the Allies first thought of leaving Germany a divided country with almost no industry so that it would be permanently weakened. However, the plan changed and the Western allies worked to rebuild West Germany's economy.

- Nazi social policies included creating a classless society based on race, with non-Germans excluded as non-citizens. All cultural activities were used as aspects of Nazi propaganda. Post-war German society was faced with the question of how to reform and move forward when the entire structure of society was permeated by Nazi Party members and the ideology of Nazism.

End notes

1   Carr, William, *A History of Germany 1815–1945*, Edward Arnold, 1969

2   Weimar constitution: Article 54

3   Weimar constitution: Article 42

4   quoted in Conway, J.S. *The Nazi Persecution of the Churches, 1933–1945*, Regent College Publishing, 1997

5   quoted in Conway, J.S., *The Nazi Persecution of the Churches*

6   quoted in Welch, D. *The Third Reich: Politics and Propaganda*, Routledge, 2008

7   Dietrich, O. *The Hitler I Knew*, translated and quoted in Kitson, A. *Germany, 1858–1990: Hope, Terror, and Revival*, Oxford University Press, 2001

8   Hitler, A. *Hitler's Table Talk, 1941–1944,* Oxford University Press, 2001

9   Strasser, G. *Work and Bread, 1932,* quoted in Noakes, J. and Pridham, G.*Nazism, 1919–1945: State, Economy, and Society, 1933–1939*, University of Exeter Press, 1994

10   Exam question from c. 1934.

4 Division to unity: the Federal Republic of Germany, 1949–91

In this section, we will consider the way that post-war German politics worked and the nature of the economic success story known as the 'economic miracle'. We shall look at opposition to government policy and the direction of German society, including terrorist activity. Finally, we will consider how the country that was divided in defeat was reunited, and what the consequences of that reunification were. We will look into:

- Political authority: Adenauer as chancellor and establishment of democracy in Western Germany; the constitution – checks and balances; the state of German democracy

- Government and opposition: governments; parties and policies; chancellors after Adenauer and coalition governments under the three-party system; the search for consensus

- Extra-parliamentary opposition and pressure: student protest; urban terrorism and the Baader-Meinhof Gang; environmentalism

- Economic developments: growth of the West German economy; the economic miracle and its aftermath; participation in the EEC; impact of the oil crisis

- Social developments: effect of the Nazi legacy; standards of living; changes to the position of women; young people; unemployment; social tensions; modern culture

- The political, economic and social condition of reunified Germany by 1991: Kohl and the drive to reunification; strengths and problems of reunification.

Political authority

The establishment of democracy in West Germany

After a dozen years of intolerant, one-party autocracy, followed by four years of rule by occupying armies, German experience of government and the state was from the position of 'subjects' not 'citizens'. The concept of a state that was a pooling of individual rights to create a collective, of a government that was accountable to the people, was a challenge. Of course, many people remembered the previous republic, but they were likely to remember instability, not accountability.

The political structure that was established in West Germany was that of a parliamentary democracy with a separation of powers into executive, legislative and judiciary:

Executive

Federal President: largely ceremonial
Chancellor: normally the leader of the largest party in the *Bundestag*; forms and leads government

Legislative

Bicameral national assembly (made up of two houses, each in its own 'chamber'):
1. *Bundestag*: elected by a mixture of proportional representation and direct mandate
2. *Bundesrat*: representing the *Länder* and so fulfilling the commitment to federalism

Judicial

Headed by the Federal Constitutional Court: guardian of the Basic Law; interprets the constitution when questions arise as to what is and what is not constitutional.

Figure 4.1: The political structure of West Germany.

At the federal elections in August 1949, the Christian Democratic Union (CDU) in coalition with the Christian Social Union (CSU) polled 31%. The partnership of the two parties was led by the CDU's Konrad Adenauer, who became the first chancellor of the new Federal Republic of Germany (FRG) (in German, the *Bundesrepublik Deutschland* or BRD). Adenauer had been a child during the *Kulturkampf* and had later been a Centre Party mayor of Cologne. His values were comparable to those of the Kreisau Circle: he wanted to see a moderate, Conservative, non-denominational Christian democracy, with a capitalist economy and a parliamentary system, fully integrated with other Western countries and defended against a manifest Soviet threat.

Close behind in second place, on 29.2%, came the Social Democrats (SPD) led by Kurt Schumacher. Schumacher had fought in the First World War, joined the SPD in 1918 and been elected to the Reichstag in 1932. He had spent much of the Nazi period in prison and concentration camps. He had opposed the 1946 enforced merger of the SPD and KPD (Communist Party) in the Soviet zone of occupation, and as part of doing so had called a meeting of Social Democrats in the western zones of occupation, which elected him leader in those areas. In the emerging West Germany, he moved the Social Democrats more into the centre ground, working for the party to appeal to a wider section of society than its working-class traditions, and emphasising patriotism. The latter course allowed him to criticise Adenauer for being too close to the Allies.

Coming a fairly distant third on 11.9% was another new party: the Free Democrats (FDP), led by Franz Blücher. It had formed the previous year from a merger of the remaining members and networks of the pre-war German Democratic Party (DDP) and German People's Party (DVP). Like the CDU/CSU it wanted an end to denazification. The following month its chairman, Theodor Heuss, was elected the first post-war federal president.

Among smaller parties, the KPD came fourth with 5.7%, while the Centre Party won 3.1%. There were also some small right-wing parties that gained representation in the Bundestag.

The federal government sat in Bonn. This did not mean that Bonn was the capital: in theory, Berlin remained the capital. But the sectors of that city that had been controlled by the Western Allies had turned into a small island entirely surrounded by East Germany (formally the German Democratic Republic or GDR; in German, the *Deutsche Demokratische Republik* or DDR). For as long as Berlin was surrounded by Soviet (and Soviet allies') forces, the seat of West German government was Bonn. This, Beethoven's birthplace, was not Germany's second city. On the contrary, it was chosen by Adenauer precisely because it was quite a small town (not like the great cities of Hamburg or Frankfurt), to emphasise that this situation was only temporary. The result was permanent traffic problems.

In theory, from early May 1955 West Germany was granted full **sovereignty**. In practice, the country was still full of the armies of the victorious Allies, albeit now under the banner of the North Atlantic Treaty Organisation (**NATO**). West Germany itself joined NATO as a full member on 9 May 1955.

With the outbreak of the Korean War in 1950, the existing tensions between NATO on the one hand and the USSR and its Warsaw Pact allies on the other had become even stronger.

Adenauer as chancellor

Chancellor Konrad Adenauer was the dominant West German politician for 14 years. During his time in office he presided over his country's 'economic miracle' (*Wirtschaftswunder*) and political restoration. He had also been instrumental in the establishment of a stable democracy and the restoring of friendly relations with France. He was credited with the return of what was believed at the time to be the last German prisoner from the Soviet Union in 1956 and the reintegration into Germany of the Saarland on the western border with France in 1957.

Adenauer was already in his seventies when he became Chancellor of West Germany and was sometimes called the Old Man (*Der Alte*). He was shrewd and experienced. A Catholic from Cologne in the Rhineland, he had been educated in Cologne and at the Universities of Freiburg, Munich and Bonn. He joined the Centre Party in 1906 and later that same year he was elected as a City Councillor in

Key term

The Warsaw Pact was a military alliance comprising the USSR (the dominant member) and other Communist-ruled countries in central and eastern Europe. It stood in opposition to NATO (the North Atlantic Treaty Organisation), which was a military alliance of democratic capitalist countries, largely in western Europe and North America.

Cologne. He became a long-standing mayor of Cologne in 1917. As a former Centre Party politician, Adenauer was permanently under suspicion from the Nazis and was arrested and even scheduled for execution more than once.

Adenauer was one of those who believed that, throughout its history, Germany had followed what was known as a 'special path' (*Sonderweg*). His own convictions on the recent past were that it was Prussian militarism that had caused the Nazi deviation from this special path. By contrast, his Social Democrat rival, Kurt Schumacher, blamed capitalism. Accordingly, in domestic policy, Adenauer consistently kept any military influence under close check. This was a clear break not just with the Nazi regime but also with the Weimar and imperial past.

Adenauer was suspicious of British intentions and went so far as to claim that the British government had given assistance to Schumacher before the federal election of August 1949. He believed that the British had done so in the expectation that an SPD government in West Germany would so mismanage the economy that an important rival to Britain would be weakened.

In his international policies, Adenauer wanted to see the FRG join NATO as a full member as soon as he could achieve it. Because of the past history of the two countries, he also prioritised improving relations with France. Given the new political realities of the world, he also worked to consolidate the already strong ties with the USA. At the same time he adopted what has become known as the '**Hallstein Doctrine**', named after a prominent civil servant in the Foreign Ministry. According to

Voices from the past

Konrad Adenauer

Konrad Adenauer had a lifelong mistrust of Prussian militarism. His biographer Hans-Peter Schwarz records him recalling his school days, saying:

Figure 4.2: Konrad Adenauer, August 1951.

I did not detect any sympathy for Prussia from my Cologne-born fellow pupils from Catholic families and this, for the first time, made me aware of the

differences among the German tribes. I can still vividly remember the day one of my school friends told me: 'We Rhinelanders are the true Germans. The Prussians are Obotrites, Wends, Slavs and the like who put together their state by theft and violence.[1]

Discussion points
1. What does Adenauer's memory tell us about German identity?
2. To what extent do you think that his, and his friend's, comments cast useful light on the divisions in German society?
3. What do you think might be the personal or political reasons for Adenauer selecting this particular memory from all the different details of his childhood and school days which were probably also quite vivid?

this doctrine, West Germany would regard as a hostile act any state recognising East Germany as an independent state. In theory, when a state recognised the GDR, West Germany broke off diplomatic relations. The exception to this was the USSR, which was too important to cold-shoulder. The Hallstein Doctrine became the guiding theme of West German foreign policy from the mid-1950s to 1970.

Adenauer was **pragmatic** about using talent where he could find it, even if it meant employing people who in the past had been part of the Nazi state. This might be distasteful, but it was both necessary and safe because he saw communism as the main enemy to the democratic, Christian, prosperous West Germany. Accordingly, he denounced the supposed excesses of the Occupying Powers before 1949 in pursuing the denazification programme. This had been overly divisive of West German society in his view and, while those proved to have committed crimes in wartime Germany deserved to be punished, the far larger number of Germans implicated should be pardoned and allowed to live and work unhindered in society. He thus brought back into politics and public life former Nazi Party members, sympathisers and employees. This was a delicate and controversial matter.

In September 1951 Adenauer made a speech in the Bundestag acknowledging the obligation of the West German government to pay reparations to the Jews who had suffered. This meant making payments to Israel as the principal representative of the Jewish people.

The CDU won the 1953 federal elections and Adenauer was re-elected chancellor. His focus was still firmly on international affairs, finally achieving full membership of NATO in 1955 and the creation of an armed force (**Bundeswehr**). His main achievement within West Germany was also remarkable – the establishment of a stable democracy. Though much credit for this must go to Adenauer, the rapid growth of the German economy, the continuing support of the West (especially of the USA) and the determination of all sections of German political society to achieve this were also important.

The Restitution Law for private persons was finally passed by the Bundestag of West Germany in September 1953, after months of discussion and tabling of amendments. (There were further restitution laws in later years which modified and expanded the provisions of the original law.) This established in law the obligation to compensate victims of Nazi atrocities. However, it was so drafted as to exclude the majority of the survivors. For example, of the 42 000 who had been interned in the Buchenwald camp during the war, just 700 were entitled to compensation under this law. Homosexuals, Roma (gypsies) and others judged 'anti-socials' were excluded entirely. Communists were also excluded initially but later were allowed to claim compensation if they could prove that they had not been politically active since 1945. As many Communist Party members had moved to the GDR, this concession only applied to a few.

A constitutional oddity in Germany at this time was the situation of Berlin. The east of the city was now the capital of East Germany. Those sectors controlled by the Western Allies had not turned into a small part of West Germany but they had a special relationship with that country. It was, in fact, technically a 'free city' (rather like Danzig (Gdansk) during the Weimar Republic). It was not under the West

Key term

Pragmatism: Moral principle favouring choices being based on the relative practicality of the options available rather than on other moral or religious principles.

German constitution or law, but the city council chose to vote in West German laws individually. Because citizens of the free city were exempt from military service, many young people moved there. They were nevertheless eligible to stand for political office in West Germany: the mayor, Willy Brandt, went on to become chancellor.

Even though the border between the two Germanies had long since been closed, in Berlin it initially remained open. Accordingly, large numbers continued to use West Berlin as an easy route to West Germany.

Then in 1961, overnight, the East German government set up a barbed-wire fence around West Berlin. This was gradually converted into a concrete wall, and the buildings near it in East Germany were demolished to allow the guards a clearer view of who was approaching it from East German territory.

To show solidarity with West Germany in general and West Berliners in particular, and also to send a powerful message to the Soviet Union confirming US support for both, West Germany and Adenauer were visited by America's young president, John F. Kennedy, close to the end of Adenauer's long term of office.

The constitution: checks and balances

The Basic Law (*Grundgesetz*) came into force in 1949 in West Germany. It treated the government of the FRG as the only legitimate representative of the German people andit assumed the eventual demise of East Germany and the reunification of Germany. Because the Basic Law was, in effect, the constitution of the FRG, it was an important document. Two provisions of this Law were specifically concerned with the possible reunification of Germany: Article 23 allowed for other parts of Germany to join the FRG and Article 146 allowed for the unification of all parts of Germany under a new constitution.

The Basic Law was thus regarded by those who drafted it as only temporary, something to use until Germany was reunited (hence the wording of Article 146). However, as time went by, it became clear that this goal was not going to be

 Voices from the past

John F. Kennedy

During his visit, US President Kennedy went to West Berlin. Close to the Berlin Wall he famously declared that:

Two thousand years ago, the proudest boast was civisromanus sum [I am a Roman citizen]. Today, in the world of freedom, the proudest boast is Ich bin ein Berliner! … All free men, wherever they may live, are citizens of Berlin, and therefore, as a free man, I take pride in the words 'Ich bin ein Berliner!'[2]

Here was an example of the dangers of using words in a language you do not speak. In German it is incorrect to use an indefinite article before a word such as 'Berliner'. He should have said 'Ich bin Berliner' instead. A small difference? Not in context: a Berliner is a type of local food, so to his German audience he was saying 'I am a jam doughnut'.

The more important message of the speech was that the USA would support West Germany in general and West Berlin in particular, by military means if necessary.

achieved in the next few months – or even years. Thus it was that the Basic Law became the FRG Constitution.

The Basic Law was designed to prevent a dictator from coming to power in Germany again. As in the case of the constitution of East Germany, it was partly based on the Weimar constitution. Central to it were the concepts of democracy, republicanism, federalism and social responsibility, including a respect for human rights and human dignity. Let's take those key concepts in order.

Democracy here meant free elections, with no prior vetting of candidates before they were allowed to stand. The only exception to this was that all participating political parties were required to conform to democratic principles and to have an internal structure to support this. This reflected an understanding of the fact that the inherently anti-democratic NSDAP had reached power through elections. In addition, the voting system was proportional representation (PR), as it had been under the Weimar Republic. However there was a 5% rule: parties earning below 5% of the vote were excluded from taking seats in the Bundestag. (The Constitutional Court did allow a notable exception to this rule not by changing it or letting it lapse but by applying it differently in 1990 in the first elections after reunification.)

Republicanism abolishes any form of monarchy. A president usually serves as head of state instead. Thus there was to be no return to imperial Germany. Absolute government and the hereditary principle were firmly rejected.

Federalism meant that Germany was made up of distinct states (*Länder*) which themselves had their own regional traditions and priorities. A number of powers were devolved to individual states. These were areas over which the local state government has complete local control granted by the national government. Education was one example, although even here central government often laid down national guidelines.

Social responsibility implied the development of a comprehensive system of welfare, education, health and social equality. The term used in West Germany was 'the social state' (**Sozialstaat**). This implied that central government would intervene to ensure:

- minimum standards of living, including a minimum income
- access to health care, housing and education, and equal treatment for all citizens in gaining access to these services.

These provisions were to be enforced by law through the courts and paid for through taxation.

The military (*Bundeswehr*) was to be kept under the direct control of an elected minister in peacetime. The chancellor was to be the commander-in-chief in wartime. The army was not to be used for riot control or any internal purpose. Although not explicit in the Basic Law, several decisions by the Constitutional Court make it clear that the military could not be deployed outside the FRG in any combat role with NATO or otherwise.

A further important aspect of the German Basic Law is that Article 116 established the right of Germans (and people of German descent) who had been living in Warsaw Pact countries or Yugoslavia to move to Germany and receive German citizenship. This was a response to the critical situation at the end of the war, where German *Aussiedler*, people whose families had lived outside the new borders of Germany, sometimes for centuries, fled to the zones occupied by the British, Americans and French. From 1992, Article 116's provisions were limited to Germans from the former USSR.

The state of German democracy

The 'ruling classes' in West Germany had been affected by each of the interlinked upheavals of the 20th century. Their relationship with political power had naturally changed during half a century and the experience of:

- Autocratic monarchical rule
- First World War
- Collapse of imperial government
- Introduction of democracy
- Hyperinflation
- Rocketing unemployment
- Collapse of democracy
- Introduction of one-party state
- Terror state
- Second World War
- Invasion
- Defeat
- Partition
- Reintroduction of democracy.

It's quite a list, and every item on it is an expression of, or relates to, how power is structured, who holds it, how it is exercised and with what underlying political, social, economic and religious values.

At each stage, some of those in positions of power before the change were still in positions of power afterwards, while others who had earlier been driven from power found their way back. Thus a number of the politicians who emerged in West Germany after 1949, including a number of members of Chancellor Adenauer's cabinets and ruling bureaucracy, had occupied positions of authority during the period of Nazi rule. Politicians, civil servants, soldiers, businessmen, civil servants, judges and lawyers, university professors and teachers: in every case the profession contained many who had sometimes been dismissed by the Allied occupation forces only to be restored to their positions following denazification or during the Adenauer years in West Germany.

Even so, there had been one massive change: in the FRG, unlike the Weimar Republic, the government had no need of the army or elite support to survive. For the first time since before Kaiser Wilhelm II was told by General Groener that the army could not be relied on to support him, the executive did not look over its shoulder at the military high command.

Key term

Aussiedler: Germans whose families had lived outside the new borders of Germany, sometimes for centuries.

ACTIVITY 4.1

In what ways was the FRG a contrast to the Nazi state that came before it?

Make notes in two columns under several headings, including: government, police, judiciary, news media, opposition parties.

In a nutshell, the democratisation (or re-democratisation) of Germany had three strands:

- Continuity: the re-emergence of pre-Nazi political parties and politicians, most notably the SPD, but also the Centre Party and the Communists
- Change: the creation of new political parties, especially the CDU and CSU, but also the FDP
- Outside forces: the imposition of democracy from outside. The Occupying Powers decided that the democratic system would defend the 'Trizone' from falling back into a right-wing autocracy on the model of the Nazi (or the imperial) era, or from being drawn into the Soviet orbit along with East Germany.

German political thinkers developed the concept of militant democracy. According to this, all parties that upheld the democratic order (or at least did not threaten it) were to be included in the workings of politics, legislation and government according to the vote they received. However, any individuals or groups committed to the undermining or overthrow of democracy were excluded as illegitimate. Direct citizen intervention was also excluded: citizens had to participate through voting and the party system. Under the constitution, and pursuant to this way of thinking, the Socialist Reich Party of Germany (*Sozialistische Reichspartei Deutschlands* or SRP), which was a Holocaust-denying party that had attracted former Nazis and campaigned for the return of Germany's former territories in eastern Europe, was banned in 1952.

Government and opposition

Governments

The 1949 elections and Adenauer's first government
In the 1949 federal elections, the Christian Democrats (taken together with their sister party, the CSU) were the strongest party. However, Adenauer's 31% was not sufficient to form a majority government. In an echo of Weimar days, he negotiated a coalition with the centrist FDP and also the smaller right-wing German party (*Deutsche Partei* or DP), which had its roots in a revived, re-launched and renamed regionalist party that dated back to even before the Kaiserreich.

Adenauer's first government faced major economic problems, but there was also a pressing key social problem which had formed part of the election campaign: denazification. Adenauer calculated that, to rebuild the country and its economy, Germany needed to rebuild its society. It couldn't do this if a large number of its citizens were being investigated for crimes dating from the 1933–45 period. In his first major speech to the Bundestag, the chancellor made a distinction between a small number of criminals, who did bear responsibility for the crimes that had occurred and should be prosecuted, and the rest of the population, who were not guilty and whom the judicial system should not trouble. This drew an immediate clear line between his government and rule by the occupying Allies between 1945 and 1949. In this he had the support of all the parties in coalition.

Adenauer's government introduced the amnesty legislation in 1951. The chancellor admitted that two-thirds of the officials in the German foreign service were former NSDAP members, but argued that without such people the state

ACTIVITY 4.2

Since 1922, the German national anthem has been the *Deutschlandlied*, or 'Song of Germany', beginning 'Deutschland, Deutschland über alles' ('Germany, Germany above all'). Since the founding of the FRG, only the third verse has been sung. Research on the full text of the song and its meaning.

- What has caused the first verse to be dropped?
- Why isn't the second verse used?
- What made the third verse appropriate for West Germany?

could not function. Both at the time and since, this approach to the issue has been controversial. It suggests that, to Adenauer, justice came a poor second to social cohesion and rebuilding.

A key element in Adenauer's rule was to make Germany part of the West. This may sound unsurprising, but it went against the long-held German conservative belief in *Sonderweg*, the idea that Germany was a case apart, a central European country which was not like the modernising capitalist UK and France, yet also not like the Russian autocracy of the tsars (and then the Soviets), a power that was neither of the West nor of the East. Adenauer dumped that entire philosophy and made plain that Germany's future lay in closer union with democratic, capitalist Western powers. He also emphasised the importance of the individual choosing to be part of the greater whole of society, not being disciplined and surrendering their individuality in a militarist autocracy. This was a project to redefine conservatism in Germany.

If the social policy was one of integration, ending the distinction between those who had voted for and supported the NSDAP and those who had voted against and opposed them, integration was the watchword of foreign policy as well. This meant that Germany needed to join the alliances and transnational institutions of the West. Prominent among these was the new military alliance NATO, founded in April 1949. But another important event was the creation of the European Coal and Steel Community (ECSC) two years later, in April 1951. Germany's partners in the ECSC included Belgium and France. This may sound like a minor matter, but there are two things to remember:

- Coal and steel had been at the heart of the conflict with France over the Ruhr occupation and were also central to France's continuing administration of the Saarland.
- The ECSC was more than an institution; it was also a step towards a wider economic and political project known today as the European Union.

In a move that again connected him to the right-wing parties of the Weimar period, Adenauer did not accept Germany's new eastern borders. For him, reunification meant the return not just of the GDR but also of those territories which had come under Polish and Soviet rule – the Germany of a 1937 atlas (though not the 1914 one).

In the case of the Adenauer government there was a clear domestic motive for this stance. The massive refugee crisis of 1945 had turned into a huge integration challenge. West Germany was now home to a substantial population of people who had left homes behind in those areas which no longer counted as German. In fact, other political parties also alleged both that they opposed the current eastern borders and that the refugees should be allowed to go home. The extent to which any of the major politicians – including Adenauer – actually thought that the lost lands would ever be German again or that the refugees would ever go home is one that historians have discussed.

Adenauer's government wanted to see German rearmament. Initially there was little stomach for such a thing among the countries that had suffered from German militarism only a few years before. The concept of a German army under proper democratic control and free of the Prussian tradition took time to establish both domestically and abroad.

In 1951 a senior civil servant was shown to have been a successful Nazi civil servant with a record of helping draft anti-Semitic legislation. Adenauer stood by him and refused to let him go; in doing so he was seen to be defending the many thousands who had held posts during Nazi rule.

The 1953 election and Adenauer's second government

The Federal Republic's second national elections (1953) took place against the backdrop of a Soviet army crushing an East German uprising. This played into the West German Conservatives' political hands and did nothing to improve the standing of any left-wing party.

The CDU/CSU alliance led by Adenauer campaigned on their record. They emphasised their economic policies of reconstruction and growth, and maintaining their social policy of Christian democracy. In foreign policy, they stood for close cooperation with the Western democracies.

Schumacher had died in 1952, so the SPD (still on paper a Marxist, albeit not a revolutionary, party) was led into the campaign by Erich Ollenhauer, with a slightly different stance from 1949. Under Ollenhauer the SPD was more positive about cooperating with the US and about the presence in the FRG of the American army.

After the count, the proportions of the vote had clearly changed. The CDU/CSU had climbed strongly from 31% to 44.7%; the SPD had changed little, moving up from 29.2% to 29.5%; the FDP had slipped from 11.9% to 10.8%. Adenauer was just one seat short of an outright majority but he chose to maintain the coalition.

The second Adenauer government passed the 1953 Restitution Law, which allowed racial, religious and political victims of Nazi prosecution to claim compensation. As defined by the law, only a few of the surviving victims were able to claim. The step was reasonable but ungenerous, and did not compare well with the generosity of the amnesty laws of 1951. Those who could not claim included:

- Foreign slave labourers, as the law limited compensation to those who were part of German society and culture
- Communists, as they were judged to have been seeking a violent seizure of power themselves
- Homosexuals, as homosexuality continued to be a crime in post-war Germany
- Roma and Sinti ('gypsies'), because the Nazi measures were judged to have been against criminality, not against a racial group
- Criminals, the homeless and the unemployed, because the Nazi measures were again judged to have been taken against criminal and anti-social groups.

After much negotiation and some false starts, West Germany received permission to form an army in May 1955. Its officers drew heavily on experienced soldiers of the old Wehrmacht, but Adenauer's own declared hostility to Prussian military traditions went some way to ensure that the new force would accept civilian control, rather than attempt to control governments as its predecessors had done throughout the Weimar period.

West Germany became a fully sovereign state in 1955. It built on its ECSC membership by joining the European Economic Community (EEC). Unemployment was low (something important to any politician who remembered the 1920s and early 1930s) and the economy was growing. In 1957 the Saarland became part of West Germany and the last of the German prisoners of war arrived home from a Soviet labour camp in 1956.

The 1957 election and Adenauer's third government

Perhaps unsurprisingly, given the fact that life was improving for many Germans, Adenauer's 1957 campaign slogan was *Keine Experimente!* ('No experiments'). The election saw the CDU/CSU strengthened again. The SPD, again led by Ollenhauer, also increased their share of Bundestag seats. The FDP slipped downwards a little more.

Between 1958 and 1960, the Nazi past haunted the chancellor on three occasions. First, his policy on former Nazis was challenged when a policeman complained that his pension had been wrongly calculated: no account had been taken of his years in the *Einsatzgruppen* (the Nazi death squads). Carried by the press, the story was a reminder of how many people who had committed what most people would regard as criminal acts had not been prosecuted. Adenauer set up a new department to investigate the matter.

Second, in 1959 the chancellor spoke at a rally for German refugees from the lost lands in the east, promising to maintain the demand for them to be allowed to return home. Calling their expulsion a crime, he declared that if West Germany were to establish diplomatic relations with Poland and Czechoslovakia, part of the negotiations would be for both countries to pay reparations. This played well in West Germany, but less well abroad.

Third, the same year Adenauer's minister of refugees, Theodor Oberländer, a spokesperson for the refugee lobby, was accused of having commanded a battalion that had committed war crimes against Jews and Poles. Oberländer agreed that he had commanded the battalion, but denied that the alleged crime had taken place. As in the 1951 case of the civil servant, the chancellor stood by his minister. Pressure was kept up though, and in May 1960 the latter resigned.

A key event in this government's term was the building of the Berlin Wall in August 1961, which overshadowed the next federal election.

The 1961 election and Adenauer's fourth government

While the CDU/CSU alliance went into the 1961 elections with the same leader, both the SPD and the FDP had a new face at the top. The contrasts between them are striking reminders of the contrasts within German society:

- CDU/CSU: Adenauer, born in 1876, was a Weimar-period Centre Party politician from the Rhineland, who retired from politics but was arrested several times by the NSDAP regime's forces.
- SPD: Willy Brandt, born in 1913 in Lübeck to a poor family (and a single mother), joined the SPD in 1930 and organisations to the left of the SPD. He spent the Nazi era and the war in exile, working as a journalist. He returned to Germany after the war and rejoined the SPD, becoming Mayor of Berlin.

- FDP: Erich Mende, born in 1916 in Silesia (which was now part of Poland), served in the German infantry in the invasion of Poland and on the Eastern Front, and had been interned by the British.

In the US there was a new, young president, John F. Kennedy, who regarded Adenauer's age as a problem. He favoured Brandt, as being younger and more progressive. When news came that the Soviets and the East German government were encircling West Berlin with a wall, it brought a slow response from the chancellor, who did not immediately fly to Berlin. This event meant that it was also a bad time to engage in personal criticism of Berlin's mayor, even if the latter was his SPD rival for the chancellorship. Nevertheless, Adenauer raised the fact of Brandt's illegitimacy.

In the event, the Social Democrats improved their position, as did the Free Democrats. While the Conservative alliance lost seats, it was still strong enough to form an alliance with the FDP. A key difference in the vote, and thus with the Bundestag that resulted, was that of all the parties standing, only the CDU/CSU, SPD and FDP had won seats. The others had lost support and were not represented. This was a clear change from 1957, when the DP had been a significant if small presence; 1953, when the DP, the Centre Party and the GB/BHE were represented; and 1949, when a range of parties were present in small numbers.

The question of the EEC's future divided the chancellor from his own deputy, the economics minister Ludwig Erhard. The latter wanted it to include more countries; Adenauer wanted to consolidate what had already been started with the existing members. As pressure mounted on Adenauer to resign, he tried to prevent Erhard from being his successor. His efforts were in vain.

Parties and policies

In the early days of West Germany, the largest political force was on the Centre Right, but confusingly it was two parties, not one. The Christian Democratic Union (CDU) was in coalition with the Christian Social Union (CSU). The CSU was founded in 1945 as a Christian, Conservative and democratic party; it only put up candidates in Bavaria, complementing the CDU, which campaigned in all the other fifteen states of the FRG, but not Bavaria.

Abolished by the Nazi Enabling Act of 1933, the Centre Party was re-founded after the war. However, its position was undermined from the beginning by the existence of the CDU and CSU, both of them avowedly Conservative Christian parties, but without the sectarian, Catholic, identity. The CDU's own leader was a former Centre Party member. Despite having been a significant force in the politics of the Weimar Republic, it gradually lost support. In 1957, the Centre Party lost its last seats in the Bundestag. However, it continued as a party in the local politics of some areas.

The Social Democratic Party was the strongest of the parties of the Centre Left, as well as being a party with a substantial history. Its approach to the politics of partition, the Cold War and diplomatic links with East Germany was different from that of the CDU/CSU, being more open to contact with the East. By contrast with

157

Adenauer's governments, the SPD leader, Kurt Schumacher, the main opposition leader to the CDU/CSU in the Bundestag, was opposed to joining NATO and much more inclined than Adenauer to look East rather than West. Although strongly anti-communist, Schumacher believed that the reunification of Germany would only take place given an improving relationship with the GDR. He wanted West Germany to stay neutral in the Cold War, whereas Adenauer regarded winning the struggle with the Soviet Union as essential, worth even a delay in reunification. Thus, an important line had been drawn in foreign policy between the CDU/CSU and the SPD. Adenauer gave the USA every assistance during the Cold War. Schumacher responded by accusing Adenauer of being 'Chancellor of the Allies'.

Founded by Liberal politicians, the FDP tended to attract the votes of more secular centre-right voters who were against the Christian agenda of the CDU/CSU. It supported the free market and, initially, an end to the denazification programme. It was in favour of human rights and civil liberties, and had an international outlook. This was a classic liberal programme – in the modern sense of the word, being different from the emphases of the 19th century.

In addition to these parties, there were several smaller parties. One of these, which exercised greater influence than its numbers might suggest possible, was the All-German Bloc/League of Expellees and Those Deprived of Rights (*Gesamtdeutscher Block/Bund der* **Heimatvertriebenen** *und Entrechteten* or GB/BHE). This was a right-wing party that had been founded to represent the views and demands of German refugees whose homes lay in the lost territories in the east. Founded in 1950 as simply the BHE, its name was a political code. The term *Heimatvertriebenen* referred to those who had lost their homeland (*Heimat*). The second term, *Entrechteten*, meant those who had been denied their rights, namely former Nazis.

The 1952 name change to GB/BHE was intended to make the party more appealing to a wider range of nationalist voters; in the 1953 federal elections, it achieved nearly 6% of the vote, giving it 27 Bundestag seats and a place in Adenauer's second cabinet. This could only be a temporary success. Adenauer's continuing social policy was integration, and accordingly the party's supporters gradually became less refugees and more simply German citizens. Involvement with the government made the party's leaders complicit in its policy of integration with Western institutions, creating a wedge between activists and deputies. Part of the leadership resigned and joined the CDU.

In the 1957 elections, the vote dropped to below the 5% threshold, leaving the party with no Bundestag seats. Like the Centre Party, the GB/BHE continued to operate in regional assemblies. In 1961 the reduced party merged with the equally reduced DP, but even the combined parties and their combined vote failed to win them 5% and thus Bundestag seats.

The importance of the GB/BHE was that it drew support away from the centre-right CDU/CSU and thus had to be cultivated and accommodated by Adenauer, while he sought all the time to undermine it. It was for these reasons that Adenauer was willing to speak at the 1959 rally of expelled Germans.

4 Division to unity: the Federal Republic of Germany, 1949–91

Among other small, right-wing parties, the DP attracted attention because for a while it was part of the Bundestag, and, indeed, the government. A conservative, market-economy party, it opposed government interference in the economy, union interference in management and federal government interference in *Länder* affairs. It thus to some extent recalled the conservative parties of the Weimar period.

Two political parties were banned by the Constitutional Court and were unable to put up candidates in elections. One was the right-wing Socialist Reich Party (SRD), which was banned in 1952 as a neo-Nazi party. In 1956 the KPD was also banned. The direct successor of the party banned under the Enabling Act, it had received nearly 6% of the vote in 1949. Perhaps the Cold War undermined the appeal of the Communists; perhaps it was the sight of events in communist-ruled East Germany that did so. Whatever the case, in 1953 the KPD support dropped to a little over 2%, so that they had no Bundestag seats.

Both the KPD and the SRD were banned because they were judged not to support the principles of democracy. In a second curious connection between extreme Left and extreme Right, the neo-Nazi SRD had secretly received financial support from the USSR because of its anti-American views.

Founded in 1980, the Green Party is one of the legacies of the environmentalist movement. It has included former left-wing activists, including Joschka Fischer and Daniel Cohn-Bendit. In 1998 it became a party of government in coalition with the SPD (it would do so again in 2002).

In the early 1980s there was an increase in far-right political activity based on concerns about immigration. In West Germany, the Republican Party ran its political campaigns almost entirely based on xenophobia (dislike of foreigners). This radical right-wing party was founded in 1983 by two former CSU members and it succeeded in getting two members elected to the European Parliament. Its domestic support was modest if noisy, at something less than 0.5% of the electorate. This was not nearly enough to gain any Bundestag seats. Its strongest support came from Baden-Württemburg and Rhineland-Palatinate but even here it only received about 1% of the popular vote.

Chancellors after Adenauer and coalition governments under the three-party system

The 1965 election and Ludwig Erhard's government
When Adenauer, in his late eighties, retired from the office of chancellor in October 1963, his successor was his CDU minister of economics, Ludwig Erhard.

The latter had been the architect of the economic success that had become known as Germany's 'economic miracle' (*Wirtschaftswunder*). What was not widely known was that Erhard, having been invited to join both the FDP and the CDU in the late 1940s, had joined neither. Despite this he had served in the Bundestag and in government and been accepted as a CDU member throughout. But he had retained the preference for the non-party independence he had shown as a young man in the Nazi period, when he had researched post-war options for Germany and shown his ideas to the economist Carl Friedrich Goerdeler, a member of

Compare the main political parties, CDU/CSU, SPD and FPD, in this period. Use a three-column format to contrast their social, economic and political policies. Then add a commentary discussing how similar or different they were from one another.

- What do these similarities and differences tell you about German politics 1949–91?
- How does this help you understand the system of coalition government?
- How does this cast light on extra-parliamentary opposition, including the Baader-Meinhof Gang?

Speak like a historian

Henry Ashby Turner

Historians have emphasised the rapidity of German growth, but also the social, political (and international) reasons behind it. American historian Henry Ashby Turner has particularly studied the economic and business context of 20th-century German history. He emphasises the importance of Erhard's role and argues that the foundations were laid even before FRG existed, during the time of the zones of occupation:

The removal of most price controls after the monetary reform of 1948 brought a flood of goods onto the market, where long-deprived consumers eagerly sought them. The stability of the new currency, which was controlled by an autonomous central bank (soon to be named the Bundesbank) spurred saving and investment. Large scale infusions of American aid under the Marshall Plan supplemented domestic capital formation. The flow of refugees from the East provided an abundant reservoir of labor to replace wartime losses. In a new spirit of cooperation organized labor and management collaborated to reduce the loss of productivity through strikes to a level far below that of other West European countries.[3]

Discussion point

Turner points to several elements that form part of the 'economic miracle'. List the causes he cites: which of them do you think were the most important? What differences and similarities do you notice with steps taken by the von Schleicher and Hitler governments in 1932–33, and the responses to the economic crises in the Weimar period (such as the contrasting actions of Stresemann and Schacht, and Brüning)?

the network of conservatives who were opposed to Hitler's rule and a former colleague of Schacht.

In the 1965 federal election, trends continued: the CDU/CSU alliance increased their percentage of the vote and their number of seats, as did the SDP under Brandt. The FDP under Mende lost further support. No other party achieved seats in the Bundestag.

The Erhard government introduced changes to policy, some of which came as a shock. The chancellor's suggestion of a massive loan to the Soviet Union as a means of bringing East Germany closer to West Germany and leading to the reunification of the country was not something that the USA was prepared to consider. The very idea went against the Cold War thinking that dominated US foreign policy at the time because it suggested a possible accommodation with the Soviet Union.

Erhard also managed to alarm the French with his belief that free trade and a united Europe would lead to a better world, which was not at all the view of the French president, Charles de Gaulle. Adenauer had long pursued a foreign policy that was perfectly acceptable in both Washington and Paris. Now Erhard seemed prepared to alienate both, a serious matter and especially dangerous with respect to the USA. This set up tensions that the Erhard government found difficult to resolve. This is not to say that Erhard rejected or replaced the Hallstein Doctrine, his predecessor's policy aimed at isolating East Germany diplomatically. However, he did seek to introduce a more nuanced interpretation of the principle.

In 1966 there came an economic recession in West Germany. In some ways this can be seen as a necessary correction to a rapidly growing economy that was already showing some signs of overheating. The economic growth rates achieved by the FRG during the 1950s (some 8.8%) shrank during the first part of the 1960s to approximately 4.5%. Inflation was on the rise. It was not clear that Erhard and the other architects of the *Wirtschaftswunder* had a clear idea about the need for changes to the labour and international credit arrangements that had served West Germany so well for a decade and a half. Growth rates slumped to zero in 1966 and West Germany faced the unfamiliar prospect of economic recession. Under these pressures, the Free Democrats, who had been coalition partners with the CDU/CSU, decided to leave government. Erhard, realising that his political friends and allies no longer supported him, stood down as chancellor.

Erhard's position had been undermined at every stage by the fact that when Adenauer left the post of chancellor, he had retained that of CDU chairman. In combination with the CSU chairman, Franz-Josef Strauss, his policies of greater cooperation with the USA were being opposed by people whom he might have expected to be his allies.

Kurt Kiesinger and the Grand Coalition

The economic crisis, coupled with student unrest, persuaded the two main political parties in the Bundestag in 1966 to unite in a **Grand Coalition** government of CDU/CSU and SPD under the new CDU chancellor, Kurt Kiesinger, who was furnished with the Emergency Acts, an amendment to the Basic Law that gave the government emergency powers. By contrast with Erhard, whose approach to foreign policy had been criticised, Kiesinger was seen as an expert on foreign affairs. He had been prominent in the CDU since the early 1950s. He made some contribution to a lessening of tension with eastern Europe by establishing diplomatic relations with Yugoslavia, Romania and Czechoslovakia but declined to go any further down this road. The Allied occupation powers in West Germany – American, British and French – were satisfied that these steps would guarantee stable democracy in West Germany and finally renounced their remaining powers.

The end of the coalition came when the proposals of the SPD economics minister were opposed by the CSU's finance minister for the domestic political reason that the measures would harm his supporters in Bavarian agriculture.

The 1969 election and Willy Brandt's government

Unusually, all the major parties in the federal election of 1969 were headed by former government ministers. The CDU was led by the former chancellor, Kiesinger, the CSU by the former finance minister in the Grand Coalition, Strauss, and the SPD by the former vice chancellor and foreign minister, Brandt, who had also served in the outgoing coalition. The FDP were led by a former Luftwaffe radio operator, Walter Scheel, who had been minister for economic development under Adenauer and Erhard. Once again the largest parties – CDU/CSU, SPD and FDP – were the only ones to win seats. This time the election was followed by a coalition between the SPD and the FDP, with Willy Brandt ending two decades of Conservative rule by becoming the first SPD chancellor since Hermann Müller's resignation in 1930.

Brandt's coalition was committed to improving relations with the country's eastern neighbours – East Germany, Poland and Czechoslovakia – and was praised internationally but raised the temperature of West German politics. This question of whether to look east towards the restoration of better relations with the GDR and with the Soviet Union, as the SPD had advocated since 1948, or to look west to the USA and France, as the CDU had long advocated, had become a major political fault line. The issue was how best to reunify Germany without at the same time endangering links with Western allies, especially the USA. The easing of Cold War tensions by the late 1960s may also have been a factor in the SPD election victory in 1969.

Brandt's policy of normalising the relationship with East Germany was called **Ostpolitik** (east policy). It led in 1970 to the Treaty of Moscow with the Soviet Union. A few months later, in Warsaw, West Germany and Poland both renounced the use of force to settle international disputes and recognised the post-war boundaries of the Oder–Neisse line. On his 1970 visit to Warsaw, Brandt unexpectedly (and perhaps spontaneously) dropped to his knees while visiting a memorial of the Warsaw Ghetto Uprising against the Nazi occupiers and remained kneeling for several minutes. This attracted enormous media attention, as it seemed to show the German chancellor (himself an opponent to the Nazis who had spent much of the Third Reich in exile) kneeling in penitence.

These steps represented a political risk for Brandt. He received the Nobel Peace Prize in 1971 for his efforts at *détente* with the GDR, but the gesture of kneeling divided the country into two halves, with more thinking it excessive than thought it appropriate. Some members of the FDP and an SPD deputy who was chair of the refugees' organisation, the *Bund der Vertriebenen* (BVD), abandoned the coalition and crossed the floor to support the CDU/CSU opposition. Brandt only narrowly won a vote of confidence.

The 1972 election and the Brandt–Schmidt government

The political crisis led to the 1972 elections, in which the SPD won its best results since the war and was the largest party in the Bundestag. The FDP also managed to improve its position, while the CDU/CSU alliance lost votes and seats under its leader, Rainer Barzel, who had come so close to being elected chancellor in the confidence debate. The SPD–FDP coalition had Scheel as vice chancellor, the future party leader, Hans-Dietrich Genscher, as minister of the interior and the rising SPD star Helmut Schmidt as economics and finance minister.

In December 1972 the Basic Treaty (*Grundlagenvertrag*) with the GDR was signed. This was in many ways the most controversial aspect of Brandt's *Ostpolitik*. It officially recognised the GDR as a sovereign state and established diplomatic relations between the FRG and GDR. Other nations, including the UK, followed

Key term

Détente is a French word meaning 'relaxation'. It refers to a diplomatic attempt during the Cold War to reduce the levels of tension. Each side still held massive arsenals of conventional and nuclear weapons. But the increased diplomatic contact meant that there was greater mutual understanding and the likelihood of armed conflict was reduced. The *détente* is usually dated as beginning in 1962, following the Cuban Missile Crisis, and it led to several conferences, summits and treaties.

suit in 1973 and so too did the USA the following year. This was a clear end to the **Hallstein Doctrine**.

In 1974 Willy Brandt was forced to resign as chancellor because of a political scandal involving a spy in his private office. Günther Guillaume was a former Nazi Party member and Stasi spy who was sent to West Germany in 1956. He rose in the hierarchy of the SPD and became a trusted aide to Brandt. Guillaume was caught, found guilty at trial and sent to prison. In 1981 he was released to East Germany in exchange for a number of Western spies; following reunification he gave evidence at the trial of his former spymaster boss.

Helmut Schmidt's governments

Brandt was succeeded as chancellor by his economics and finance minister Helmut Schmidt. Unlike events when the chancellorship passed from Adenauer to *his* economics minister, Schmidt came to power with Brandt's support.

The years after 1973 were dominated economically by a world financial crisis triggered by a sharp rise in oil prices. Schmidt's main concern was to ensure that the West German economy coped well with this crisis, and by common consent it did. He was also active in promoting social reforms at home, though his room for state generosity was limited by the economic situation. In terms of foreign policy, his priorities were international, helping to establish a series of world economic summits.

By the time of the 1976 election, Brandt, Barzel and Scheel had all stood down under different circumstances. As a result, all three main parties were being led by men who had not headed a federal election campaign before: Schmidt for the SPD, the former interior minister in the coalition, Genscher, for the FDP, and the new CDU/CSU leader, Helmut Kohl. The governing parties both lost votes and seats, but the improved CDU/CSU position in the Bundestag was not sufficient to take power.

Schmidt won again in 1980 when the CDU/CSU were led by Strauss, the CSU's leader, the first time that the Bavarian party had led the coalition. This time the CDU/CSU lost seats. Strauss's style, which worked so well in Bavaria, appealed less in the rest of West Germany: he was seen as aggressive and uncompromising whereas Schmidt succeeded in seeming moderate, reasonable and practical.

Schmidt was a staunch supporter of both the European Union and the USA. His reputation both domestically and abroad was as a manager, rather than as a political visionary. In this he contrasted strongly with his well-liked predecessor Brandt and also with the orator Schumacher. Making a virtue of what he saw as a weakness, Schmidt mocked political visionaries, saying that people who saw visions should take medical advice.

Schmidt governed throughout in coalition with the FDP, and Genscher was consistently his vice chancellor and foreign minister. The latter had fought in the Wehrmacht in the Second World War and had gone to university as an East German citizen before fleeing to the West.

In 1982, the differences between the coalition partners over social and economic policy were such that the Free Democrats left the coalition and voted with the CDU/CSU. As a result the latter's leader, Helmut Kohl, was elected chancellor in a coalition with the FDP. Recognising that this was a government for which the nation had not voted, Kohl called for a second confidence vote in which his own deputies did not vote. The vote being lost, the president scheduled fresh federal elections.

Helmut Kohl's governments

In West Berlin and the Ruhr a majority voted SPD but nationally their vote dropped under the party's new leader, Hans-Jochen Vogel. The FDP vote also dropped: perhaps they were being punished for switching sides. In contrast, the Conservative vote climbed. They were strongest in southern Germany (including the CSU vote in Bavaria) and in more rural areas away from the big cities. They were able to form a government, though only with the FDP as coalition partners. Genscher was thus vice chancellor and foreign minister again, just as he had been with Schmidt.

A striking result in the 1983 elections was the first showing in the Bundestag of the Green Party, with 5.6%, a mark of the growing profile of environmental issues in West Germany in the 1980s. This new party thus went from no seats to 28. Putting this number into context, the FDP had dropped to 35 seats yet were still able to act as a party of government, albeit as a junior partner. The arrival of a new party of the Left was clearly a threat to the SPD, as the Greens were capable of attracting voters who might otherwise have backed the Social Democrats. Would this lead to endless SPD defeats? Were the new arrivals capable of turning into a junior party of government, as the FDP had so long been?

The new chancellor, Helmut Kohl, had been born and brought up in Ludwigshafen on the Rhine (then in Bavaria, now in the *Land* of Rhineland-Palatinate (*Rheinland-Pfalz*)). Like Adenauer's, his was a Roman Catholic household and his parents had been members of the Centre Party. He was educated at a local primary school and then at the Max-Planck-Gymnasium in Ludwigshafen. He was active in politics even as a young man and joined the recently formed CDU (rather than the Centre Party) in 1946. In 1950 he studied law in Frankfurt and history and political science at the University of Heidelberg from 1951.

Kohl was elected as Minister President of Rhineland-Palatinate in 1969 after being active in the CDU locally and a prominent member. In the federal election of 1976 he was the CDU/CSU candidate for chancellor and did well (49%), but the SPD and FDP coalition did even better and Helmut Schmidt, the SPD leader, remained chancellor. However, in 1982 the FDP switched sides to enter a coalition with the CDU and Kohl was elected Chancellor of the FRG.

As chancellor he presided over a West Germany which had an economy that was becoming the strongest in Europe. Like his CDU predecessors, he maintained good relations with France. In partnership with the centre-right President Valéry Giscard d'Estaing and his successor as French president, the socialist François Mitterrand, Kohl put his weight behind the movement for European integration that led the essentially economic EC to become the more overtly political EU. When he met Mitterrand in September 1984 it was at Verdun, the place where a decisive battle between Germany and France had been fought in 1916. The symbolic handshake between the two was a powerful sign of a mended relationship.

Kohl also recognised relations with West Germany's main supporter and sponsor, the USA, as vital to the country's interests. He visited the USA to meet the US president, Ronald Reagan in 1985.

In the federal elections of 1987 Kohl led the CDU/CSU to victory, but with a slightly reduced majority. Later that year, the East German leader Erich Honecker became the first GDR leader to visit the FRG. Kohl now seemed to be pursuing a policy very similar to the *Ostpolitik* of successive SPD governments in the 1970s that he and the CDU had loudly condemned.

Kohl was both politically and socially conservative. In social policy, he resisted calls to extend the preschool childcare provision in West Germany. He saw it as a threat to the traditional family unit, but also as a left-wing policy that extended the role of the state into private life, where the state had no place. In this attitude, he was aligned with the US presidents Ronald Reagan and George Bush. However, he impressed politicians outside the right wing: the Democrat president Bill Clinton called him 'the greatest European politician of the second half of the 20th century'.

Helmut Kohl's chancellorship was confirmed in the 1987 election, but with losses for both the biggest parties. The FDP improved their position to have 48 seats, but the Greens were chasing them on 44 seats.

The CDU/CSU and FDP coalition government survived any grumbling in the West with new supporters in the East. In the first election held for a reunited Germany in December 1990 – the first federal election covering the whole of Germany since 1933 – the governing coalition led by Chancellor Helmut Kohl gained nearly 44% of the popular vote, with the SPD in second place with 33.5%. This was a comfortable victory for Kohl and his party, much the same as the election results for the FRG in January 1987. The SPD did slip back a little in the 1990 election but even so some 15.5 million Germans voted for them, while around 2.4 million voted Green. Indeed, the SPD won a majority of votes in some of the western parts of Germany, especially around the conurbations of Frankfurt and Stuttgart and in the Saar region on the French border. A majority in Berlin voted CDU but in the city of Hamburg the SPD gained an absolute majority. These results indicate a division of opinion in Germany about the future. For the time being, however, the CDU remained as the government, in coalition with the FDP, and Helmut Kohl remained Chancellor of Germany.

For the post-unification election of 1990, 150 seats had been added to the Bundestag to allow for the *neue Länder* ('new states'), the former East Germany. The big losers were the Greens, whose share of the vote dropped below 5% and who therefore lost all their seats. From a high point of 44 seats in 1987, this was a major comedown for the Greens. A Green voice was retained because of the presence of their allies from the former East Germany, the new Allianz 90, who took eight seats in the *neue Länder*.

The big news story in many ways, however, was the arrival of the *Partei des Demokratischen Sozialismus* (the Party of Democratic Socialism or PDS). This had been formed by younger, reform-minded members of East Germany's ruling Communist Party. The PDS made little impact on the former West German electorate but managed to poll quite well in the former East. The temporary

ACTIVITY 4.4

What do you think were Helmut Kohl's achievements as chancellor? Make notes as though preparing for a debate. List specific achievements and comment on each item on the list. Remember that, both at the time and since, Kohl was a controversial figure, so make sure you show both sides to any question.

relaxation of the 5% rule allowed by the Constitutional Court meant that they were able to arrive in the Bundestag as a group of 17 deputies, led by Gregor Gysi, who quickly became a nationally recognised politician. (It was this same relaxation of the 5% that allowed Allianz 90 to gain representation in the Reichstag.) Given the 1956 West German ban on the KPD, this was a significant political event: the Bundestag had not had communists (or even former communists) sitting in it for some years. This development reopened the question of the SPD's future. Did they now have a second left-wing competitor for votes?

Kohl's 16-year term of office as chancellor was the longest since Bismarck's, and both were in office when the map of Germany was redrawn. Unsurprisingly, historians have drawn attention to similarities and differences in their terms of office and achievements. Kohl's high-water mark was around the time of reunification. His standing went down gradually as euphoria was followed by the discovery that the process was an expensive one for tax-payers.

The search for consensus

In his essay 'Does Germany Have an Efficient Secret?', the British political scientist Gordon Smith examined Germany's post-war economic success and decided that the national commitment to consensus was a major contributing factor. The country's leadership – not only political but also in industry – continually sought the widest possible agreement.

An aspect of this is to be found in the formation of governments. Every single federal government since the formation of the FRG has been a coalition. There have been no single-party governments and no minority governments either. Even when Adenauer might have formed a Conservative government, he chose to retain a coalition. Adenauer's second government included no fewer than five parties: CDU, CSU, FDP, DP and GB/BHE. Later, the CDU/CSU also worked with the SDP, in Kiesinger's Grand Coalition.

Commenting on Smith's analysis, Kaevan Gazdar has since added that, in such a situation, political leaders themselves act as moderators and the approach can lead to all change being slow. This may appear to an onlooker like a static or change-averse process. But, says Gazdar, when change comes it can be profound and is rarely reversed.

The commitment to consensus in political decision-making is clearly linked to the policy of social cohesion, which in the hands of Adenauer drove the prioritising of integration over justice. Smith argues in the same essay that Germany had succeeded in depoliticising politics, by which he means moving away from a clash of ideologies towards parties competing to show managerial competence.

One of the expressions of this has been the position of the chancellor. Although Germany's chancellors have come from the major parties, they have never considered themselves bound by party loyalties or even party policy. Brandt's declaration *Wir wollen mehr Demokratie wagen* ('We must risk more democracy') might be taken as a break with this tradition. But even he told an SPD conference that he would listen to the party and its debates and resolutions, but in office he would take decisions according to his judgement of the country's needs. Adenauer before him and Schmidt after him would have said much the same. Indeed, when

Schmidt later did say that he was not good at towing the party line, it was a not dissimilar point. German chancellors have thus not seen themselves as in office principally to carry forward their party's views and agendas. As a result, German policy in different areas has varied less from government to government than one might have expected.

Jonathan Story's analysis of post-war German politics (in his edited volume, *The New Europe: Government, Politics and Economy since 1945*, Blackwell, 1993) emphasised this element of continuity. According to Story, the SPD–FDP coalition largely maintained the economic policies of the preceding CDU/CSU–FDP coalitions. Even though the political parties in government changed, the commitment to (for example) avoiding too much government interference in the economy and the workings of business remained a point of agreement. The area where Story argues that there was a real change of approach was in foreign policy. Here, Brandt's *Ostpolitik* approaches to the Soviet Union and the countries of eastern Europe was a real break with the preceding 20 years.

There are thus five 'c' words that describe some of the interrelated domestic factors that have made possible West Germany's success:

- Consensus
- Coalition
- Competence
- Chancellors
- Continuity.

However, in recognising the success, it is important to notice as well that the state – its structures, methods and values – has been subject to criticism, some of it very hostile and violent criticism, and it is to this that we turn next.

Extra-parliamentary opposition and pressure

In theory, West Germany in this period was a politically tolerant state. A plural, liberal democracy, it had (among other things):

- Different political parties
- Elections
- A balancing of local and national assemblies
- Legislation to protect the citizens' right to protest
- Majority rule
- Protection for minorities' rights.

There was an efficient internal police system that kept the government of the day well informed, but its relationship with political dissent bore no resemblance to the attitudes and activities of the Gestapo in the past or even the Stasi in East Germany.

All the mainstream politicians of the post-war republic, and all the major parties to which they belonged, were committed to a break with Germany's dark past. None of them would find an oppressive authoritarian regime acceptable. FRG governments recognised that both privately expressing and publicly demonstrating disagreement were essential elements in the democratic process, a process which cannot be limited to participating obediently in periodic elections.

In addition, West German tolerance made a political contrast with East German intolerance, which was useful for sending a Cold War message. This message – of democracy and civil rights – was one that their major supporter, the USA, particularly wanted to broadcast in the years of Soviet domination of much of central and all of eastern Europe. However, there developed in West Germany a difference in political priorities between older and younger citizens.

For those who had lived through the Second World War and the post-war economic collapse, and who had perhaps had their views formed by the experience of living under an authoritarian government or had memories of short-lived governments during the Weimar Republic, political priorities tended to relate to stability and order: economic security, law and order. These people also emphasised traditional moral values.

By contrast, younger West Germans had more experience of stability, prosperity and democracy. They were often better educated and better informed about the world outside Germany. Their demands were different and tended to include environmental concerns, sexual politics and the desire to increase participation in decision-making – perhaps they would have echoed Brandt's call, *Wir wollen mehr Demokratie wagen*.

This generational change is studied by Ronald Inglehart in his book *The Silent Revolution*. He reports on the changing way in which Germans responded to a set of questions first asked in 1949 and then repeated at intervals until 1970. In 1949, when asked whether they preferred a government that guaranteed economic security or one that guaranteed freedoms of speech, suffrage, press and religion, 62% chose economic security. These people also chose 'freedom of want' as the most important from a short list of possible freedoms. When the process was repeated in 1954 and 1957, the figures were changing. By 1970, more people chose 'freedom of speech' than voted for all the other choices put together.

Student protest

In the late 1960s, new social movements emerged, notably the student movement. This aimed to change public perceptions about social behaviour, including the tolerance of minorities and the purposes of education. It was international in character and had no central organisation. Its participants felt a strong unity of purpose with students throughout the world. In Europe it was most strongly developed in France, West Germany and Italy, although it also appeared in other European democracies and in some totalitarian states of eastern Europe, as well as the USA, South America and Asia. Beside the well-established process of street demonstrations, it developed new methods of expressing protest, such as the issuing of provocative statements meant to shock a conformist society, and 'happenings' (events modelled on street theatre that were intended to startle and stimulate those who witnessed them to question the political and social system). The student movement was loud and organised without being regimented. Irreverent and anarchic, it contrasted with the predominantly Marxist structures of the conventional Left, which largely showed little patience with it. Many traditional citizens (even including many on the Left) found it alarming.

A generation growing up in the post-war world, accustomed to increasing prosperity and rising living standards, gave this student movement a strong impetus, in West Germany and elsewhere. So too did the first stirrings of an easing of tension between the Warsaw Pact and NATO. The example from the success of the US student movement and the civil rights campaign in making their views known and changing social attitudes may well have been an inspiration in Europe. Indeed, social attitudes were changing fast in the second half of the 1960s. The post-war generation rejected the deference and obedience to established authority that many of their parents accepted without question. There was an increased willingness to discuss historical matters that had previously been subject to a strong taboo, in particular Germany's Nazi past. This was a challenge to the longstanding policy, both public and private, of *Schlußstrich* (drawing a line, closure) by which Germans and the governments had preferred to put the past behind them.

As part of this there was an increasingly critical analysis of Germany's political partners, especially the USA. The US at this time was a belligerent in the Vietnam War (1955–75). This war was the first to be covered live on US television and so get beamed into millions of US homes. The coverage contributed to a greater awareness of the war and also the way in which it was conducted and the cost in American and Vietnamese lives. This generated huge protests in the USA. Opposition, expressed in demonstrations, spread to several other countries, including Germany. There was considerable student hostility to the war.

In West Germany the student movement has been credited by some historians with contributing indirectly to the downfall of the CDU government led by Chancellor Ludwig Erhard in 1966, and directly to the Social Democratic government of West Germany in 1969. Student leaders in West Germany included Joschka Fischer, later a leader of the Green Party and the united Germany's foreign minister and vice-chancellor, and Gerhard Schröder, a future SPD chancellor. Other historians regard the student movement as a failure because no sweeping changes can be attributed to it compared with its stated objectives.

Urban terrorism and the Baader-Meinhof Gang

There were limits to the liberality of German laws on civil rights, however, and of course there was considerable public support for political orderliness. Where state security was judged to be at risk, the forces of the FRG acted. The best-known of the terrorist groups active in West Germany was the Red Army Faction (*Rote Armee Fraktion* or RAF), sometimes called the Baader-Meinhof Gang after one of its founders, Andreas Baader, and a prominent journalist who joined, Ulrike Meinhof. It was founded in 1970 and acts committed in its name continued well after unification. Despite the group killing 34 people, a measure of support for the RAF persisted on the Left, as they were perceived by some to be active in their criticism of the Vietnam War and the inadequacy of denazification, where other critics merely made speeches.

ACTIVITY 4.5

'The student movement in West Germany in the second part of the 1960s was a left-wing luxury which centre-right governments had made affordable.'

- Prepare for a debate on this motion. Gather evidence and arguments for both sides. Each time you think of an argument on one side, make sure you consider how the other side of a debate would counter it.

Many have described Gudrun Ensslin, Andreas Baader's girlfriend, as the real leader of the RAF in its first phase (1970–72). The daughter of a pastor and very intelligent, she became a student radical in 1968 and then moved from protest to direct action in 1970. Ulrike Meinhof was also radicalised in the student protest movement of 1968 and outraged by the lack of action taken against the perpetrator after the student leader Rudi Dutschke was shot in 1968. It is evidence for the persistence of a small but influential radical political group growing out of the student protest movement that the RAF continued to operate after the deaths of the founders of the violent movement, right up to 1998.

The leadership of the RAF was arrested in 1972 and held in a specially built prison. In April 1975, while Baader, Meinhof, Ensslin and others were awaiting trial, the German embassy in Stockholm was attacked by RAF members. Two hostages were killed when the government refused their demands. In 1976, Meinhof was found hanged in her prison cell, apparently a suicide, although conspiracy theories abound. In April 1977, Federal Prosecutor Siegfried Buback was killed by the RAF, as were his driver and bodyguard. In July of the same year, Jürgen Ponto, the head of the Dresdner Bank, was shot and killed during a botched RAF kidnap attempt. Later in 1977, Baader was found shot dead in his cell and Ensslin hanged in hers; the state concluded that these were coordinated suicides, but again this conclusion was disputed. In 1990 it was shown (or perhaps claimed) that the RAF had been given financial and logistic support by the Stasi, the security police of East Germany. A second and then a third generation of RAF activists continued to commit other terrorist acts under new leadership.

The whole story astonished and horrified most Germans. The journalist Stefan Aust, in his book *The Baader Meinhof Complex*, emphasised the historical context in seeking to explain what had occurred. Those who were in charge of the West German police, schools and government were too often the same people who had been in those roles during Nazi rule. The chancellor in the late 1960s was Kiesinger,

Voices from the past

Ulrike Meinhof

Ulrike Meinhof was born in 1934. Her father died in 1940 and her mother in 1949. As a student she became involved in opposition to the formation of a German army and to nuclear weapons, and joined various left-wing groups including the KPD. She married in 1961, had twins and divorced in 1968.

Meinhof worked as a journalist but was sympathetic to the actions of Gudrun Ensslin and Andreas Baader, as were many people on the political left in Germany at this time. Persuaded by Gudrun Ensslin to help Baader escape from prison, Meinhof seems to have taken an instant decision not to write about the event but to flee with him and join the gang.

Journalist Stefan Aust, whose 1985 book *The Baader-Meinhof Complex* was turned into a feature film of

the same name in 2008, draws on interviews and the published writings of members. Here he explains the steps by which the group moved into violence and quotes Ulrike Meinhof:

'Indignation turned to protest, protest to resistance, resistance to violence. And from the first, parallels with the Third Reich were drawn. Ulrike Meinhof said, "In the moment when you become serious about solidarity with the Vietnamese, when you become intent on weakening the American position everywhere in the world, so that the Vietnamese people derive some benefit, then I know, then I really don't see the difference between the terrorism of the police that we have already experienced in Berlin and are threatened with now and the stormtrooper terror of the Thirties."'[4]

who had been a Nazi. These were issues that Germany had coped with by not discussing them. As a result, older Germans had little experience of describing their personal experiences of Germany between 1933 and 1945. In addition, younger Germans' lack of education regarding the period meant a difficulty in distinguishing authority from autocracy. Aust noted that any violent or even rough behaviour by the police was instantly seen as comparable with the SS. Some radicals thus saw the Federal Republic as the heir of Nazi Germany. In this way, the much-valued political virtues of 'continuity' and integration became unforgivable vices in their eyes. Although only a few people actually engaged in terrorist acts, many more offered some degree of support and far more – very large numbers – were willing to say that they sympathised and would offer support if asked.

The RAF's goals included:

- the removal of former Nazis from positions of power and authority
- opposing the influence of the USA in Germany and the wider world, as America was seen as a fascist-imperialist state
- ending the war in Vietnam (seen as an example of US imperialism)
- ending Western support for the Shah in Iran (viewed as a fascist dictator propped up by the US and its allies, including Germany).

These were goals that older Germans found it difficult to identify with or even grasp. It was an unfamiliar kind of politics both in its programme and in its campaign.

Environmentalism

Unlike the student movement of the later 1960s, the environmental movement of the 1970s was able to draw in people of all ages. Also unlike the student movement, it was not associated with a specific, recognisable political ideology. However, in common with the students, environmentalists felt a strong community of interest with their counterparts in other countries.

The environmental movement emerged especially strongly in West Germany, partly because of the rapid pace of economic development and industrialisation. An increasing concern for pollution in both rural and urban areas added a strong sense of urgency among supporters.

The environmental movements that began to emerge in the 1970s were largely a reaction to a series of reports indicating the significant environmental damage caused by the modern economy, notably the 1972 publication D.L. Meadows's book *Limits of Growth*. This book in turn gave the results of an authoritative report of the Club of Rome, an influential global think-tank founded in Rome in 1968 to deal with a variety of international political issues. It brought together industrialists, academics, diplomats and politicians from many countries.

The environmental movements that sprang up in many countries used similar techniques of mass mobilisation to the student movements of the time – demonstrations, marches, petitions and so on. There were numerous organisations, some campaigning against nuclear weapons, some against nuclear power, some concerned with biodiversity, farming practices, pollution and so on.

ACTIVITY 4.6

Historians draw attention to certain specific events and circumstances in contributing to the rise of the Baader-Meinhof Gang (RAF). These include: the shooting of Rudi Dutschke, the June 1967 visit of the Shah of Iran and the shooting of Benno Ohnesorg, the presence of former Nazis in senior positions in West German government and society, and the *Schlußstrich* mentality.

Research on these, making notes and assessing how they radicalised certain individuals.

ACTIVITY 4.7

- In two columns, make notes contrasting the student movement with the environmental movement.

- As part of this, note the differences in approach, goals and achievements between the Baader-Meinhof Gang and the Green Party.

This movement may be credited with changing attitudes in Germany towards environmental issues among the general public, politicians and business leaders. Legislation designed to protect the environment did follow and influential organisations such as Greenpeace emerged at this time. Another of the legacies of the environmental movement was the Green Party.

Economic developments

The growth of the West German economy

Ludwig Erhard had avoided being drawn into the Nazi state, and had maintained contacts with anti-Nazi groups and individuals. After the war he became an economics consultant. The allies saw a memo that he had written on post-war economic options for Germany and identified him as a suitable person with whom to work. In 1947 he was appointed by the American and British occupation administrations to head a commission to recommend currency reform. The following year he was elected as director of economics in the Bizone (the US and British zones of occupation). He also abolished the production and price controls that had been established by the occupation administrations. These bold measures prepared the ground for Germany's later economic recovery and growth.

Erhard became minister of economics in Adenauer's first government in September 1949 and was able to put his plans for economic Liberalism, with minimum government regulation, into practice. Germany in those years still had major economic problems to deal with, of which war damage and the integration of millions of refugees from eastern Europe were the two most urgent. The economic surge in Germany in the 1950s and 1960s meant that both these and other difficulties could be managed at the same time as West German living standards rose. The purchasing power of wages increased by over 70% between 1950 and 1960. In addition, the government of the day spent heavily on such things as schools, hospitals, libraries and underground rail networks.

As finance adviser to the Trizone occupying powers, Erhard had already abolished the Reichsmark, the currency used in Germany since 1924, in the summer of 1948 and replaced it with a new currency, the Deutsche Mark (commonly called the 'Deutschmark' in English). The arrangement was that, for prices and wages, DM1 = RM1. However, for savings and government debt, DM1 = RM10. At the same time, Erhard abolished a number of economic controls which had been introduced by the NSDAP government. He said afterwards that he had done this on a Sunday, knowing that the Allied offices of administration were closed, so reducing the chance of his orders being countermanded by the Allies. The difference in the value of the exchange of Reichsmarks for Deutschmarks meant that the relationship between 'current account' activities (earning and paying) and 'deposit account' activities (saving and borrowing) had been rebalanced.

The new currency was stable and became respected internationally, fuelling the growth of the West German economy. Government spending on social welfare in West Germany increased roughly tenfold from 1950 to 1970. The result of all this was a sustained period of economic growth in West Germany in the 1950s and 1960s. Growth rates of 8%–10% were achieved, overtaking the economy of the UK, a nation that, unlike West Germany, was wary of accepting reconstruction funds and advice from the US Marshall Fund.

The contribution of the Marshall Plan to this remarkable economic growth is open to debate. The Marshall Plan operated from 1948 to 1952. Many historians point to the fact that the economic revival in West Germany was well established before US loans for reconstruction became available. Others note the great advantage enjoyed by the German economy even before the flow of US financial aid in terms of general American support and the international confidence and creditworthiness that this meant. Yet others emphasise the quality and determination of the German workforce and in particular their willingness to work for relatively low wages until times improved.

Establishing West German prosperity, so that it could be contrasted with Soviet-supported East Germany, became an important Cold War issue. The building of the Berlin Wall by East Germany in 1961 to halt the flow of emigrants to West Berlin underlined the success of this US strategy.

The economic growth model pursued by the Adenauer government was a great success, dubbed the *Wirtschaftswunder* ('economic miracle'). There is still debate among historians about the contribution of major US financial backing to this success. Much credit no doubt belongs to the West Germans themselves, but superpower backing did restore the country's position commercially and financially on the international scene. Some have argued that the main cause of the rapid economic growth experienced by West Germany in the 1950s and 1960s was the liberalisation of the economy marked by Ludwig Erhard's adoption of the social market economy (**Soziale Marktwirtschaft**) concept put forward by Alfred Müller-Armack, a member of his economic ministry. Others have argued that the key driver of the boom was the massive need for reconstruction because of the need to rebuild the war-damaged cities of West Germany and destroyed infrastructure.

This rebuilding of the German built environment took two main forms. The first was restoration: the reconstruction of historic cities on the pattern of their pre-war state, such as in Dresden and Leipzig in East Germany, and Hamburg, Cologne and Frankfurt in West Germany. Berlin was also badly damaged but was, as ever, a special case.

Second, the complete rebuilding of devastated cities provided an opportunity for the design and construction of many fine new buildings. Many leading architects were employed from around the world: the Brazilian Oscar Niemeyer, the Swiss-French Le Corbusier and Germany's own Walter Gropius and Ludwig Mies van der Rohe, designed new buildings for West Berlin.

In many cases both approaches were used – a faithful reconstruction of a historic city centre and complete rebuilding elsewhere. Berlin had been especially badly damaged by bombing and invasion. Major German port cities such as Hamburg were also badly bombed, as was the Ruhr valley, the industrial heartland of German industry.

ACTIVITY 4.8

Research the factors that allowed the West German economy to grow so rapidly in the 'economic miracle'. Create a mind map showing the different elements, how they related to one another and what they caused.

The 'economic miracle' and its aftermath

The West German economy had grown rapidly, fed by:

- Erhard's reforms
- the Marshall Plan
- willingness of the workforce to accept relatively low wages
- demand created by the domestic programme of reconstruction
- demand created by the Korean War (1950–53).

All of these were important, but an extra element was the revival of confidence. Germans increasingly believed that the government could solve problems, and that their country was capable of recovering and prospering.

A growth rate for industrial production of 25%, which Germany saw in 1950, is highly unusual. Rates of growth did drop off, but they continued to be high for most of that decade. The Gross National Product (GDP) shot up and unemployment fell in the same period from over 10% to a little over 1%.

As the country became clearly more prosperous, so employees' demands for pay rises also grew. Wages and salaries climbed and there was increased state investment in social programmes.

In 1957 the country established the Bundesbank, a central bank for West Germany. It was given authority over monetary policy. The intention was to depoliticise these aspects of the economy and thus achieve a continuity of policy that would not be affected by elections and the changes of government.

Urbanisation in West Germany was also remarkable. The Rhine–Ruhr area was already home to over 8 million in 1950 but in a generation this had grown to over 12 million, the largest such concentration in Europe. Berlin (taking West and East together) more than doubled its population in the same period (1950–75), from 1.6 million to 3.8 million. Hamburg and Munich had a more modest growth at the same time, while Stuttgart actually had a smaller population in 1975 than in 1950, although this may have been the result of urban boundary changes.

This growth of cities was not unexpected, given the rapid growth in the economy of the FRG, but even so it meant a continuing shrinkage of the rural population and a decline in the importance of rural production, although increased mechanisation in the countryside on farms ensured that growing cities were fed. However, even before the First World War broke out in 1914 Germany could not grow enough to feed its population, so that imports were crucial for the country. Fortunately, much industrial development in West Germany was export-led, so that the balance of payments for West Germany (the difference between the cost of imports and the revenue from exports) was comfortably positive.

Taken together, urbanisation and prosperity (and, one might add, increasing car ownership) meant almost continuous infrastructure building (roads, rail, sewers and so on) and with that a growth in urban pollution. The latter became a political issue when the environmental movement began to have an impact on mainstream politics.

This economic growth was not entirely even, as might be expected over two decades. There were times of relative faltering, such as the zero growth of the economic recession of 1966. But overall the living standards of West German workers rose steadily, and by the time of the formation of the single European market in 1957 with the creation of the European Economic Community (EEC), the West German economy was one of the strongest in the world.

Growth in the 1960s was slower. Perhaps no country could have continued at the previous rate, but in any case the building of the Berlin Wall meant that the workforce was no longer growing at the same rate, as migrants from the east were no longer able to travel west.

The response in government was to increase political interference in the economy, something that Erhard had always avoided. The Kiesinger government decided that the federal government should influence the economy. In 1967 the Bundestag passed a law that declared that federal, *Land* and local budgets should be coordinated; the intention was to give the government's fiscal policy (how it raises money through taxes and what it spends that money on) greater impact. The finance minister in the new government, Karl Schiller, assured industrialists and others that he was not interested in dictating the details, but that government should provide *Globalsteuerung* (global management), meaning a set of framework guidelines.

Brandt's SPD–FDP alliance invested more in social programmes. Then, under Schmidt, the economy grew again, recovering from the problems created by the oil crisis. However, Germany was building up a fiscal deficit: government had become better at spending money than at raising it.

Under Helmut Kohl, the federal government rediscovered Erhard's priorities and set out to reduce its role in the economy by:

- Reducing restrictions and regulation
- Selling government shares in state-owned enterprises and institutions.

It also aimed to reduce government spending and to cut the federal deficit. This remains a controversial area, but we should note that the state role in the West German economy shrank during the 1980s from 52% to 46% of GDP. Rapid growth did not return to the West German economy until the late 1980s. With growth came a fall in the unemployment rate.

Participation in the EEC

One of Adenauer's goals was to reintegrate Germany into European politics, and to do so in such a way that further wars on the model of the previous world wars became unthinkable. The creation of trans-European political, social, economic and cultural organisations was a key element in this policy.

There were obvious hurdles to be overcome. The Second World War had generated many tensions between European nations, and the Cold War after 1950 increased these tensions markedly. However, despite these barriers, some sort of European civil society did emerge, cautiously at first.

The European Coal and Steel Community (ECSC) formed in 1951, comprising Belgium, France, Italy, Luxembourg, the Netherlands and West Germany. In 1957, the same six countries also established the European Atomic Energy Community. This was an umbrella organisation: it had no members of its own and exercised little influence on European politics. Even so, with the ECSC it represented the early stages of the emergence of transnational civil society.

In 1957, the six countries also founded the EEC. This was a free-trade area with political oversight, and institutions to create and enforce trading rules. Germany's negotiator was Walter Hallstein, who was conscious of the difference of opinion in his own government between Adenauer and Erhard over the questions which the possibility of EEC membership raised. When Hallstein returned with the details of what was being agreed, Erhard was unenthusiastic. Adenauer regarded the process as essential to European integration and of an improved and stabilised relationship with France. Erhard took the view that the EEC was a necessary stage, but wanted to see it enlarged.

The EEC was created by the 1957 Treaty of Rome. The plan was to make trade within the EEC as straightforward as trade within any member state. In 1962, the EEC agreed that the prices paid for agricultural products would be the same across the EEC. In 1968, tariffs affecting trade between member states were abolished.

Matching these developments, the European Trade Union Confederation was founded in 1973 as an umbrella organisation campaigning for better pay and conditions throughout Europe. It made only a modest impact, as employers were largely not willing to engage in bargaining at this level.

In addition to European-wide initiatives, the relationship with France was clearly understood as vital to a stable, peaceful Germany. In this context, the Élysée Treaty of 1963 was both practically and symbolically important. It was signed by Adenauer and the French president (and former wartime leader), Charles de Gaulle. It established the principle that:

- France and West Germany would consult one another on all matters of significance.
- Ministers and officials would meet regularly.
- The two countries would always attempt to agree a common approach to transnational problems and questions.

From this grew a youth organisation, connections between individual schools and towns (twinning), and later (in 1987) the Franco-German Brigade, a military formation combining units from the two countries' armed forces.

Part of the background to the treaty was a distrust of Britain which de Gaulle and Adenauer shared. For the latter, the treaty was part of the same forward drive for peace and prosperity as EEC membership. Erhard and critics of the chancellor didn't see it that way: to them it looked more like the creation of an alliance to limit the EEC's size.

The impact of the oil crisis

In the 1970s, the German economy was hit by the 1973 oil crisis. This was a sudden increase in the price of oil, caused by the concerted actions of the Arab members of the Organisation of Oil Producing Countries (OPEC), who responded to American support for Israel, particularly during the 1973 Yom Kippur War, by launching an oil embargo against the US, along with certain allies.

These price increases affected countries beyond those targeted. In Germany, the Helmut Schmidt government witnessed GDP fall by more than a percentage point, something that the Federal Republic was not used to. With the price of imported oil so much higher, the balance of payments became less benign. In addition, individual households were paying more. The cost of fuel at the pumps, for both urban and rural users, became a major political factor. Oil for domestic and commercial heating also became more expensive. However, it was not just the price of fuel, but the price of everything that needed transporting that went up. Accordingly, trade unions demanded pay rises for their members to keep up with inflation. Those pay rises themselves contributed to inflation. Government costs (as a large-scale employer) went up. Unemployment went up.

Social developments

The effect of the Nazi legacy

The most obvious legacy of Nazi rule was the widespread destruction. An estimated 7 million Germans had died during the Second World War. The country's economy and infrastructure was in ruins. Diplomatically, the country had many enemies and few friends.

In addition, a dozen years of intolerant, one-party autocracy, followed by four years of rule by occupying armies, had given Germans the experience of being the 'subjects' of the government, not the 'citizens' of the state. The concept of a state which was a pooling of individual rights to create a collective, of a government which was accountable to the people, was a challenge. Of course, many people remembered the previous republic, but they were likely to remember instability, not accountability. Meanwhile, many people held the authorities in awe and were reluctant to criticise, let alone oppose. The views which had been continually taught and reinforced through Nazi propaganda did not disappear overnight.

In the early 1950s, during the first Adenauer government, nearly half of West Germans said that they would prefer an autocratic to a democratic political system. It was more than a decade before there was general agreement that democracy was the best form of government. Germans in the early 1950s also tended to respect the earlier autocratic governments. Bismarck was seen as the figure in German history most to be admired; the Kaiserreich and the period of Nazi rule were seen as the best times for Germany. Hitler continued to have admirers and there was a notable measure of support for the restoration of the monarchy. These were all matters which West Germany's politicians had to take account of when writing the constitution, forming governments and taking forward the day-to-day business of politics.

ACTIVITY 4.9

Research the factors that caused the West German economy to go into recession in 1966 and 1974/75. Create a mind map showing the different elements, how they related to one another and what they caused. Compare it with the one you drew to study the 'economic miracle' and the period of growth. What connections do you see and what do they tell you not just about the West German economy but also about its society and politics?

The Nazis had infiltrated every aspect of German society. By the end of the Nazi regime, more than 10% of the population were NSDAP members; that is 8 million people. The percentage among the professions – teachers, lawyers and above all civil servants – was higher because party membership influenced career development. Clubs, organisations and associations had been either closed down or Nazified or in some way signed a deal with the NSDAP. For example, when he was 14, the church youth group to which Joseph Ratzinger (the future Pope Benedict XVI) belonged was merged with the Hitler Youth; this left him a member of the HJ. No part of German society had been left untouched.

A telling example is that of the principal Protestant and the Roman Catholic churches, which had made agreements with Hitler's regime in order to continue their work unmolested. The nature of these agreements is still hotly debated, but in any event the prestige of the churches in West Germany after 1949 was high, partly because of their perceived resistance to the Nazi regime. Attendance at churches in West Germany enjoyed something of a revival after 1949 and a significant number of educational, medical and social welfare institutions were established or re-established. The income of these churches was largely because of individual voluntary donations by church members, traditionally up to 10% of their income. As living standards rose in West Germany and individual prosperity increased, so too did church income. This was partly spent on maintaining the many church buildings, partly on the salaries of pastors and priests, and partly on their various welfare, educational and medical activities.

The response of some Germans was to found political parties; others established newspapers. The weekly newspaper *Die Zeit* was first published in February 1946. The publishers included a judge with a Jewish wife (who had fled to the UK in 1933) who joined the CDU and worked as a journalist, and a Conservative architect who had been removed from his position by the Nazis. The first edition of the daily *Frankfurter Allgemeine Zeitung* appeared in November 1949; its staff included people who had worked for a newspaper which had been shut down in 1943. Both newspapers are centre-right in their politics. Both were intended to make a contribution to the re-establishing of civil society, part of a recognition that rebuilding Germany could not happen in the political sphere of parties and elections alone.

Standards of living

The Sozialstaat and the social market economy

A key aspect of German management of the economy is the concept of the *Sozialstaat* (social state). This ensures that there are labour laws protecting workers from unfair dismissal and promoting job security. There are provisions for employee participation in company decision-making. The legal code also offers the means to distinguish between lawful and unlawful eviction, and between reasonable and unreasonable rent increases. In some ways, the *Sozialstaat* was not unlike aspects of East Germany's socio-economic path. However, Alfred Müller-Armack's social market economy (an important aspect of Ludwig Erhard's economic approach) was to be achieved through democratic means, without the levels of state intervention and totalitarianism to be seen over the eastern border.

The term 'social market economy' underlined the importance of the social dimension of economics. After the bitter experience of Nazi rule, an economy relatively free from government control was appealing to business and trade unions, as well as being good for the country, in the opinion of Erhard and Müller-Armack. The social aspect was also highlighted by generous social-welfare spending.

Initially, West German workers were prepared to accept low wages, optimistic that they could catch up with their counterparts abroad over time. Living standards rose. Cities and towns were reconstructed, as were factories, often equipped with the latest machinery and informed by the most modern manufacturing ideas. Overseas trade, on which the strength of the German economy had for so long depended, steadily revived.

With rising prosperity came rising car ownership. This increased dramatically, from a little above zero in 1950 to 400 per thousand of the population by 1990. All these cars demanded roads and petrol stations, and created pollution. Initially accepted with little thought, the latter became a political issue with the rise of the environmental movement.

Trade unions began to re-form after the war. To support this process, coordinate activity and give a voice to unions on the national political stage, the Confederation of German Trade Unions was founded in 1949. Union membership reached a peak in the 1950s and 1960s: in West Germany from 1950, trade union members formed a fairly constant percentage of the total employed, at over 30%. This gave the trade unions considerable influence in society and politics. They were a very visible force, with their noisy rallies and marches, especially every 1 May, and their banners and slogans. Their most effective weapon by far was the strike, and this threat encouraged employers to take their demands seriously.

The unions in West Germany did more than negotiate pay settlements; they also formed housing associations and cooperative retail operations. And they campaigned for better conditions at work as well as higher wages. Nevertheless, they realised very well that pay restraint was necessary for some years if the West German economy was to recover. By the 1960s, however, there were signs that this restraint was starting to fray and the economic crisis of 1966 was in part caused by the need for adjustments in the labour market in West Germany as the 'economic miracle' began to falter.

Emigration and immigration

West Germany experienced both emigration and immigration in this period. In 1949 alone, some 270 000 people emigrated from the country, most to the Americas, especially to the USA but also to Canada, Brazil and Argentina. Motives for emigration vary and are notoriously difficult to judge. Some had Nazi pasts that they were trying to leave behind. Others were simply economic migrants, wanting to leave war-ravaged Europe and seek a new life with better prospects. However, this year of 1949 was the peak of such emigration from West Germany. It began to slow in the early 1950s and by 1990 was very small indeed, perhaps because the FRG itself had begun to offer more attractive prospects.

ACTIVITY 4.10

Research West Germany's social market economy and list the elements that it was made of. Comment on these elements, showing connections and causes. Show what some of the consequences of this policy were.

Immigration gradually became the more pressing social and economic issue. It comprised two distinct processes – forced migration and labour migration – and Germans themselves were a major element in both.

Part of the FRG's response to the situation was to include Article 116 in the Basic Law, so that the estimated 9 million ethnic Germans who were evicted from other countries in central and eastern Europe, plus a further 9 million Germans from the provinces that Germany had lost in the redrawing of borders after 1945, had a status in West German law, were given citizenship and were resettled. In addition, people continued to cross over from East Germany.

Germans had lived in East Prussia, the Sudetenland and Silesia for centuries. Many fled the advancing Red Army and took refuge in West Germany, where they were housed in displaced person (DP) camps. Others stayed put initially but left following the 1945 redrawing of national borders in central and eastern Europe. In addition, there were forced political migrations, relatively small in number but of significant individuals. These were political, cultural and scientific migrants, including technicians, intellectuals and artists of all kinds. Altogether, these forced migrations brought over 12 million people into West Germany. Their absorption represents a major achievement for the occupying forces in the immediate post-war period and for the FRG governments after 1949. Their numbers meant that the GB/BHE was for a few years a significant force in FRG politics, having its own deputies in the Bundestag.

East Germany continued to be a source of immigrants. Before the construction of the Berlin Wall in the summer of 1961, some 3.5 million Germans had crossed into West Germany from the East. This represented more than 15% of the East German population. A number of these migrants came during the early and mid-1950s, especially around 1953, when the death of Stalin aroused particular concerns about the effect on the USSR's satellite states, of which East Germany was one. Many of the migrants were younger people who saw their chance for a better life in the West. These were often well-educated, entrepreneurial people whom East Germany could ill afford to lose.

The pull was clear enough. For enterprising, young, educated East Germans the West seemed to offer excellent prospects. The West German economy in the 1950s experienced rapid growth. There were many opportunities for engineers, designers, technicians, scientists and other skilled workers in the FRG. The fact that these immigrants spoke German gave them an added value compared to the foreign workers who were also attracted by the opportunities. For creative persons, the liberal freedoms of the FRG offered an environment where they could flourish as they could not in the GDR. The free-trading, minimally regulated economy of West Germany also offered a standard of living to migrants and their families that East Germany could not match.

Changes to the position of women

During the 1970s, the women's movement in West Germany grew more prominent. It was not a new phenomenon, as it had its roots in the 19th century. However, unlike its predecessor, this new social movement did not have to fight for the vote, for access to education and jobs, or for entry into public life. In common with its sister movements in other Western countries, its concerns were above all to change social assumptions about the role of women at work and in the home. It also addressed such issues as divorce, abortion and sexuality. The movement staged spectacular media events, as well as using the marches, rallies and demonstrations employed by other social movements. Like the environmental movement it attracted supporters of all ages, not just young adults. It was local in character and did not develop any national or international organisation. A growth in gender studies in universities is further evidence of concern about the issues.

The employment of women did not change a great deal from 1950 to 1990, rising from about 33% of women of working age in 1950 to just 36% in 1990. There were several reasons for this:

- In general, these were decades of growing prosperity for most West Germans. Families were better off and jobs continued to be available, so fewer women felt pressured into working by their husbands' circumstances.
- The retirement age for women dropped significantly towards 60 in this period, so older women left the labour market.
- There was a considerable expansion of higher and further education, so many young women entered the labour market a few years later.

In part these factors were balanced in the FRG by the desire to work of both married and unmarried women. Working mothers were increasingly able to take advantage of preschool facilities.

After 1970 the pace of change in the employment of women gathered pace in West Germany. Whereas in 1970 around 65% of women aged between 20 and 50 were employed, this percentage had risen to 80% by 2000.

Changing concepts of the family

The traditional structure of the family was changing. German society was essentially a conservative one before 1945. The unprecedented freedoms of the Weimar period in the 1920s, including sexual ones, had delighted some Germans but at the cost of outraging many others. The Nazis insisted on a family model where the woman stayed at home and looked after her man and their children, as well as keeping the house clean and tidy. This model was popular with some sections of German society, especially in the more conservative rural areas.

After 1950 this family model began to break down, if slowly at first. The increased employment of women and better preschool and welfare provision were major factors here and so was the wider acceptance and availability of contraception.

The government's attitude to social policy limited intervention by the state into the world of marriage and the family. Nevertheless, arm's-length policies promoted the idea of a male-breadwinning, family-based social structure with different gender-based roles for men and women. This was advanced through wages, marriage-based benefits and tax allowances. For example, the federal government responded to the fifth Family Report in 1994 by insisting on a clear distinction between public obligation and private family arrangements. For many years, this principle inhibited the establishment of full-time preschool childcare arrangements. Social welfare provision was still based on the married unit in 1991.

ACTIVITY 4.11

Create a mind map showing how the changes in employment, education and family life in the FRG after 1950 affected women in West Germany.

Changes to the position of young people

Education and training

In 1949, the Basic Law devolved authority of educational policy to the states, so that there was some variation across the FRG. This variation had in fact begun even before the formation of the country, as the occupying powers had each put systems in place in their own zone that mirrored their experience at home. In one area of education, however, all occupying powers, and all parts of West Germany, were agreed: Nazi ideology disappeared from the school curriculum.

After 1949 the federal government prioritised investment in education, and this was a politically uncontroversial policy. A well-educated, well-trained workforce was seen by the government as essential if the economy of West Germany was to grow as they hoped. The new curriculum was especially strong on technology, physics, mathematics and engineering.

Many kindergartens (for ages two to six) in West Germany after 1950 were run by charitable foundations and were therefore outside the control of the state. The use of such preschools was slow to develop, however: even by the mid-1970s take-up was only about 50%. Although the numbers remained modest for some time after that, the increasing tendency of women to return to work while their children were still young caused a growth in preschool provision.

Free primary education was offered by the state throughout this period, and there were also various independent schools, many of them linked to the Protestant or Catholic churches, which some parents preferred.

During this period lower-secondary education was a universal provision. With rapidly rising standards of living, the potential loss of family income because of secondary-school attendance by pupils became less important. There was also a steady growth in the numbers attending upper-secondary school, with the wish to go on to some form of higher education. Attendance at upper-secondary level by the mid-1970s was around 25% of the total and growing.

The increasing availability of white-collar jobs in industry, the service sector and the civil service encouraged this educational growth in West Germany. Meanwhile, the demand for unskilled workers with just an elementary education fell sharply. Successive FRG governments continued to invest in education – in school buildings and salaries for teachers – even in the 1970s, when the economic revival faltered in West Germany.

Germany had several respected universities dating from the 14th to 19th centuries. One of these was in the Soviet sector (the future East Berlin). In 1947, some Berlin University staff and students expressed discontent at the rule of the Soviet occupying authority. This led to arrests, imprisonments and executions. Part of the university staff and students then asked for American support in founding a Free University in the western part of the city in 1948.

Higher education expanded throughout West Germany in the 1960s, with the founding of many new universities. These educated and trained the kinds of entrepreneurial figures with great technical or scientific expertise that the country needed at the time.

The percentages of 20- to 24-year-olds attending university speak for themselves:

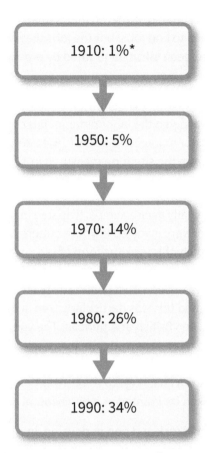

(*The 1910 figure is for the Kaiserreich, the 1950-90 figures are for the FRG.
This means different borders and different population numbers. As a result,
percentages are significant; actual numbers of those attending would mean less.)

Figure 4.3: Flow diagram showing the percentages of young people attending university.

This rapid expansion provided West Germany with the increased number
and quality of engineers, designers, mathematicians and scientists required
for economic expansion. Similar growth occurred in the availability of
apprenticeships, offering a wide range of courses.

Youth employment and unemployment

In its first years the Federal Republic had high growth. This, combined with a
low birth rate during and after the war meant that it was not difficult for young
people to be in full-time education, training or work. Unemployment tended to
be infrequent, unusual and short-term or seasonal. Young people in 1950s West
Germany expected to go out to work: in 1953, 17% of 17-year-olds were in the
labour market; for 18- to 20-year-olds, the figure was 85%.

High levels of employment largely remained the case until the 1970s, when the
number of apprenticeships available began to decline in both public and private
sectors. The 1974/75 recession reduced the number of jobs on offer. At the same
time, the higher birth rate of the 1960s, compared to the 1940s and 1950s, meant
that more teenagers were coming onto the labour market, so there was more

competition at the same time that there were fewer opportunities. The resulting youth unemployment figures were the highest for a quarter of a century. Those with the poorest qualifications suffered, but even graduates saw their early career prospects reduced. They tended to find jobs, but the jobs they found were less high-flying than those that had been taken for granted by previous university leavers.

Nevertheless, the state's commitment to widening and lengthening education meant that more young people joined the labour market later. By 1984, only 19% of 17-year-olds were in the labour market and 56% of 18- to 20-year-olds: the figures mark a major change from the situation measured in 1953.

Youth culture

Some young people were politically aware and participated in the youth movement. Far larger numbers were involved in youth culture, which was dominated by light music. Initially this took the form of jazz, but from the late 1950s it became rock and roll, another American import. Many Germans, especially younger ones, looked outside their own country for their cultural influences and entertainment and this was particularly true in the area of music. The best-selling groups were often British or American. The young people who followed this music made a point of wearing denim jeans, a form of clothing previously sold as overalls for people in manual work. This costume choice emphasised informality and was a challenge to the convention of politeness and smartness that society had taken for granted as a behavioural norm.

It took time for a German form of rock and pop to develop, in a market where local light music had been characterised by the cheery banalities of *Schlager*. This German-language pop music was consistently optimistic and sentimental, with simple melodies, an unvarying beat and well-laundered, ceaselessly smiling performers; little had changed since the merry operettas of decades before. Nevertheless, the domestic music industry did manage to create German stars based on American models: Peter Kraus was marketed as a German Elvis Presley, but the image created was milder and did not have Presley's sullen rebelliousness.

Another form of German pop, called *Krautrock* by British journalists, dates from the 1960s. The groups combined conventional pop forms and production values with a more experimental approach, and used electronic instruments including synthesizers. Kraftwerk and Tangerine Dream are probably the most successful groups from this time and style.

Regardless of style and format, numerous bands continued to write their lyrics in English rather than German.

Social tensions

The 1950s and 1960s were decades in which the most significant immigration was Germans leaving the former eastern territories, and then East Germany, for the West. West Germany concentrated on developing political stability through this process and experienced a period of rapid economic growth. However, the 'economic miracle' of these years required a continuing influx of labour and here a second main type of migration – non-German labour migration – became much more significant over time.

Immigration numbers rose sharply in this period. Government policies on immigration to the FRG in the 1950s and 1960s were relatively relaxed but this changed somewhat from the early 1970s, when between 1973 and 1974 most EEC member countries, including West Germany, in a coordinated way, sharply cut the levels of immigration from outside the EEC. At the same time, such barriers as there were to the free movement of labour within the EEC were reduced to almost zero.

Such was the rapid pace of industrial development in the 1950s and 1960s that West Germany became short of labour. Any international opposition to buying German goods because of the recent past had faded and the Korean War (1950–53) produced a shortage of goods that the FRG was only too ready to supply. To cope with this increase in demand and consequent labour shortage, the country signed treaties with various European countries from 1955 enabling it to recruit *Gastarbeiter* (guest workers). The term made clear that they were not expected to stay and apply for citizenship or naturalisation. These workers came mostly from the less-prosperous southern Europe – Greece, Italy, Spain and Turkey.

Gastarbeiter made a major contribution to the automobile manufacturing industry, itself a prominent sector of the German economy. The combination of an adequate and well-trained workforce and German engineering expertise, proved to be a winning formula. *Gastarbeiter* provided an increasing percentage of the workforce in this sector, rising to as high as 25%.

Immigration became an important political issue in the EEC, including the FRG. In particular, the question of the social integration of immigrant communities developed into a prominent political question. The virtual ceasing of new immigration did not mean that immigrant-origin communities no longer grew – they did. There was by now a second generation whose parents were immigrants in the 1950s or even 1960s. Some of these communities were better able to integrate with existing societies than others.

Another concern was the question of illegal entry. This became even more of an issue as borders in eastern Europe and China opened up and as the economic gap between most African countries and Europe continued to widen, not to mention the contrast between peace within the EEC and war in some parts of the world.

Despite problems of integration, it was clear that West Germany, and Europe as a whole, could not continue to develop economically without these communities, and government policies on immigration and social policies reflected this.

Modern culture

West Germany developed a lively cultural scene. Creative and performing artists were given more freedom than other citizens. Many used this freedom to criticise the government and its policies. For example, the painter Joseph Beuys and his pupil Jörg Immendorff produced work in the 1960s and 1970s that was overtly political. However, it would be a mistake to think of Beuys as a communist propagandist. He had been a Luftwaffe pilot and he explored ecological issues by questioning how humanity fitted into the natural world, arguing that the artist was a kind of shaman. He created various fictions about his life, but an anecdote about his having crashed in the Crimea and his life being saved by Tatar tribesmen is widely accepted as true, and formed the seed of several of his art works.

Beuys's pupil Sigmar Polke also sought to offer a critique of West Germany that was not merely praise of East Germany. His paintings used some of the appearance of commercial art; he called his style 'capitalist realism', itself a pun on the 'socialist realism' which was the official art of the USSR and all its clients states, including the GDR.

Gerhard Richter reacted to the Baader-Meinhof Gang, and the deaths of several of its leaders, in a series of 15 ambiguous photo-paintings entitled *October 18, 1977* (1988). In them he painted not so much the individuals as the way in which they had been represented in newspapers and police photographs. In these and other works, he drew attention to the extent to which the media create the way in which we see and understand our world.

The actor and theatre manager Ida Ehre was Moravian by birth (in 1900) where her father was cantor at the local synagogue. She studied acting in Vienna before touring in Austria and Germany. From 1930 she made regular appearances at the Lessing Theatre in Berlin. As a Jewish actor she was not allowed to work after the Nazis came to power in Germany and she was briefly interned by the Gestapo in a concentration camp. After the Second World War she opened the Hamburg Kammerspiele theatre in 1945. Before the war, Hamburg had been one of the largest seaports in the world but it had been badly damaged by Allied bombing. Ehre opened the theatre amid ruins. By 1960, however, the city had been extensively rebuilt and was a flourishing commercial centre again, with a reputation for crime and prostitution. At the Kammerspiele Ehre established a strong reputation as a successful theatre manager, putting on modern plays and introducing foreign ones for the first time in Germany. She continued as manager until her death in 1989.

Another artist attracted by the FRG cultural regime was the writer Günter Grass, who had arrived in West Germany as a homeless refugee. Grass is best known for his novel *The Tin Drum* (*Die Blechtrommel*, 1959), the first of his Danzig Trilogy. All three of these books concern the rise of Nazism in Danzig (now Gdansk, in Poland) and record the interactions of the unique cultural mix then to be found in that city. Apart from his novels, Grass was also prominent in West Germany as a poet, sculptor, playwright and graphic artist. He was a strong supporter of the SPD and of its then leader Willy Brandt. When he revealed in a magazine interview that as a teenager he was conscripted into the Waffen-SS, this was controversial in part because he had himself been critical of the responses of prominent individuals and institutions to their Nazi past.

In classical music, the contemporary music scene in the FRG was dominated by two composers: Hans Werner Henze and Karlheinz Stockhausen. Both were highly influential on music composition both within and outside Germany.

Born in Westphalia, Central Germany, in 1926, Henze studied music in Heidelberg from 1946 to 1948. At first he composed in a neo-classical style like his fellow

Russian, Igor Stravinsky, but he also experimented with serialism and remained open to many influences, including expressionism and jazz. He never lost his affection for the musical styles of the past. A left-winger in politics and a homosexual, he did not feel comfortable with the attitudes and political beliefs of the FRG in the early 1950s and he left for Italy in 1954. There he composed music that was more sensuous and lyrical. He died in 2012 in Dresden and is buried outside his home in Rome. He is remembered for his combination of rigour and lyricism.

Stockhausen was especially known for his experiments in serial, aleatoric (music with an element left to chance) and electronic music. Unlike Henze, he maintained a style of composition all his life that rejected classical harmony. He was born in a village near Cologne in 1928 and studied music at the University of Cologne and then with the influential French composer Olivier Messiaen in Paris in the early 1950s. From 1953 he taught music in Darmstadt, where the Darmstadt School of composition had its centre. He died near Cologne in 2007. He was a prolific composer, teacher, performer and writer. He declared that his experience of hearing Nazi marching songs on the radio when young had left him with a lifelong detestation of regular rhythm, preferring to write music in which 'players are floating freely'.

Among musical performers, some had careers dating back to the Third Reich. The conductor Herbert von Karajan and the soprano Elisabeth Schwartzkopf had been members of the Nazi Party. In contrast, the conductors Otto Klemperer, Fritz Busch and Erich Kleiber had chosen to leave Germany in the same period. Unsurprisingly, the contrast has attracted a good deal of discussion in the media. Younger performers, such as Karajan's protégée Anne-Sophie Mutter (born 1969), have been free of this issue.

In cinema, Edgar Reitz wrote and directed *Heimat* (*Homeland*), a 32-episode series of films set in a village in the Rhineland between 1919 and 2000. It tells the story of Germany over this turbulent period by examining one small community. The title was in part an ironic reference to the popular types of film in 1950s Germany called *Heimatfilm*. These were usually sentimental films with a simple morality set in an improbably cheerful rural setting. The series was first released in 1984. It gave a strong signal that Germany's past, including the Nazi period of the 1930s and 1940s, once a taboo area, could now be actively discussed by a new generation.

The political, economic and social condition of reunified Germany by 1991

Helmut Kohl and the drive to reunification

The existence of East Germany as a state, and the dominance of its politics by the Communist SED, was made possible by the power of the USSR and its army. As Soviet support reduced and disappeared, the weakness of Communist rule in East Germany was exposed.

Despite the fact that reunification had been an article of faith among politicians since the founding of the FRG – and despite the fact that this event was predicted

---

ACTIVITY 4.12

Create a spider diagram showing what the key changes in West German society in the period 1949–91 were. Show the causes, the connections, the way in which the changes took place and what consequences they had.

and legislated for in the country's Constitution – the swift demise of the Communist government took many Germans, in both east and west, by surprise.

The opening of borders between Hungary and Austria allowed large numbers of East Germans to emigrate. A series of demonstrations in East Germany showed that the government there could no longer command the situation. One day in 1989 the state had been celebrating the 40th anniversary of the founding of East Germany; 11 days later, in October, its leader, Erich Honecker, had been pushed out of office by colleagues trying to regain control of the situation. In November, amid some political confusion, the gates in the Berlin Wall were opened and still more people left the GDR. Deputies in the Bundestag rose on hearing the news and sang *Einigkeit und Recht und Freiheit* (the West German national anthem) – predictably misreported in the UK press as *Deutschland, Deutschland über alles*. Individual citizens began demolishing the Wall.

Helmut Kohl, aware of his obligations under the FRG Constitution, visited Moscow in February 1990 and received assurances that the USSR would not stand in the way of unification. Furthermore, reunification would not be a merger but a takeover, East Germany being absorbed into West Germany under the West's constitution. In addition, the new Germany would retain its membership of NATO. Kohl willingly agreed that Germany would have no atomic, biological or chemical weapons, that its armed forces would be limited to 370 000 people and that it would make a substantial contribution to war-damage reparations. It was like a re-run of the Allies' deliberations of 1945 at Potsdam or of 1919 at the Palace of Versailles – but this time Germany was present and negotiating her own future.

In May 1990 Kohl signed an economic, monetary and social union treaty with East Germany to prop up its ailing economy and to ease the process of integration. Unification was to be under Article 23 of the Basic Law, the simplest and speediest process because no new constitution had to be drafted and only a simple majority vote was required in the Bundestag and its GDR equivalent, the *Volkskammer*. Despite some objections from the Bundesbank and others, Kohl proposed parity between the West German Deutschmark and the East German Mark (the Ostmark). This meant a 1 : 1 exchange rate between East and West German Marks for rent, wages and interest. Karl Otto Pöhl, the Bundesbank president, had advised against this but there were fears that lack of parity would mean an even greater flood of people and capital heading west.

A reunification treaty was signed in September 1990 and approved by both parliaments the following month. On 3 October 1990, East Germany ceased to exist and the two parts of Germany were reunited 45 years after the Occupying Powers had divided the country.

The fall of the Berlin Wall in late 1989 was a powerful symbolic moment for many in the unification process. It generated an understandable euphoria, especially for those in West Berlin at the time, but unification has to be seen as a process lasting many months and requiring preparation.

Some in the east mourned the loss of the GDR, with its highly centralised economy, its relatively full employment and its generous social-welfare provision. Some citizens had spent all or most of their lives in the GDR. For them the readjustment was neither easy nor instant nor even possible. In German, this is punningly called *Ostalgie*.

There were apprehensions concerning the likely cost of unification. How would the obviously necessary building of infrastructure and restructuring of the ailing East German economy be paid for? The generous terms offered to the GDR by Kohl only added to the sense of doubt among critics.

Figure 4.4: The Brandenburg Gate, 1989, after the fall of the Berlin Wall.

Strengths and problems of reunification

The absorption of East Germany by West Germany was never going to be easy. The FRG was characterised by its free-market economy and its minimal government control over many aspects of everyday life. The now-defunct GDR had had a centralised economy, high levels of central government control and widespread police surveillance.

A reunited Germany was faced with numerous practical difficulties. The party was over and now the bills began to come in. Some of them were bigger than expected. The costs of reunification were many. The old industrial areas in the former GDR, places such as Chemnitz, were known to be badly polluted but the costs of an adequate clean-up were higher than anticipated. Many industries and firms in the former GDR were found to be in bad shape – inefficient and poorly equipped by West German standards. The potentially more profitable ones were taken over or bought up by companies in the west. The rest were allowed to dissolve.

Infrastructure costs soared. The costs exceeded budgets for the construction of the new roads and rail links that were to knit together the formerly divided Germany. For example, in September 1988 the governments of the GDR and FRG had begun negotiations on the construction of a new 258 km high-speed railway line (ICE) between Hanover in the west and Berlin in the east. Eventually in June 1990 an agreement was reached between the two transport ministers for a line between Hanover and Berlin on a northern route through Wolfsburg (home of Volkswagen). This was the shortest, most direct and least expensive option. It would run hourly high-speed train services, joining the existing north–south ICE network at Hanover. The dream was that Berlin citizens could travel by high-speed train to Munich in the south or Hamburg and Bremen in the north via Hanover. Construction did not begin until November 1992 with the new bridge over the Elbe River.

When the costs reached the German tax-payer, there was some resentment, especially in the west. The decision taken to offer parity of currency put great strain on the financial system of a reunified Germany as it vastly increased the number of Deutschmarks in circulation.

There were social pressures also. Many former residents of the GDR moved west in search of better jobs and living conditions. Some met with a cool reception. Those from the east – sometimes called 'Ossies' – were resented by some 'Wessies' as they competed for jobs, housing, social benefits and services.

Stasi files were opened, so that people found out about the extent of surveillance in the GDR. The names of those who had collaborated actively with the Stasi were often revealed. Inevitably, many individuals discovered that colleagues, friends or family members had been betraying them to the secret police. There was indignation, for example, among academics and others as the extent of the system of Stasi spying on university campuses in the east became known. Lothar de Maizière, the man who, as the only elected prime minister of East Germany, had signed the unification agreement with Kohl, was regarded as a man with a bright political future after reunification. A year later he had to resign, following reports in the press that he had secretly worked for the Stasi.

However, despite all these pressures and problems, few in the now reunited Germany questioned what was for them the fundamental principle that a nation divided in 1945 must be united again, whatever the cost.

The CDU/CSU and FDP coalition won the elections that followed reunification. The surprise in many ways was that the balance between CDP, CDU/CSU and FDP was not dramatically altered by the changes in the electorate. The political condition of a reunified Germany by 1991 was remarkably stable given the magnitude of the recent changes: continuity remained the watchword.

For many West Berliners, the tearing down of the Berlin Wall early in November 1989 was an unforgettable time, laden with the most powerful symbolism. Although the formal process of reunification had to wait for nearly a year, this was the moment that stayed in the memory. As late as the 1980s, the Wall still divided the city; a major European city had a line of floodlights, barbed wire and observation towers manned by soldiers with automatic weapons. By the early 1990s, the wall had gone and Potsdamer Platz, which had been a wasteland, was once again a central open space in an undivided city in an undivided country.

Historians offer competing interpretations as to who or what should take the credit for the reunification of Germany in 1990:

- Helmut Kohl liked to be thought of as the principal architect of a reunited Germany, a 20th-century Bismarck. He certainly steered the FRG in the final phases of the process and personally negotiated directly with the Soviet leader, Mikhail Gorbachev, held reconciliation talks with France and won the support of the USA.
- Willy Brandt can claim to have pursued with vigour a policy of *Ostpolitik*, looking east rather than west that, it can be argued, unfroze relations with the GDR.
- Konrad Adenauer ensured in 1949 that the eventual reunification of Germany was a major aim of FRG policy.

There is also a case for saying that the causes were circumstantial, not political. According to this interpretation, the collapsing Soviet economy drove Gorbachev to seek ways to modernise. The Cold War, which had been as dominant an issue in the 1950s and 1960s as the fear of Russian-style revolution had been in the 1920s, no longer dominated political and diplomatic discussions by the 1980s. With tensions lowered (through *détente*), the Soviets were able to engage in further dialogue with the West. Gorbachev was willing to lose a military-economic system of client states that had ceased to be useful. This made the break-up of the Warsaw Pact inevitable and, with that, the collapse of the SED rule in East Germany. Reunification thus became inevitable.

Timeline

1945	Germany surrenders
	Christian Social Union (CSU) founded
1946	February: *Die Zeit* first published
1947	Ludwig Erhard appointed by the American and British occupation administrations to prepare currency reform
1948	Erhard appointed director of economics in the Bizone (US and British zones of occupation); production and price controls abolished
	Summer: Erhard replaces Reichsmark with Deutschmark
	Free Democrats (FDP) founded by Liberal politicians
1949	Basic Law (*Grundgesetz*) comes into force
	Confederation of German Trade Unions founded
	April: NATO founded
	August: federal election; Konrad Adenauer leads CDU/CSU to victory
	September: Erhard became minister of economics in Adenauer's first government
	November: *Frankfurther Allgemeine Zeitung* first published
1950	League of Expellees and Those Deprived of Rights (*Bund der Heimatvertriebenen und Entrechteten* or BHE) founded

1951	April: creation of the European Coal and Steel Community (ECSC)
	September: Adenauer's speech in the Bundestag acknowledging the obligation of the West German government to pay reparations to the Jews who had suffered
	Adenauer stands by senior civil servant shown to have been a successful Nazi civil servant and drafter of anti-Semitic legislation
1952	Socialist Reich Party of Germany (*Sozialistische Reichspartei Deutschlands* or SRP) banned by Constitutional Court
	SPD leader Kurt Schumacher dies
	BHE changes name to All-German Bloc/League of Expellees and Those Deprived of Rights (*Gesamtdeutscher Block/Bund der Heimatvertriebenen und Entrechteten* or GB/BHE)
1953	September: federal election; CDU wins and Adenauer is re-elected chancellor
	September: Restitution Law finally passed by the Bundestag
1955	May: West Germany granted full sovereignty; West Germany joins NATO as a full member; formation of *Bundeswehr* (army)
1956	What were thought to be the last of the German prisoners of war arrive home from a Soviet labour camp. Many others in fact remain; one is released as late as 2014
	KPD banned by Constitutional Court
1957	Reintegration of the Saarland into Germany
	September: CDU remains largest party in Bundestag following federal election
	Establishment of the Bundesbank
	European Atomic Energy Community established
	Germany becomes a founder member of EEC, created by the Treaty of Rome
1959	Adenauer speaks at rally of expelled Germans
1961	August: building of the Berlin Wall by East Germany
	September: federal election; SPD now largest party but CDU/CSU remains in coalition government
1963	June: US President John F. Kennedy's speech in West Berlin
	Élysée Treaty signed by Adenauer and French President Charles de Gaulle
	October: Adenauer retires as chancellor; succeeded by Ludwig Erhard

1965	September: Erhard leads CDU/CSU to victory in federal election
1966	Economic recession
	Grand Coalition government of CDU/CSU and SPD under Chancellor Kurt Kiesinger
1967	June: visit of the Shah of Iran sparks demonstrations; Benno Ohnesorg shot dead by police
1968	April: student leader Rudi Dutschke shot and severely injured
	May: Grand Coalition passes Emergency Acts, an amendment to the Basic Law
1969	September: federal election won by SPD under Willy Brandt
1970	Treaty of Moscow
	Brandt visits Warsaw and kneels during visit to memorial of the Warsaw Ghetto Uprising
	Foundation of Red Army Faction (RAF *Rote Armee Fraktion*), known as the 'Baader-Meinhof Gang'
1971	Brandt receives Nobel Peace Prize
1972	September: SPD wins federal election under Brandt
	December: Basic Treaty (*Grundlagenvertrag*) signed with GDR
	Baader-Meinhof Gang leadership arrested and imprisoned
1973	European Trade Union Confederation founded
	Oil crisis
1974	Willy Brandt resigns as chancellor because of Günther Guillaume spy scandal; succeeded by Helmut Schmidt
1975	April: while Baader, Meinhof, Ensslin and other leaders of the Baader-Meinhof Gang await trial, the German embassy in Stockholm is attacked by Baader-Meinhof Gang members
	May: Meinhof found hanged in her prison cell
1976	October: SPD wins federal election under Schmidt
1977	April: Federal Prosecutor Siegfried Buback killed by the Baader-Meinhof Gang, as are his driver and bodyguard
	July: Jürgen Ponto, head of Dresdner Bank, shot and killed during kidnap attempt by the Baader-Meinhof Gang
	Baader found shot dead in his cell and Ensslin hanged in hers
1980	October: federal election won by SPD–FPD coalition
	Green Party founded
1982	FDP leave coalition and vote with CDU/CSU; Kohl elected chancellor

1983	March: CDU/CSU wins federal election under Kohl; Green Party enters Bundestag
	Republican Party founded
1987	January: CDU/CSU wins federal election under Kohl
	East German leader Erich Honecker became the first GDR leader to visit the FRG
	Formation of Franco-German Brigade
1989	Celebrations of 40th anniversary of the founding of West and East Germany
	October: Erich Honecker pushed out of office
	November: gates in the Berlin Wall opened; fall of the Berlin Wall
1990	February: Helmut Kohl visits Moscow
	September: Treaty on the Final Settlement with Respect to Germany (*Vertragüber die abschließende Regelung in bezug auf Deutschland*) signed
	3 October: East Germany ceases to exist; Germany is reunited 45 years after the Occupying Powers had divided it
	December: first federal election covering the whole of Germany since 1933; PDS enters Bundestag
	December: Lothar de Maizièrere resigns from government
	It is revealed that Baader-Meinhof Gang had been financed by the Stasi

Practice essay questions

1. 'Adenauer's period in government was one of stability and success.' Assess the validity of this view.
2. The Federal Republic of Germany was successful in its policies to immigration in the period to 1989'. Assess the validity of this view.
3. To what extent were the SPD governments led by Willy Brandt and Helmut Schmidt from 1969 to 1982 a break with the past?
4. With reference to these extracts and your understanding of the historical context, which of these two extracts provides the more convincing interpretation of the response made by FRG to its Nazi legacy?

Extract A

The Chancellor was, then, more than well aware that he governed a nation of 'turncoats', as it was put later. Everyone knew, including Adenauer, that it was best to keep quiet about the twelve-year period of Nazi rule. This attitude was controversial and not without its problems. But Adenauer succeeded with it. In the decades after 1945, the question of the Nazi past had a similar subordinate political status as during the 1950s. In 1960, however, the stench of the Nazi past could again be smelled at home and abroad and Adenauer had to do something about it in the last years of his Chancellorship.

Source: Schwarz, Hans-Peter, Konrad Adenauer: From the German Empire to the Federal Republic, 1876–1952, Berghahn Books, 1995

Extract B

When a war ends, coming to terms with its violence and its victims is one of the most important and urgent tasks postwar society must perform. After 1945 Germany had to cope with the deaths of about seven million soldiers and roughly half a million civilians, many killed in air raids. In addition, there was an unknown number of refugees and prisoners of war. At the same time, the German people were confronted with the moral and political consequences of a military catastrophe, the destruction of many towns, occupation and the undeniable crimes that the Nazi regime and the Wehrmacht had committed during the war.

In the context of these crimes and the experience of total war, the former interpretation of the fallen soldiers as heroic and patriotic warriors, serving in a just and noble cause, could no longer be maintained as a master narrative. Looking back at the years before 1945, most Germans had very ambivalent emotions: They remembered rather good times for themselves - compared to the postwar years the 1930s appeared normal - but no longer could deny the horrible times for the victims of German aggression and persecution. In this respect, it is of great interest to ask what period Germans perceived as the era of violence, who was seen as victims and who as perpetrators of violence. In short: What was the legacy of war in the German mind?

Source: Between Pain and Silence by Sabine Behrenbeck, in Richard Bessel and Dirk Schurmann (eds) Life after Death: Approaches to a Cultural and Social History of Europe During the 1940s and 1950s. Cambridge University Press 2003 p.33-64

Chapter summary

You should now understand the steps by which the western part of this defeated country was able to rebuild its economy, create a new political system and re-establish the agencies of civil society. Part of this was achieved by Germany putting its past behind it as quickly as possible. However, the past had a habit of coming back to haunt not only politicians but also civil servants and the leaders of society and the economy. Meanwhile, changes in international diplomacy and the collapse of the East German state created the opportunity for reunification. Remember that:

- When the war ended, the task of establishing democracy in Western Germany was partly achieved by an older generation of politicians and revived political parties, partly by a new generation and the creation of new political parties

- West German politics was dominated for a generation by Adenauer but also by coalition governments, which were themselves dominated by three political parties

- German politics and wider society favoured consensus over debate, and as part of this sought to integrate refugees from the lost territories in the east, but also to allow former Nazi supporters to build new lives

- Partly in responses to these tendencies, extra-parliamentary opposition grew from protest to terrorism, while politics moved on from being class-based to examine issues of gender and the environment, as well as to reopen questions regarding the recent past that an older generation had sought to close down

- Germany's politics and society were dominated by the 'economic miracle', and later by the various recessions and crises that followed, including the oil crisis, as well as by a debate regarding participation in Europe and the wider world, especially membership of the EEC

- German society had to cope with the Nazi legacy, but was also affected by rising living standards and changes to the position of women and young people, as well as the arrival first of large numbers of Germans from outside West Germany and then of foreign economic migrants

- The final major event in this period was the collapse of the East German political system and the country's reunification, something that had immediate as well as longer-term consequences for every aspect of Germany.

End notes

1 Schwarz, Hans-Peter, *Konrad Adenauer: From the German Empire to the Federal Republic, 1876–1952,* Berghahn Books, 1995
2 US President John F. Kennedy in a speech in West Berlin, 26 June 1963
3 Turner, Henry Ashby, *Germany from Partition to Reunification*, Yale University Press, 1992
4 Aust, Stefan, *Baader-Meinhof: The Inside Story of the R.A.F.,* Oxford University Press, 2009

Glossary

A

Abdication
renouncing a position of power or authority; stepping down from such a position

Anti-Semitic
hostile to Jews

Aristocrat
a member of the nobility, from a family with a tradition of owning land and holding political power

Aryan
south-central Asian tribe which is believed by some historians to have invaded both northern India and Europe in pre-history; pseudo-scientific classification for pure German

Autarky
self-sufficiency

Authoritarian
a political point of view or system in which the government has the authority to take decisions without consultation and the power to enforce them, and the population is expected to obey instructions from the government without questioning them

Autocracy
a political system in which a single figure possesses unrestrained power

B

Bekennende Kirche
churches and church members who opposed the Nazi regime and argued that the allegiance of the Church should be to God and scripture not to a worldly Führer

Bizone
the merged UK and US zones of occupation after 1945

Black-marketeer
someone who buys and sells goods on the 'black market', dealing in goods in a way that breaks the law such as not paying an import tariff or without taking account of a rationing system

Blockade
a campaign to disrupt trade and communication in order to prevent the movement of imports in such a way as to deprive the targeted place of necessary supplies

Bourgeois
French word originally meaning 'town-dweller' but now meaning capital-owning middle class; feminine: bourgeoise

Bundesrat
the Federal Council that formed part of both imperial Germany's central government and that of the Federal Republic of Germany; members nominated by the various member states or *Länder*, not directly elected. A similar body called the *Reichsrat* existed in the Weimar Republic

Bundesrepublik
German expression meaning 'Federal Republic'

Bundestag
the West German parliament, a democratically elected national assembly

Bundeswehr
the West German army

Burgfriedens politik
German word meaning 'town peace' or 'castle peace'; a policy of agreeing to end domestic disputes when faced with a foreign enemy

C

Camarilla
President Hindenburg's group of advisers

Casualty
dead or injured person, especially in war

Coalition
a government including members of more than one political party and thus committed to implementing more than one political programme or set of ideas

Communist
a left-wing political point of view or party, believing in the working class taking political and economic power through revolution

Concentration camp
a prison created by a barbed wire fence and containing huts; a more temporary structure than a traditional prison; built to hold large numbers of prisoners chosen for their membership of specific groups rather than in response to their own specific (criminal) actions

Conservative	a political point of view that political and other changes should be avoided, postponed or minimised, especially revolutionary or radical changes	**Environmentalism**	the belief that the condition of our natural surroundings is the most important issue facing politicians and voters
Constitution	the written set of rules for how a country is governed; laws can only be passed if they do not conflict with the principles set out in the constitution	**European Economic Community (EEC)**	an association of separate European states in a free-trade area with political oversight and institutions to create and enforce trading rules; created by the 1957 Treaty of Rome
Coup	French word meaning 'blow'; an attempt to change government by force rather than persuasion; a Putsch	**Extra-parliamentary**	activities that take place outside parliament, such as demonstrating or holding public meetings
D		**F**	
Death camps	concentration camp where the intention is to kill all prisoners	**Federal Republic of Germany (FRG)**	West Germany after 1949
Decree	a law issued by a head of state, not formulated by an elected government and debated by an elected assembly	**Federalism**	a belief in federations, political units made up of member states in which each member surrenders some responsibilities and powers to the central authority but retains others
Demilitarisation	taking armed forces out of an area		
Democracy	a political system in which all citizens are able to choose their government, usually through an electoral process	**Four-Year Plan**	Nazi project for the development of the German economy in readiness for war, with specific production targets; led by Göring
Denazification	a programme of removing from German society the influence of Nazi individuals and ideas following the Second World War	**Franco-Prussian War**	a war fought between France and Prussia, 1870–71, which Prussia won
Deutsche Christen	German expression meaning 'German Christians'; Protestant churches and church members who accepted or supported the Nazi regime	**G**	
		Gastarbeiter	German expression meaning 'guest workers'; people who came to West Germany from other countries, e.g. Turkey, but were not expected to stay and apply for citizenship or naturalisation
Divine right	a right to exercise power believed to have been conferred on a monarch by God		
Dreadnought	heavily armed early 20th-century battleship	*Gauleiter*	German word meaning 'District Leader'
E		**German Democratic Republic (GDR)**	East Germany after 1949
East Germany	a state created in 1949 out of the Soviet zone of occupation	**Gestapo**	acronym for *Geheime Staatspolizei*; German expression meaning 'secret state police'
Edelweisspiraten	German expression meaning 'Edelweiss Pirates'; groups of young Germans who imitated American fashions by wearing American clothes and playing American music		
		Ghetto	area or district where only members of a specified race live
Emigration	movement of people out of a country to live in a different country	**Grand Coalition**	a government based on two large parties rather than one large and one or more small ones
Enabling Act	1933 Nazi law abolishing political parties and democratic process	*Grundgesetz*	German word meaning 'Basic Law'; the West German Constitution

H

Hallstein Doctrine a political principle named after a prominent civil servant in the foreign ministry under Adenauer, according to which West Germany would regard as a hostile act any state recognising East Germany as an independent state; guiding West German foreign policy idea from the mid-1950s to 1970

Hansa an association of trading cities on Germany's coast

Harzburg Front a campaigning group including several right-wing groups and parties

Heimatvertriebenen German word meaning 'those who have lost their homeland'

Hitlerjugend German word meaning 'Hitler Youth'; Nazi paramilitary youth movement

I

Ideology set of ideas and ideals that underpins and gives shape to, for example, a policy or political programme

Immigration movement of people into a country to live there rather than in their country of birth or previous home

Industrialisation the development of industry and the increasing dependence of a country on industry as opposed to agriculture for income and employment

Infrastructure the services and systems which underpin the economy and society of a state, including bridges, power-distribution networks, railways, roads, telecommunications and water supplies

Iron Front a German left-wing campaigning group including several left-wing groups and parties

J

Jesuit informal name for the member of a Roman Catholic religious order called the Society of Jesus

Junker land-owning Prussia nobility with tradition of joining the officer class in the army and the government's bureaucracy

K

Kaiser German word for emperor

Kaiserreich German empire, 1871–1914

Kreisau Circle group of opponents to the Nazi regime, especially from army and aristocratic backgrounds, largely social conservatives, monarchists, Liberals and Christians

Kristallnacht German word meaning 'crystal night' but often translated as the 'Night of Broken Glass'; a night in 1938 when Jews were killed and arrested and their property seized and destroyed

Kulturkampf German word meaning 'culture struggle'; a conflict between the German state and the Roman Catholic Church during Bismarck's chancellorship

L

Landtag elected assembly for any of the *Länder* (German states)

Lebensraum German word meaning 'living space'; territory claimed by Hitler's Germany in eastern Europe

Liberal political point of view that originated as a 19th-century reform movement which emphasised free trade and a process of constitutional political change

Luftwaffe German air force

M

Mark German currency or money; its name changed after each of a series of currency reforms, e.g. Goldmark, Reichsmark, Rentenmark, Deutsche Mark

Marshall Plan familiar name for the European Recovery Plan, after the US Secretary Of State George Marshall; plan to rebuild the economies of European countries damaged by war including Germany's; loan of funds to support the recovery process

Mefo abbreviation for Mefo-Wechsel, the German name for a form of government promissory notes; certificates of borrowing

Middle class	a social group possessing less property and political power than the nobility but more than the working class and so in the middle of society; dependent on working to earn a living but working in employment requiring higher levels of education (professions and management of business)
Militarism	a belief in the importance of the army; a tendency to depend on the army to solve diplomatic problems
Monarchist	political point of view or party believing in a monarch, e.g. a king, being head of state or head of government
Morgenthau Plan	initial plan for German economy after Second World War put forward by US Treasury Secretary Henry Morgenthau; plan to destroy Germany's military strength by disarming, destroying the industrial support for the armed forces and leaving the country poor and largely agrarian
Mutiny	refusal by armed forces personnel to obey an order or orders
N	
Nationalism	a political point of view or tradition whereby one's country is prioritised above competing demands on one's time and resources; the belief that one's own country is special (which can take the form of believing it is always best or always right or both)
Nationalsozialistische Frauenschaft (NS Frauenschaft)	German expression meaning 'National Socialist Women's League'; Nazi women's association
Nationalwerdung	German word meaning 'becoming a nation'
NATO	acronym for the North Atlantic Treaty Organization; a military alliance of democratic capitalist countries largely in western Europe and North America
Nazi	acronym for the *Nationalsozialistiche Deutsche Arbeiterpartei* (NSDAP), the National Socialist German Workers' Party

O	
Ostpolitik	German word meaning 'east policy'; policy of Willy Brandt's government, intended to increase the trust of east European countries in West Germany
P	
Pan-Germanist	political point of view that all Germans or German-speakers belong together in a single political entity or state, and that all land occupied by Germans or German-speakers should form part of a German state
Parish	a unit of a country served by a specific local church, in theory each with its own priest
Productivity	the amount that workers produce in a given time
Profiteer	someone who takes advantage of a crisis such as a war or famine to make money
Propaganda	communication, especially in politics, intended to persuade through emotional appeal not through explanation, information or argument
Protectionist	an economic approach designed to protect the producers in one country against the import of competing produce from any other country, usually through imposing tariffs
Protestant	relating to a group of Christian churches stemming from a church-reform movement in the 16th century, with a tendency to be more closely linked to individual nationalities and states than, for example, the Roman Catholic Church
R	
Reactionary	a right-wing point of view created in reaction to a left-wing expression or course of action; conservative; wishing to re-establish a set of circumstances which have been changed
Reform	change that takes place over the course of time, usually with widespread agreement, usually by constitutional means

Reichsbanner	a paramilitary group dedicated to the protection of the Weimar Republic and parliamentary democracy	**Socialist**	a left-wing political point of view or party believing in universal adult suffrage, a welfare state and the workers controlling the means of production; different schools of thought believe political change can be achieved through constitutional reform or revolution
Reichskanzler	German word meaning 'imperial chancellor'		
Reichstag	the elected federal assembly or parliament of unified Germany; the building where that assembly met		
Reichswehr	the imperial German army	**Sovereignty**	the ability of a state to make decisions about itself and its future without other countries imposing policies or programmes on it without consent
Remilitarisation	put armed forces back into an area		
Reparation	payment made by, for example, a state as punishment for wrongdoing, e.g. war crimes		
Republicanism	a political point of view preferring an elected or appointed head of state (e.g. a president) to a hereditary one (e.g. a king)	*Soziale Marktwirtschaft*	German expression meaning 'social market economy'; a political approach to the economy of a country in which government intervenes in the economy and society to protect employees' wellbeing
Revolution	change that takes place suddenly and unexpectedly, often despite opposition, usually by violent means	*Sozialstaat*	German word meaning 'the social state'; a state in which central government intervenes with legislation to ensure various minimum standards, e.g. for conditions in the workplace
Roman Catholic	relating to the largest of the Christian churches, with its administrative centre in Rome		
S		**SS**	abbreviation of *Schutzstaffel*, German word meaning 'protection squadron' or 'defence corps'; Nazi paramilitary organisation
SA	abbreviation for *Sturmabteilung*, German word meaning 'storm detachment' or 'assault division'; the original paramilitary wing of the Nazi Party		
		T	
		Tariff	a tax applied to goods when they are imported
Second Boer War	a war fought between Great Britain and Dutch-speaking settlers in southern Africa, 1899–1902	**Terrorism**	a political campaign to achieve ends by violence and instilling fear, rather than by constitutional means such as debate, demonstration or standing for election
SED	East German Communist party		
Social Democracy	a left-wing political movement campaigning for political reform especially allowing all men, or all adults, to vote in elections; influenced by the ideas of Karl Marx; contains both constitutional and revolutionary traditions	**Third Reich**	partial translation of Dritte Reich ('Third Empire'), an expression coined to show Nazi rule as coming third, following the Holy Roman Empire (which began in the early Middle Ages and ran until the beginning of the 19th century) and the Kaiserreich of 1871–1918
		Total war	a war in which every part of the economy prioritises the war and the needs of the military
		Trizone	the merged UK, US and French zones of occupation after 1945

Tsar	Russian word for emperor
U	
Urbanisation	the growth of towns and cities and the movement of population from the countryside to them
V	
Volk	German word meaning 'nation' or 'people'
Volkssturm	German word meaning 'people's storm'; a civilian defence force
W	
Weisse Rose	German expression meaning 'White Rose'; an anti-Nazi student group which in 1942–43 campaigned for the end of the war and the end of Nazi rule
Wirtschaftswunder	German word meaning 'economic miracle'; the sudden recovery and rapid growth of the West German economy despite ruin in the Second World War
Women's rights	women's civil rights as citizens; usually discussed in the context where it is argued that women ought to possess the same civil rights and the same status of citizenship as men, but do not
Z	
Zollverein	a customs union such as the one introduced in Germany in 1834

Bibliography

Chapter 1

Abrams, Lynn, *Bismarck and the German Empire, 1871–1918*, Routledge, 2006

Barnett, Corelli, *Britain and Her Army 1509–1970: A Military, Political and Social Survey*, Faber and Faber, 1970

Bunsen, Maria von, *The World I Used to Know,* Thornton Butterworth, 1930

Cecil, Lamar, *Wilhelm II* (volume1: *Prince and Emperor 1859–1900*; volume 2: *Emperor and Exile, 1900–1941*), University of North Carolina Press, 1989and1996

Mann, Golo, *The History Of Germany Since 1789*, Pimlico, 1996

Pflanze, Otto, *Bismarck and the Development of Germany* (volume 1: *The Period of Unification, 1815–1871*; volume 2: *The Period of Consolidation, 1871–1880*; volume 3: *The Period of Fortification, 1880–1898*), Princeton University Press, 1990 and 2014

Röhl, John C.G. *The Kaiser and His Court: Wilhelm II and the Government of Germany*, Cambridge University Press, 1996

Steinberg, Jonathan, *Bismarck: A Life*, Oxford University Press, 2012

Trebilcock, Clive, *Industrialisation of the Continental Powers 1780–1914*, Routledge, 1982

Chapter 2

Clark, C. *Iron Kingdom: The Rise and Downfall of Prussia, 1600–1947*, Penguin, 2007

Davis, Belinda J. *Home Fires Burning*, University of North Carolina Press, 2000

Evans, Richard J. *The Coming of the Third Reich: How the Nazis Destroyed Democracy and Seized Power in Germany*, Penguin, 2004

Keynes, John M. *The Economic Consequences of the Peace, Macmillan,* 1919

Lutz, *Ralph Haswell, The German Revolution, 1918–1919,* Ulan Press, 2012

Mantoux, Etienne, *The Carthaginian Peace: The Economic Consequences of Mr Keynes*, Oxford University Press, 1946

McElligott, Anthony, *Rethinking the Weimar Republic: Authority and Authoritarianism 1916–1936*, Bloomsbury, 2013

Merkel, P. *Political Violence under the Swastika,* Princeton University Press, 1975

Meyer, G.J. *World Undone*, Random House, 2006

Röhl, John C.G. *Wilhelm II: Into the Abyss of War and Exile, 1900–1941*, Cambridge University Press, 1996

Schuker, Stephen A. *The End of French Predominance in Europe: The Financial Crisis of 1924 and the Adoption of the Dawes Plan*, University of North Carolina Press, 1976

Seeckt, Hans von, quoted in Wheeler-Bennett J, *The Nemesis of Power*, Macmillan, 1967

Stark, Gary D. *Entrepreneurs of Ideology: Neoconservative Publishers in Germany, 1890–1933*, University of North Carolina Press, 1981

Stevenson, David *1914–1918: The History of the First World War*, Penguin, 2012

Taylor, A.J.P. *The Origins of the Second World War*, Penguin, 1991

Watt, Richard M. *The Kings Depart: The Tragedy of Germany: Versailles and the German Revolution*, Weidenfeld and Nicolson, 2003

Weitz, Eric D. *Weimar Germany*, Princeton University Press, 2007

Winkler, Heinrich August, *The Age of Catastrophe 1914–1945*, Yale University Press, 2015

Ziemann, Benjamin, 'Germany1914–1918: Total Warasa Catalyst of Change', in Helmut Walser Smith, ed., *Oxford Handbook of Modern German History*, Oxford University Press, 2011

Chapter 3

Carr, William, *A History of Germany 1815–1945*, Edward Arnold, 1969

Conway, J.S. *The Nazi Persecution of the Churches, 1933–1945*, Regent College Publishing, 1997

Crewe, David, *Nazism and German Society, 1933–1945*, Routledge, 1994

Dietrich, O. *The Hitler I Knew*, translated and quoted in Kitson, A. *Germany, 1858–1990: Hope, Terror, and Revival,* Oxford University Press, 2001

Finney, Patrick, ed., *The Origins of the Second World War: A Reader*, Bloomsbury, 1997

Hitler, A. *Hitler's Table Talk, 1941–1944,* Oxford University Press, 2001

Kershaw, Ian, *The 'Hitler Myth': Image and Reality in the Third Reich*, Oxford University Press, 1985

Kershaw, Ian, *The Nazi Dictatorship: Problems and Perspectives of Interpretation*, Hodder Arnold Publication, 2000

Mason, Timothy, *Nazism, Fascism and the Working Class*, Cambridge University Press, 1995

Mason, Timothy, *Social Policy in the Third Reich: The Working Class and the National Community*, Bloomsbury, 1993

Overy, Richard, *War and Economy in the Third Reich*, Oxford University Press, 1995

Strasser, G. *Work and Bread, 1932,* quoted in Noakes, J. and Pridham, G. *Nazism, 1919–1945: State, Economy, and Society, 1933–1939*, University of Exeter Press, 1994

Welch, D. *The Third Reich: Politics and Propaganda*, Routledge, 2008

Chapter 4

Aust, Stefan, *Baader-Meinhof: The Inside Story of the R.A.F.*, Oxford University Press, 2009

Berghahn, V.R. *Modern Germany: Society, Economy and Politics in the Twentieth Century*, Cambridge University Press, 1987

Gazdar, Kaevan, *Germany's Balanced Development: The Real Wealth of a Nation*, Quorum, 1998

Judt, Tony, *Postwar: A History of Europe since 1945,* Penguin, 2005

Laqueur, Walter, *Europe since Hitler: The Rebirth of Europe*, Penguin, 1985

McAdams, A. James, *Germany Divided: From the Wall to Reunification*, Princeton University Press, 1994

Moeller, Robert G. *West Germany under Construction: Politics, Society, and Culture in the Adenauer Era*, University of Michigan Press, 1997

Schwarz, Hans-Peter, *Konrad Adenauer: A German Politician and Statesman in a Period of War, Revolution and Reconstruction* (volume 1: *From the German Empire to the Federal Republic, 1876–1952*; volume 2: *The Statesman, 1952–67*), Berghahn Books, 1995 and 1997

Smith, Gordon R. 'Does Germany Have an Efficient Secret?', in William E. Paterson and Gordon R. Smith, eds., *The West German Model: Perspectives on a Stable State*, Routledge, 1981

Story, Jonathan, ed., *The New Europe: Government, Politics and Economy since 1945*, Blackwell, 1993

Turner, Henry Ashby, *Germany from Partition to Reunification*, Yale University Press, 1992

Williams, Charles, *Adenauer: The Father of the New Germany*, Abacus, 2003

Willis, F. Roy, *France, Germany, and the New Europe, 1945–1967*, Stanford University Press, 1968

Acknowledgements

The authors and publishers acknowledge the following sources of copyright material and are grateful for the permissions granted. While every effort has been made it has not always been possible to identify the sources of all the material used, or to trace all copyright holders. If any omissions are brought to our notice, we will be happy to include the appropriate acknowledgements on reprinting.

The publisher would like to thank the following for permission to reproduce their photographs (numbers refer to figure numbers, unless otherwise stated):

Chapter 1 opener TopFoto: ullsteinbild. **1.2** Johan Hamman. **1.3 akg-images. 1.4 akg-images:** picture-alliance/dpa. **1.5** Scan of image from the book *Deutschlands Wehrmacht*, published in 1913. **1.6 Alamy Images:** Chronical. **1.7 TopFoto:** World History Archive. **Chapter 2 opener akg-images. 2.1 akg-images. 2.2 Alamy Images:** Interfoto. **2.3 TopFoto:** ullsteinbild. **2.4 Alamy Images:** Interfoto. **2.5 akg-images. 2.6 Mary Evans Picture Library:** Photo Researchers. **2.7 akg-images. 2.8 Alamy Images:** Novarc Images. **2.9 The Kobal Collection:** UFA/Karl Ewald. **Chapter 3 opener akg-images. 3.3 Getty Images:** Keystone/Stringer. **3.4 Alamy Images:** Photos 12. **3.5 TopFoto:** ullsteinbild. **3.8 TopFoto:** The Granger Collection. **3.9 Alamy Images:** Pictorial Press. **3.11 TopFoto:** ullsteinbild. **3.12 Getty Images:** Bachrach. **3.13 REX Shutterstock:** Weiner Library. **Chapter 4 opener Fotolia:** BlackMac. **4.2 Getty Images:** Roger Voillet. **4.4 Fotolia:** Sean Pavone Photo.

The publisher would like to thank the following for permission to reproduce their texts:

Extract Chapter 1 Bismarck and the German Empire, 1871-1918 by Lynn Abrams, Routledge (11 April 2006) reproduced by permission of Taylor & Francis Books UK; **Extract Chapter 1** Hildegard von Spitzemberg reprinted with permission of The Historical Commission of the Bavarian Academy of Sciences; **Extract Chapter 1** Otto von Bismarck, Reden 1847-1869 [Speeches, 1847-1869], ed., Wilhelm Schüßler, vol. 10, Bismarck: Die gesammelten Werke [Bismarck: Collected Works], ed. Hermann von Petersdorff. Berlin: Otto Stolberg, 1924-35, pp. 139-40. Translation: Jeremiah Riemer; **Extract Chapter 1** August Bebel. First edition written and published in German in 1879; Authorized Translation by Meta L. Stern (Hebe);

Copyright 1910 by the Socialist Literature Company. New York; **Extract Chapter 1 from** Kaiser Wilhelm II, My Early Life; **Extract Chapter 1** A Young Noblewoman is Presented at Court (1882-83) - Source: Marie von Bunsen, Die Welt, in der ich lebte. Erinnerungen 1860-1912 [The World in Which I Lived: Memories 1860-1912], new edition. Biberach, 1959, pp. 90ff. Translation: Erwin Fink; **Extract Chapter 1** Correlli Barnett, "Britain and her Army 1509–1970: A Military, Political and Social Survey" (1970); **Extract Chapter 1** Rosa Luxemburg. Written: February–April 1915 (while in prison). First Published: In Zurich, February 1916, and illegally distributed in Germany. Source: Politische Schriften, pp.229-43, pp.357-72. Translated: (from the German) by Dave Hollis Copyleft: Luxemburg Internet Archive (marxists.org) 1996, 1999, 2003; **Extract Chapter 1** Lynn Abrams, Bismarck and the German Empire, 1871-1918, Routledge (11 April 2006) reprinted with permission Taylor & Francis; **Extract Chapter 1** The Kaiser and his Court: Wilhelm II and the Government of Germany by John C. G. Röhl. Cambridge University Press, 1996; **Extract Chapter 2** Wilhelm II's letter of abdication as translated and appearing in the 1923 Source Records of the Great War, Vol. VI, edited by Charles F. Horne; **Extract Chapter 2** Weimar Germany: Promise and Tragedy by Eric D. Weitz. Princeton University Press (September 24, 2007); **Extract Chapter 2** Political Violence Under the Swastika: 581 Early Nazis by Peter H. Merkl. Princeton University Press (March 8, 2015); **Extract Chapter 2** The crisis in the German social-democracy (the "Junius" pamphlet) by Rosa Luxemburg. Published 1919 by Socialist Publication Society in New York; **Extract Chapter 2** Sir John W. Wheeler-Bennett, Richard J. Overy. Nemesis of Power: The German Army in Politics 1918-1945, 2nd Edition Paperback – 1 Sep 2005. Palgrave Macmillan reproduced with permission of Palgrave Macmillan; **Extract Chapter 2** From ENTREPRENEURS OF IDEOLOGY: NEOCONSERVATIVE PUBLISHERS IN GERMANY, 1890-1933 by Gary D. Start. Copyright © 1981 by the University of North Carolina Press. Used by permission of the publisher. **Extract Chapter 2** from HOME FIRES BURNING: FOOD, POLITICS, AND EVERYDAY LIFE IN WORLD WAR I BERLIN by Belinda J. Davis. Copyright © 2000 by the University of North Carolina Press. Used by permission of the publisher; **Extract Chapter 2** John Maynard Keynes, The Economic Consequences of the Peace, Macmillan, 1919; **Extract Chapter 2** J. M. Keynes The Economic Consequences of the Peace, Macmillan, 1919; **Extract Chapter 2** Christopher

Clark, Iron Kingdom: The Rise and Downfall of Prussia, 1600–1947, Penguin, 2007; **Extract Chapter 2** Ralph Haswell Lutz, The German Revolution, 1918–1919, Ulan Press, 2012; **Extract Chapter 3** A History of Germany 1815-1990 4Ed by William Carr. 10 (Hodder Arnold Publication) Paperback – 17 Oct 1991. Bloomsbury Academic; 4 edition (17 Oct. 1991), Reprinted with permission of Bloomsbury Publishing Plc; **Extract Chapter 3** (Article 54) (Article 42) From Documents of German History © 1958 by Louis L. Snyder. Reprinted by permission of Rutgers University Press; **Extract Chapter 3** The Hitler I Knew: Memoirs of the Third Reich's Press Chief by Otto Dietrich, introduction by Roger Moorhouse. Pen and Sword Books and Skyhorse Publishing; **Extract Chapter 3** Hitler's Table Talk, 1941-1944 by Adolf Hitler Paperback – February 1, 1988. Introduced by Hugh Trevor-Roper. Publisher: Oxford Univ Pr (Sd) (February 1, 1988); **Extract Chapter 3** Nazism, Fascism, and the Working Class: Essays by Tim Mason, ed. Jane Caplan. Cambridge University Press, 1995; **Extract Chapter 3** Henry Ashby Turner, German Big Business and the Rise of Hitler. Oxford University Press 1985; **Extract Chapter 3** Banks And Business Politics In Nazi Germany by Harold James: BUSINESS AND INDUSTRY IN NAZI GERMANY Edited by Francis R. Nicosia and Jonathan Huener. Berghahn Books; **Extract Chapter 3** The Nazi Dictatorship and the Deutsche Bank by Harold James. Cambridge University Press 2004; **Extract Chapter 3** The Third Reich: Politics and Propaganda by David Welch, 2nd Ed Routledge (25 April 2002) reproduced by permission of Taylor & Francis Books UK; **Extract Chapter 3** Nazism 1919-1945 Volume 2: State, Economy and Society 1933-39 (A Documentary Reader) Paperback – 1 Aug 2000, by Jeremy Noakes|G. Pridham. Reprinted by permission of Liverpool University Press; **Extract Chapter 3** Nazism, Fascism, and the Working Class: Essays by Timothy Mason, edited by Jane Caplan, Cambridge University Press; **Extract Chapter 4** German Empire to the Federal Republic, 1876-1952 v. 1: German Politician and Statesman in a Period of War, Revolution and Reconstruction by Hans-Peter Schwarz. Berghahn Books Inc. Reproduced by permission of Berghahn Books Inc; **Extract Chapter 4** US President John F. Kennedy in a speech in West Berlin, 26 June 1963; **Extract Chapter 4** German Empire to the Federal Republic, 1876-1952 v. 1: German Politician and Statesman in a Period of War, Revolution and Reconstruction by Hans-Peter Schwarz. Berghahn Books Inc. Reproduced by permission of Berghahn Books Inc; **Extract Chapter 4** Baader-Meinhof: The Inside Story of the R.A.F by Stefan Aust and Anthea Bell. OUP USA; Revised edition (16 April 2009) Published by Bodley Head, part of Vintage Publishing (Random UK); **Extract Chapter 4** Germany from Partition to Reunification: A Revised Edition of The Two Germanies Since 1945. Henry Ashby Turner. Extract Chapter 4 Yale University Press; **Extract Chapter 4** Between Pain and Silence by Sabine Behrenbeck. Life after Death: Approaches to a Cultural and Social History During the 1940s and 1950s: Richard Bessel and Dirk Schurmann. Cambridge University Press; First Edition edition (26 Jun. 2003)

Index compiled by Indexing Specialists (UK) Ltd.

Index

Lightning Source UK Ltd.
Milton Keynes UK
UKHW051607120719
346024UK00008B/71/P

9 781107 566088